Contents

5   Learning Principles 88

6

Processing Information from Lectures 124

10   Managing Stress   248

11   Information Literacy   262

Preface

Having taught learning strategies for more than 25 years now, I can honestly say that not a semester has passed that I have not learned from my students. They are innovative, resilient, and want to be successful in college. Many need guidance in the strategies that will help them do their best and efficiently use the time they have. As a professor, writer, and researcher, I have written this text to share what I have learned about learning how to learn and strategies for being a successful student. I'm especially excited about the Sixth Edition's increased focus on skills students need to be successful. Four completely revised chapters in this edition offer:

- Strategies needed on day-one for success in college and resources available on campus, at home, and in the community (Chapter 1).
- Ways to process and transfer information into long-term memory and strengthen connections that allow for learning (Chapter 5).
- Reading strategies that help students adjust to the amount reading required in college (Chapter 7).
- Critical thinking strategies needed for researching and evaluating sources. (Chapter 11).

Put Your Students in the Driver's Seat

Take a minute to consider the following situations. How many of these can you relate to?

- Planning out your route carefully on a map before you get in your car
- Driving in an unfamiliar city with confusing signs
- Getting stuck in traffic on your way to an important meeting
- Unexpected road construction that forces you on a detour
- Carpooling with people you don't know

Now, think about these common issues that college students face:

- Choosing a major and the classes to take next semester
- Navigating around the college campus and finding where classes are
- Managing time in and outside the classroom
- Meeting new people and experiencing new things
- Managing stress and unexpected life events

See any similarities between the above lists? Brain research has found that one of the most powerful ways to learn is by using analogies The analogy used throughout the Sixth Edition is that college is a journey or road trip and each student must be the driver if the student is to be successful. A passenger may come along for the ride, but the driver is in control and accepts responsibility. The driver does whatever is necessary in order to reach the destination: chooses the route, follows the road signs, steps on the gas and the brakes, fuels up, and asks for directions. The driver fights fatigue and stress and experiences the confusion of driving in an unfamiliar place. But the driver also owns the whole experience of the drive, every curve and bump and every complex intersection. We will use the driver analogy to think critically about student responsibilities in each chapter of the text.

In the journey through college, students will discover that learning involves more than getting information. It involves examining new information, making it personal, and determining where it fits into their own experiences. It then requires converting comprehension into a plan or strategy and actively testing the strategy. Learning requires full participation and keeping eyes on the road. The Sixth Edition of *Practicing College Learning Strategies* models this learning process by clearly and concisely presenting the essential information students need to successfully navigate their way through their college education. Structured activities and exercises will guide them in the reflection process to make the information personal and useful and provide practice in developing strategies for learning and in testing those strategies.

The straightforward, brief explanations and structured activities modeling the learning process make this text especially useful for first-time college students or returning adults. However, the brain-based academic orientation makes it valuable for anyone who wants to get the most out of their college journey.

Brain-Compatible Learning

The text and activities in *Practicing College Learning Strategies*, Sixth Edition, are thoughtfully constructed using brain-compatible strategies. Brain-compatible learning is based on how research in neuroscience suggests our brain naturally learns best.

In his book, *Human Brain and Human Learning* (1983), Leslie Hart argues that teaching without an awareness of how the brain learns is like designing a glove with no sense of what a hand looks like—its shape, how it moves. Brain-compatible, or brain-based, learning is the central focus of the Sixth Edition of *Practicing College Learning Strategies*.

In keeping with the straightforward style of the text, the discussion of learning principles in Chapter 5 includes enough explanation of neurological research on memory to empower students. It provides them with a basic understanding of how to make maximum use of their memory and thereby improve their job performance, school achievement, and personal success. Students' idea of learning has often been limited to memorizing or comprehension of a new concept.

The Sixth Edition continues to expand use of what James Zull calls "four essentials of learning." Students gather new information and analyze it, and many students think their learning is complete with the completion of these two steps. However, students must learn to go further and use this new information to form ideas and hypotheses. The learning process is not really complete until these ideas have actually have been tested with some action. In each chapter, students are guided through all four steps of the process with the exercises and activities and debriefed at the end of each chapter with the "Modeling the Learning Process" feature so that they become more aware of the process they just used. They see that the effect is ownership of information, not just memorization. They move from receivers of knowledge to producers of knowledge. By modeling the process repeatedly, students should be able to more easily transfer the learning model to their other classes.

Brain research has confirmed that when we experience something new, the brain looks for an existing network into which the information will fit, and the brain works best through analogy and metaphor, constantly looking for similarities and differences or relationships between old and new information. In addition to the driving analogy, the Sixth Edition includes "Making It Concrete," a feature that guides students through the process of how new concepts they learn may be similar to concepts they already know. "Making Connections" helps students analyze how new concepts relate to concepts already covered in the text and helps them to see how those new concepts or strategies can be used in other courses or situations.

Learning Outcomes

Clearly defined "Learning Outcomes" (learning objectives) form a framework for learning by providing instructors and students with standards and expectations for every lesson. In addition, these learning objectives are helpful when funding, accreditation, or institutional effectiveness plans require instructors to provide evidence of student learning and the effectiveness of a course or program. With this in mind, the Sixth Edition begins each chapter with measurable "Learning Outcomes" and concludes with an "Evaluating Learning Outcomes." These "Learning Outcomes" should be the basis for selecting content, classroom activities, and assessment measures such as chapter or unit tests and final projects or exams.

New to the Sixth Edition

- **New!** Chapter 1, "Making a Smooth Transition to College," provides the most basic skills that students need to be productive from "day one."
- **New!** Chapter 5, "Learning Principles," teaches students the learning principles used as ways to process or transfer information into long-term memory and to strengthen connections that allow for learning. For

us to learn something new, we must make a connection to something that is already in our brain.

- **New!** Chapter 7, "Processing Information from Textbooks," serves as a reading guide to help students adjust to college-level content and reading requirements.
- **New!** Chapter 11, "Information Literacy," highlights important critical thinking strategies for evaluating sources.
- **New!** Practice exercises in Time Management, Goal Setting, Critical Thinking, and more!
- **Updated!** Newly designed chapter opener maps provide for an easy-to-follow guide of the chapters' main topics.
- **Updated!** "Brain Bytes" throughout the text now include research on our ability, or lack thereof, to multitask!
- **Updated!** Revised "Virtual Field Trips" include more activities and videos.

Additional Features

The Sixth Edition includes additional features that help focus student learning.

Student Tips

Because students want proof that the strategies really work, each chapter includes tips from students who have actually tried the strategies and who have found unique ways to use them in the college setting. My students jumped at the chance to share their experiences with other students. I have included a few of these "Student Tips" in each chapter. You may want to make this a feature on your website, discussion board, or wiki, or simply post them in your classroom. Although instructors see learning strategies at work in successful students, students who have a better concept of what will work for them can more easily modify strategies for maximum effectiveness. Giving advice about using strategies successfully helps give students ownership of new concepts and confidence to apply them to new situations.

Parallel Parking

Each chapter in the Sixth Edition ends with a critical thinking exercise that applies the driving analogy to concepts learned in the chapter. Brain research confirms that using metaphors or analogies is one of the best ways for students to demonstrate that they understand a new concept. We know that the brain needs to know that it knows something. We also know that the only way new learning is processed into long-term memory is to make new connections to connections that are already in the brain. The "Parallel Parking" exercise at the end of each chapter promotes this kind of critical thinking. The analogy that students need to assume the responsibilities of drivers runs throughout the text. The "Parallel Parking" feature is a natural extension of this analogy, which encourages students to think critically about how the strategies used in each chapter and their experience as college students parallel various driving terms.

Virtual Field Trips

Updated for the Sixth Edition, the "Virtual Field Trip" features provide opportunities to expand textbook information, without adding to its length, and give students more opportunities to adapt, personalize, and evaluate strategies. Many of the "Virtual Field Trips" in the Sixth Edition include more activities and videos. These guided Internet activities help students find useful and reliable resources, engage in purposeful Internet searches, and build both confidence and skill in using Internet resources. The "Virtual Field Trips" also allow students to apply the learning model to student success topics such as campus safety, health issues, and budgeting. In addition, these features allow flexibility to use this text as the core for a student success course and, at the same time, include other important student success issues. A list of "Virtual Field Trip" features is found on the inside cover of the text. Access these Virtual Field Trips via College Success Course Mate at www.cengagebrain.com or via the author's website at http://frank.mtus.edu/~studskl/6evirtua; fieldtrips.html

Case Study: What's Your Advice?

Each chapter summary, with the exception of Chapter 1, is followed by a case study exercise in which students synthesize and evaluate what they have learned in the chapter so that they can provide advice to a fictional fellow student.

Brain Bytes

"Brain Byte" features appear in the margin throughout the text, providing bite-sized factoids relevant to the chapter material. Updated for the Sixth Edition, these features highlight topics that brain researchers have discovered.

Order and Content of Chapters

The first four chapters of the Sixth Edition help students adjust to the new environment of college.

- **New!** Chapter 1, "Making a Smooth Transition to College," places emphasis on the tools for success in college, as well as resources available on campus, at home, and in the community. This chapter provides the most basic skills that students need to be productive from "day one." Key words that every college student should know are boldfaced in the chapter and encourage students to be active in the reading process. (Previous users will note that this new chapter combines the Survival Kit and Chapter 10 from the Fifth Edition and places this important information at the forefront of the text.)

- Chapter 2, "Applying the Principles of Time Management," addresses time-management problems inherent in a college student's schedule and sets in place an individualized time-management plan to help each student meet the demands of a college schedule.
- Chapter 3 introduces students to the critical-thinking skills that they will need to be successful in college. Each subsequent chapter has critical thinking activities to allow students to practice the new techniques.
- Chapter 4 gives students guidance on setting goals and determining their locus of control. The Sixth Edition has updated exercises and activities.

Chapter 5 is the core chapter on brain-compatible learning. It introduces some basic functions of the brain so that students understand not only what they need to do to aid memory, but also why the principles work. The 10 learning principles act as a guide for students to begin the learning process and as a foundation for developing learning strategies that work. The Sixth Edition shifts the term from "memory principles" to "learning principles" to more accurately describe the principles and to emphasize that memorizing is not the same as learning. Building on what they have learned about learning, students then develop strategies for taking notes, reading textbooks, and taking tests in Chapters 6–9. These chapters support students' discovery about how they learn and process information and highlight the need for students to use the strategies that work for them.

Chapter 6 includes a guided "Modeling the Learning Process" exercise that uses what James Zull calls the "four essential functions of the brain." This exercise helps students establish ownership of the information in the first five chapters and then apply that information to develop strategies for processing information from lectures and textbooks in Chapters 6 and 7. The Question in the Margin system introduced in these chapters, a modified Cornell system, employs the learning principles from Chapter 5 and helps students understand why such a systematic approach works. Chapter 7, "Processing Information from Textbooks," now includes basic reading strategies to help students who may be struggling with reading college textbooks, to remove some "rust" from adult students, and to act as a guide to help all students adjust the amount of reading required in college.

Chapter 8, "Learning Styles," introduces sensory modes, hemispheric dominance, and multiple intelligences—three elements that brain researchers agree are necessary for optimal learning. The three approaches to learning styles are consistent with the learning process of gathering information, processing it, and activating it. This chapter includes inventories to help students determine their preferences and practical strategies for using those preferences.

Although students experience stress and need to know specifics about their higher education environment during the first days of school, the chapters on these subjects are purposely placed toward the end of the text. It has been my experience that students get a bit "antsy" at the beginning of the semester and want to learn skills they can use immediately. Having addressed those skills in Chapters 5–9, they are now seeking ways to practice them and to deal with the stress that higher education presents (Chapter 10). **New!** Chapter 11, "Information Literacy," covers a systematic approach for information literacy and research to help students have the tools they need to be an effective student in an information age. The chapter highlights important critical thinking strategies for evaluating sources. Appendix A addresses some unique strategies needed for studying math. It is common for students to believe that they are not good at math. The appendix begins with an inventory evaluating students' math study skills, and here many students discover that it may not be math that is the problem; rather it is their approach to studying math that prevents them from being successful. Appendix A walks students back through each textbook topic to discover ways to fine-tune strategies they have already learned and to apply them to the math classroom.

Additional Resources

The Sixth Edition offers additional resources to both instructors and students.

Instructor Companion Site

The Instructor's website provides access to the online *Instructor's Resource Manual*, a transition guide for the Sixth Edition, sample syllabi, quizzes, Virtual Field Trips, strategies for using the student website in your course, and PowerPoint presentations to aid in lectures. To present a more accessible view of the concepts, presentations are broken down by topic within each chapter. Access the Instructor Companion Site by logging into your account at http://login.cengage.com.

Instructor's Resource Manual

An online *Instructor's Resource Manual* (IRM) accompanies *Practicing College Learning Strategies*, Sixth Edition. Following the structure of the main text, the IRM provides teaching suggestions, additional activities, and exercises by chapter, in addition to the answers to the text's chapter summary questions. Access the IRM on the Instructor Companion Site by logging into your account at http://login.cengage.com.

College Success CourseMate

New! College Success CourseMate for *Practicing College Learning Strategies* provides online interactive quizzing, Video Skillbuilders that combine video clips featuring discussions with students, instructors, and experts, with articles and activities, glossary and flashcards, Virtual Field Trips, Student Survival Kit, PowerPoint Presentations to aid in study, and more! With CourseMate, you can use the Engagement Tracker to assess student preparation and engagement in your course. Students will need an access key to use the College Success CourseMate. To package this with your textbook, talk to your Cengage Learning sales representative or log on to www.cengagebrain.com.

College Success Factors Index 2.0

New! College Success Factors Index (CSFI) 2.0 is an online survey that students complete to assess their patterns and behavior in 10 factors that are specific to succeeding in the classroom/campus: Responsibility/Control, Competition, Task Planning, Expectations, Wellness, Time Management, College Involvement, Family Involvement, Precision, and Persistence. The CSFI is a perfect assessment tool for demonstrating the difference your College Success course makes in your students' academic success.

Study Skills Help Page

You may also want to log onto The Study Skills Help Page, the website I developed for the course I teach using this text: http://www.mtsu.edu/~studskl/.

TeamUp

An additional service available with the text is access to TeamUp; an unparalleled suite of services provided by Cengage Learning that offers you flexible and personalized assistance for using our programs and integrating them with your course materials. Whether online, on the phone, or on campus, TeamUp will strive to deliver high-quality service and support via faculty programs, training, and media support.

The TeamUp consultants have a wide variety of experience in teaching and administering the first-year course. They can provide help in establishing or improving your student success program. They can assist in course design, instructor training, teaching strategies, annual conferences, and much more. Learn more about TeamUp today by calling 1-800-528-8323 or visiting http://www.cengage.com/teamup/.

Acknowledgments

I am indebted to many people for the preparation of this book. This text is the result of suggestions from students and faculty involved in the Academic Enrichment courses at Middle Tennessee State University (MTSU), as well as colleagues I have met across the country at workshops and conferences. The success of the learning strategies program at MTSU has been very much a team effort. I have benefited greatly from my association with the talented and caring members of the University College faculty and staff. I give thanks specifically to my colleagues, Tom Tyner, Andrea Bell, and Carla Hatfield, who can be credited with many of the ideas found here, and whose understanding of how crucial it is for students to "learn how to learn" has made the course successful for thousands of students.

And much of the credit for this text goes to the students in the learning strategies classes at MTSU, who continue to keep me fascinated with their development and help me grow in my understanding of how students learn.

Each revision has been student-driven. The longer I teach, the more I learn from my students. Revision has been a direct result of students demonstrating the learning process. They have taken suggestions from the text and processed that information, tried it, adjusted it, and made it work for themselves. Then they have made suggestions to me about how to clarify or adjust the information to perhaps make it easier for other students in the path of learning how to learn. They truly demonstrate that the learning process moves students from being receivers of knowledge to producers of knowledge.

I particularly want to acknowledge the insights given to me this year by my granddaughter Chelsey Elliott who, as a freshman at MTSU this year, gave me a fresh perspective on the needs of college students entering higher education.

I am particularly indebted to the research of Dr. James Zull at Case Western Reserve University. His book, *The Art of Changing the Brain* (Stylus, 2002), provides concreteness to that which is complex and validity to what I teach and share with colleagues. I owe the online version of the hemispheric dominance inventory to Mark Templeton's expertise and patience.

Authors Eric Jensen and Karen Markowitz, Pierce Howard (*The Owner's Manual for the Brain*), and Eric Chudler (Neuroscience for Kids, http://faculty.washington.edu/chudler/neurok.html) were generous in granting permission to share their research about what brain research says about learning. A special thanks to Ralph Hillman, the Voice Doc (and friend), for sharing the BREATHE System. The brief introduction included in Chapter 1 in this text does not do justice to this system. I hope you will examine it further at http://thebreathesystem.com/. Ralph Hillman reminds me that no exercise in the text should begin without the Big 3 of the Breathe System: Check your posture, relax your shoulders and neck, and breathe! Thanks to Laurie Witherow and Ginger Corley, who once again granted permission to use their wonderful "All I Ever Needed to Know I Learned from My Advisor."

I can't begin to thank the wonderful staff at Cengage for their vision, suggestions, and persistence. Thanks to Shani Fisher for her continued support and thoughtful input. Joanna Hassel's perception and creativity made the creation of the Sixth Edition fresh and exciting for me. Special thanks as well to Julia Giannotti, Jessica Rasile, and Sarah Turner for their work on this revision, and to the TeamUp Consultants for their continued support.

I would like to extend a special acknowledgment to the following instructors for their reviews of the text and suggestions for the improvement of this edition:

Alicia Cawley, Central New Mexico Community College
Victoria Dixon, Washtenaw Community College, MI
Sally Firmin, Baylor University, TX
Tom Flagg, Central New Mexico Community College
Carla Hatfield, Middle Tennessee State University
Carlotta Hill, Oklahoma City Community College
Norma Letinksy, Moorpark College, CA
Margaret Puckett, North Central State College, OH
Becca Seul, Middle Tennessee State University
Karen Welch, Tennessee Technology Center at Jackson

Carolyn H. Hopper

Practicing College Learning Strategies

1 Making a Smooth Transition to College

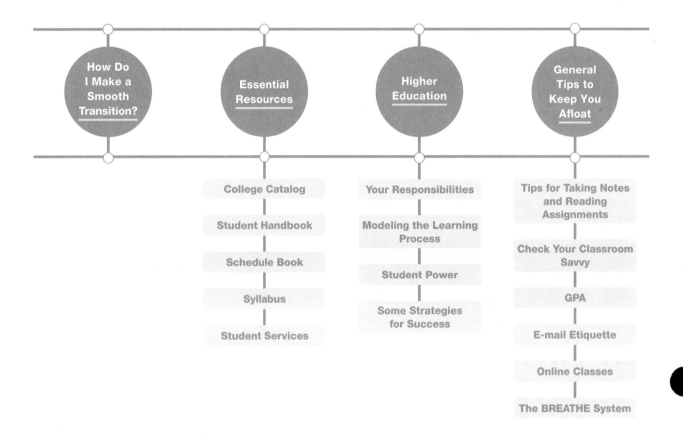

How Do I Make a Smooth Transition?	Essential Resources	Higher Education	General Tips to Keep You Afloat
	College Catalog	Your Responsibilities	Tips for Taking Notes and Reading Assignments
	Student Handbook	Modeling the Learning Process	Check Your Classroom Savvy
	Schedule Book	Student Power	GPA
	Syllabus	Some Strategies for Success	E-mail Etiquette
	Student Services		Online Classes
			The BREATHE System

Brain research says that we may learn best through analogies, comparing something new to things we already know and understand. The primary analogy we will use throughout this text is that your college education is a journey. However, you can't hop on a plane, look out at the clouds, read a book, watch a movie, eat and drink a bit, have a casual conversation with your seat mates, catch a nap, and be at your destination. Nor can you get there as a passenger on a bus or train. College education is a rough road trip, and you are the driver. You choose the route, you follow the road signs, you step on the gas and the brakes, you fuel up, and you ask for directions. You fight fatigue and stress. But you also take in the whole experience of the drive, every curve and bump, every complex intersection, and every flat tire or fender bender.

If this is your first semester at college, you have already discovered it is difficult to drive in a place that is unfamiliar. You are definitely out of

Learning Outcomes
for Chapter 1 Making a Smooth Transition to College

Here is your destination for Chapter 1. When you complete Chapter 1, you are expected not only to understand the material presented, but also to be able to:

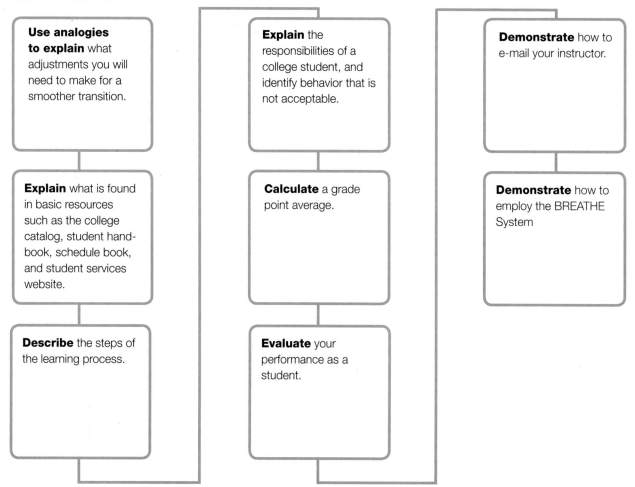

Use analogies to explain what adjustments you will need to make for a smoother transition.

Explain what is found in basic resources such as the college catalog, student handbook, schedule book, and student services website.

Describe the steps of the learning process.

Explain the responsibilities of a college student, and identify behavior that is not acceptable.

Calculate a grade point average.

Evaluate your performance as a student.

Demonstrate how to e-mail your instructor.

Demonstrate how to employ the BREATHE System

your comfort zone. You may make a few wrong turns. You may not take the shortest route. Even when you use Mapquest or a GPS instructors or other students to help you navigate, driving in a new territory requires concentration. Right now everything is new: the campus, the instructors, the amount of work required, and the speed with which things are covered—the entire college environment with **credit hours**, **general education requirements**, choice of which classes to take, and what time to take them. It's all pretty overwhelming.

Beginning your college education is a lot like traveling to a foreign country. Your entry into college transports you to a place that is foreign to you too. The surroundings, the culture, the customs, and even the language are unfamiliar and may be a difficult adjustment. Let's carry this analogy a bit further and say that you have just arrived at the airport of a foreign city. Each traveler brings different expectations and experiences. Some of you have visited this place before. You may have some idea of what you want to see again and perhaps you might want to change some things from your last visit. Some of you have carefully planned your trip. You have talked to those who have lived and worked here. You have read the guidebooks and have studied the culture and the language. You have prepared to make the most of the experience. Some travelers have arrived with little idea of where they are and the opportunities available here. Some of the travelers are here for a visit. Most of you, however, are here to take a job. You will become a resident of this place for a while and so you will want discover all you can to make your experience meaningful and your job rewarding.

Your approach as you begin college may be the same approach that you would take if you were moving to a foreign city to do a job. You can get irritated because you don't understand the language. You can become frustrated because you are constantly getting lost. You can be confused or unaware that you have offended the local residents. This first chapter can become your travel guide; and although it can't tell you everything you need to know, it will give you a heads up on the language, the people, the customs, and expectations; your responsibilities in your new job; and some tools to help you make the most of your experience and to make your transition to college smoother. You have chosen to come here. This is your new job. You will be spending a great deal of time, money, and effort trying to be successful in a foreign place. The good news is you can soon be acting like a native.

As you read this chapter, you will find several bold print words. These are words that are frequently used in college that you may not be totally familiar with. At the end of the chapter, you will be asked to list at least five of these words and define them as they are used on your campus. When you get to a word, you may want to turn to the end of the chapter and record it as you read.

This is a learning strategies text, a manual with tips to help make your drive smoother, your experience better. This text is about more than how to study. The focus of the text is on *learning how to learn*. The world is changing at an amazing pace. We are able to access more and more information using more and more technology. In fact, the job you will be doing ten years from now probably doesn't exist now in the form you will be performing it. I really think that the most important thing you will learn in college may be *learning how to learn*. You will learn how to maximize your memory, your note taking, your textbook reading, your test taking, your critical thinking, your time management, and your information literacy. The attitude with which you approach this course will make the difference in more than just passing a course and discovering skills to make your life better.

You are a college student. This is your job! Many of you are still working your old job; however, beginning college is the same as beginning a new job. Each semester is a promotion and brings new responsibilities. Think of your first days on other jobs. In fact, jot down some things you remember about your first few weeks on the job. I'm sure you didn't just choose a place to work and say, "I think I'll work here today." Many of us may have approached college this way, however. For your job, someone interviewed you; and when you were hired, someone explained *exactly* what was expected of you, what procedures to use, how to work necessary equipment, and where to go to find out information you did not know, or who to report to. Often this is not the case at the beginning of college. Some of us plunged right in. You should approach college as you would a new job. Don't just wander in and begin work without knowing essential information. This is not your high school, the job you left or currently work, or the world you were immersed in six months ago. Find out as much as you can about this new work environment, both what is expected of you and what resources are available. If you have not already done so, meet with an **academic advisor**. Discover how to register for each term in the most efficient manner and which courses you really need to take. You are spending too much time, effort, and money not to do it right!

Essential Resources

At most colleges and universities, there are some essential resources that will provide your "job description" as a student, in addition to explaining how to get "promotions," or better grades. The first essential resource you need is the **college catalog.** Because it is changed periodically, the catalog for the year you enroll becomes your contract with the university. Containing the rules, regulations, and procedures you are expected to follow, the catalog corresponds to a company's policy manual.

Most degree or certificate programs require a certain numbers of **credit hours** to graduate. The catalog will spell out which classes you are required to take. In addition, the catalog lists a detailed description of each course. You need to know what is in the catalog for your college. Similar to how you would use a reference book, you will probably not read the catalog cover to cover. However, it's a good idea to put it in a place where you will look at it often, both to become aware of policies and procedures and to understand your **degree requirements**. If you have declared a **major**, you should also study that section carefully. If you don't have a major yet, the catalog is a good source of information to help you decide on one. What majors are offered? What does each require? What major would you really like to take classes in? When you register for classes, you should consult the catalog for a description of the course you are registering for. These course descriptions may help you determine some possible majors to consider.

Exercise 1.1

Using Your College Catalog

Consult your college catalog and find the following information (insert page numbers so you can find this again; you may need to use a separate sheet of paper for some of the questions). You may also find that there is an online version that is easier to use.

Locate the **academic calendar**: (a) What are the holidays for this semester? (b) When are your final exams?

_____

_____

How do you **drop or add** a course?

_____

_____

What is the significance of **course numbers**?

_____

_____

What **degrees** are offered at your institution?

_____

_____

What are the requirements for the degree you seek?

_____

_____

Find the course description of one course that you are required to take, and write a brief summary of that course.

_____

_____

What **grade point average (GPA)** do you need to graduate?

_____

_____

General Education, or Core Curriculum, Courses

One of the most important uses of the catalog is determining which courses to take and when to take them. Most colleges and universities have a required **core curriculum**, often called *general education* or *general studies* courses. No matter the major, any student who graduates from that college or university must complete a required number of courses covering a broad area. According to the Association of American Colleges, college graduates should:

> possess the marks of a generally educated person—that is, having such qualities as a broad base of knowledge in history and culture, mathematics and science, the ability to think logically and critically, the capacity to express ideas clearly and cogently, the sensitivities and skills to deal with different kinds of people, sophisticated tastes and interests, and the capability to work independently and collaboratively.[1]

College education should be both specialized (a major) and broad (general education), because we experience the world whole, not in isolated

[1]*Strong Foundations: Twelve Principles for Effective General Education Programs* (Washington, DC: Association of American Colleges, 1994, pp. ii–iii).

parts such as history or biology. We find that as many as two-thirds of college graduates work in areas unrelated to their majors. General education provides students with adaptive skills for an uncertain future.

The requirement of general education courses allows students to build a base of general knowledge even before they decide on a major. But here's where you may need to be careful in your choices of classes. Although there are usually many choices in an area of general studies, your major may require a particular class. By seeing an advisor, you can avoid taking extra courses.

What follows is a copy of a poster loaded with useful things you can learn from your advisor. Students sometimes avoid seeing their advisor when, in fact, an advisor's services may be one of the biggest bargains included in your tuition. Study "All I Ever Needed to Know I Learned from My Advisor." Circle at least four things you might ask your advisor about.

All I Ever Needed to Know I Learned from My Advisor

What classes to take this semester, and next semester, and the next semester, and . . . • *Why I can't take 40 hours if I can work 40 hours* • **That I should study a minimum of two hours outside class for every hour in class** • How many credits I need to graduate • *Information about graduate schools* • **How to get an overload** • Why I must take general studies classes that have nothing to do with my major • *"Mr. Staff" isn't the hardest-working instructor on campus* • **How to withdraw from a class** • An advisor writes a good recommendation letter • *How to change my major* • **What minors might be good for me** • Scholarships offered by my department • *Why I shouldn't take all my classes in a row* • **When and where to file my upper-division and intent-to-graduate forms** • What employers in my field are looking for • *What campus organizations would benefit me* • **Career information** • My advisor cares

—Laurie B. Witherow and Ginger A. Corely

A second resource you should have is your institution's **student handbook.** Handbooks usually list specific student resources and student organizations, in addition to rules and regulations. Many colleges and universities have the handbook online or incorporated into the college plan book or agenda.

Exercise 1.2

Using Your Student Handbook

Consult your student handbook and find the following information (be sure to insert page numbers so you can find this again):

Where do you get a parking permit?

_____

_____

Where can you replace a lost ID?

_____

_____

Name two student organizations you might be interested in joining.

1. _____

2. _____

Where can you go for career counseling?

_____

_____

Name three other things in the handbook, and explain a situation for each that might arise where you would need to know this information.

1. _____

2. _____

3. _____

A third resource that you should keep is the current **schedule** or **registration book**. Some colleges have a printed version of the schedule book, others have a website or both. The schedule book will have the class schedule for that **semester** or **term,** payment instructions, important dates for that semester such as drop-and-add dates, and the **final exam schedule**. Don't think that because you have registered, you are finished with this book. Like the catalog, the schedule book contains information that you are not likely to find elsewhere. Read it carefully, and save it for future reference. Because changes in classes or instructors may be made after the schedule is printed, you should double-check offerings online whenever possible.

There are some basic strategies you should follow when you register for a new semester. When choosing classes:

- Consider your responsibilities outside college that may put constraints on your choice of classes. (List things you should consider.)
- Given these constraints, what is a reasonable course load for you? Will this make a difference in when you can take classes?
- Carefully study your options. Read the catalog to see what your logical choices are both in general education and in requirements for your major. (List the options you have.)
- Taking the right mix of classes is also important. You don't want all courses that require a great deal of reading. If math is difficult for you, you don't want all math-related courses. What classes are you considering for next semester? Is there a mix of types of classes and time required for each course?
- If possible, talk to other students who have taken the classes you are considering. Many students say this is the best way to get a feel for

what the classes will be like. Remember, however, your learning style preferences and work ethic may be different from the students you ask.

- Seek the opinion of experts. Consult with your advisor. Your time and money are too valuable to just take the advice of another student or to guess. (Who is your advisor?) What are some questions you should ask? If you are in doubt about what is involved in a course you are considering, talk with the professor.
- The time classes are offered may be important if you are working or have other responsibilities.

Exercise 1.3

Using Your Schedule Book

Consult your schedule book for the following (be sure to insert page numbers so you can find them again):

How much did this class cost to take?

_____

_____

When is the final exam for this class?

_____

_____

What are some important things you should consider when choosing classes?

_____

_____

How will you get your grades at the end of the semester?

_____

The fourth resource to keep handy at all times throughout the semester is the **syllabus** for each class. The syllabus gives you a picture of what will be expected of you during the semester. The syllabus contains the rules and policies for that particular class. Not all classes will have the same **grading scale**, **absence policy**, or **make-up policy**. In addition, a syllabus will contain overall course requirements and perhaps class-by-class assignments. The syllabus should contain your instructor's office hours and telephone number. Students forget most of what goes on the first day of class, so it's important to take notes and read your syllabus carefully, both to refresh your memory and to understand policies that perhaps weren't discussed. The syllabus is your contract with your professor. It is a good idea to go through the syllabus of each class and mark assignments and tests. You may also want to list them in your calendar, your plan book, agenda, or mobile devices.

Exercise 1.4

Using Your Syllabus

Consult the syllabus for this class to determine the following:

What is the absence policy?

_____

_____

How is your grade determined?

_____

_____

Is late homework accepted? Is there a penalty for late work? Can a missed test be made up?

_____

_____

What are your instructor's name, telephone number, and office hours?

_____

Student Services

Are you missing out on some valuable resources just because you don't know they exist? Although most colleges try to keep the campus community aware of what they offer, it is difficult to keep up with all options. Take the Virtual Field Trip to identify some of those resources.

VIRTUAL FIELD TRIP

Your College Homepage

This is the first of many Virtual Field Trips you will take during this course. To access this material, you will need to login to the College Success CourseMate for your textbook with your access key at www.cengagebrain.com. If your book was not packaged with a passkey, you will have the opportunity to purchase access online. Once you login you will find all of the Virtual Field Trips from *Practicing College Learning Strategies*, Sixth Edition. Your destination and itinerary is just a click away. Bookmark or add this site to your Favorites for easy access.

Some Frequently Asked Questions (FAQs) by First-Year College Students or Transfers

The Student Affairs Office on many campuses offers "one-stop shopping," a place where you can find the answers to most of the questions below. You might also search your college homepage or ask other students, your advisor, or your professors for information.

I don't own a computer. Where can I use one?

Can I buy or rent one at a student rate?

Are there workshops or classes I can take to become more computer literate?

I don't have any financial aid. Where can I go to see if I qualify?

What if I get sick? What kinds of health services are available?

I am having trouble with my math, chemistry, and history. Are there tutoring services available?

Is there affordable child care available on or near campus?

I think I may have a learning disability. Is there a place I can get help?

My professor suggested group study. Are there group study areas available?

I am having nonacademic problems. Is there help available on campus?

I need a part-time job. Where can I find out what kind are available?

Is tutoring available on campus?

My professor says the more involved I get on campus, the more sense of belonging I will have. She says that this will contribute to my success as a student. What clubs or activities are available?

Where can I cash a check or use an ATM?

Where can I get photocopies made?

Is there public transportation available?

What is there to do on the weekends?

Higher Education

You have already discovered that there is a great deal of difference in the demands made on you as a high school student or an employee and the demands made on you as a college student. Stop and make a list of the differences you have found that affect you. Then examine and compare against what other students have said.

 Critical Thinking About Higher Education

Following is a list of differences students have noted both between higher education and high school and between higher education and work. Choose at least four of these and comment on how you have learned to handle them. Be specific. If you have not been able to handle these differences, set specific goals for improvement.

1. There is more reading to do.
2. The campus is larger. It's hard to know what's available and who to see.
3. College classes are larger, and classmates are more diverse.

4. I have less free time in college.

5. I have more responsibilities in college.

6. College seems more impersonal.

7. I have more financial pressures in college.

8. College professors give fewer tests and are less tolerant of excuses.

9. There are so many courses offered at the college that I don't know what to take or when to take them.

10. Most classes at the college last for only one term (semester or quarter).

What difference *not* noted in the list has been most difficult for you?

BRAIN BYTE

In *How People Learn*, John Bransford says that the goal of education today should be "helping students develop the intellectual tools and learning strategies needed to acquire the knowledge that allows people to think productively about history, science and technology, social phenomena, mathematics and the arts." He suggests that fundamental understanding about all subjects, including how to ask questions about many subject areas, is a major factor in understanding the principles of learning that people need to develop in order to become lifelong learners.

VIRTUAL FIELD TRIP

College Life

 Visit the College Success CourseMate at www.cengagebrain.com.

Your Responsibilities?

You can't just attend college and expect to be successful. Less than 26 percent of Americans over the age of 25 have earned a college degree. It's not easy. There are certain expectations and responsibilities that go hand in hand with higher education.

You may have already noticed that your idea of learning and your professor's idea of learning are not always the same. Recognizing the difference and adjusting to it may be one of the most difficult but most important transitions you make as a first-year student. As you begin your drive toward success as a college student, here is the basic model for learning.

Modeling the Learning Process: Your Map for Learning How to Learn

In his book *The Art of Changing the Brain*, Dr. James Zull reminds us that first and foremost, learning causes a physical change in the brain and that this change takes time. Dr. Zull says that there are four essentials of learning[2]:

Gathering. New information enters the brain through the senses. We hear, read, see, or interact with new information. *(Some of us would like to think that listening to a lecture or reading an assignment is enough. It's not.)*

[2]James Zull, *The Art of Changing the Brain* (Sterling, VA: Stylus Publishing, 2002). Reprinted by permission of Dr. James Zull.

Analyzing. If we are to use this information in the future, we must understand it and look for relevance and meaning. *(Now, if I understand it, can I stop? Not if you are to own the information.)*

Creating New Ideas. When we as learners convert comprehension into ideas, hypotheses, plans, and actions, we take control of the information. We have created a meaningful neural network and are free to test our own knowledge.

Acting. The testing of the knowledge requires action for the learning cycle to be complete. Writing, speaking, drawing, or other action will identify a strategy that works for us and provides a way that we can test the newly learned information.

We are used to being *receivers* of knowledge, gathering new information and trying to make meaning of it. Learning occurs when we take that knowledge and become *producers* of new knowledge. In the following chapters, as you learn how to be a more successful student, watch for the process of how you take ownership of the knowledge content. In each chapter, we will follow this cycle; and at the end of each chapter, we will identify what we have done so that you will be well on your way to understanding what your professors mean by *learning*.

With the learning model in mind, let's look at what professors say they wish their students understood about learning in college.

- I think the biggest adjustment first-year students have to make is understanding and taking responsibility for the amount and quality of work it takes to be successful. Professors are there to lead the class, but you must make the effort to learn.
- Most learning actually takes place outside of the classroom when you are analyzing, creating, and acting on information you gathered in class.
- The connections in your brain are like no one else's. You must take it upon yourself to do whatever it takes (required or not) to learn the material.
- It may seem like an obvious statement, but the work you do will result in the grade you get.
- When you miss a class, whether you are sick; have a family emergency, a court date, a doctor's appointment, or a sick child; are called in to work; or have transportation failure; you are still responsible for what went on in class. Usually turning in a homework assignment is not enough. You should have a partner in each class you can depend on to help you re-create what you missed.
- You are expected to read your email daily.
- You are expected to ask questions if you don't understand something and actively participate in class.

Your professors are human, so they are always forming opinions. You need to be aware that the impression you make can have an effect on your grade. Even the way you sit and where you sit communicate something to your professor. The quality of your work is also important.

Your assignments and the way you turn them in tell the instructor a great deal about you, how much you care about the course and how serious you are about being successful in college. Whatever the assignment is, you should make an effort to complete it on time and fully. The more information you can give on an assignment, the higher your professor's opinion of you as a student will be. Getting by is not good enough in college. Not understanding is never an excuse in college, nor is not having enough time.

Try to get to know the professor personally; that way, when you do have a question or an emergency, you are able to relate better. Most of your professors have responsibilities other than teaching your class. If you wish to get extra help or get clarification on an assignment, you should probably make an appointment during office hours. The professor's office hours are usually included in the syllabus. Check with each professor to see what his or her policy for student appointments is. If you just drop by, you may be disappointed to find another student has scheduled an appointment.

Student Power

You hold more power in the classroom than you may realize. Ask any professor and they will tell you that the students in the class significantly affect the delivery of information. By coming prepared, sitting up front, paying attention, taking notes, making eye contact, nodding when you agree or understand, asking questions when you are confused, and actively participating in class activities, you actually are able to affect the professor's enthusiasm and approach to the class. Think about classes that you are taking now. The best professors have the best students. I can't be an exciting professor without your cooperation.

Some Strategies for Success

At the end of each semester, I ask students what they wish they had known at the beginning of their first semester that would have made the journey easier. Below is a list of general survival tips that former students say you should know.

General Survival Tips to Make Your Transition Smoother

If you haven't already registered, try not to schedule back-to-back classes. You'll wear yourself out, besides missing the best times to study—right before and right after class.

1. Begin the first day of class. Know what's expected of you.

Take notes on the first day even if it's routine stuff you think you already know.

2. Take notes in class. Don't depend on your memory.

3. Read directions carefully before you begin an assignment. Don't assume you know what to do.

4. Establish a routine time to study for each class. For every hour you spend in class, you will probably need to study two hours outside class. Study for each subject at the same time and in the same place if possible. Studying includes more than just doing your homework. You will need to go over your notes from class—questioning, editing, and making sure you understand them. Study your syllabus daily to see where you are going and where you have been. Be sure to do reading assignments. (Don't put them off just because there's no written assignment.) Read ahead whenever possible. Prepare for each class as if there will be a pop quiz that day.

5. Establish a place to study. Your place should have a desk, a comfortable chair, good lighting, all the supplies you need, and so on; and of course, it should be as free of distractions as possible. It should not be a place where you routinely do other things. It should be your study place.

6. Do as much of your studying in the daytime as you can. What takes you an hour to do during the day may take you an hour and a half at night. If possible, avoid long blocks of time for studying. Spread out several short study sessions during the day

7. Although it may seem obvious, your grades, your preparation for class, and class attendance are directly related to your success as a student. Once you miss a day or an assignment, it is very difficult to ever get caught up.

8. Keep a list of what is due in each class, and try to get as much done ahead of time as you can. You will have major assignments and tests due on the same day.

9. Make use of study resources on campus. Find out about and use labs, tutors, videos, computer programs, and alternative texts. Sign up for an orientation session in the campus library and computer lab. Get to know your professors and advisors. Ask questions. "I didn't know" or "I didn't understand" is never a good excuse. Get involved in school activities in general. And become a part of some group, so that when the unexpected happens (and it will), you have support.

10. Find at least one or two students in each class to study with. Research shows that students who study with someone routinely make better grades. You will probably find yourself more motivated if you know someone else cares about what you are doing in the class. Teaching a concept or new idea to someone else is a sure way for you to understand it. However, because studying in a group or with a partner can sometimes become too social, it is important to stay focused.

11. Study the hardest subject first. Work on your hardest subjects when you are fresh. Putting them off until you're tired compounds their difficulty.

12. Be good to yourself. Studying on four hours of sleep and an empty stomach or a junk-food diet is a waste of time. Avoid food and drink containing caffeine just before or just after studying.

BRAIN BYTE

Dr. Judith Wurtman of M.I.T. says that proper nutrition can boost thinking and learning. The brain's most basic need is oxygen, but ingredients found in protein are critical to the brain. For mental alertness, three or four ounces of protein-rich foods should be a regular part of your diet.

Notes That Save Time

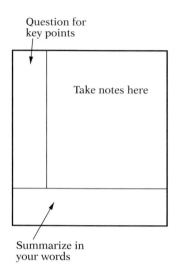

QUESTION IN THE
MARGIN SYSTEM

Reading That Saves Time

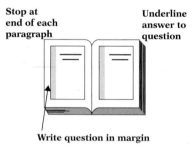

Tips for Taking Notes and Reading Textbooks

- It's the first day of class. You need to know that short-term memory can hold only five to seven bits of information at a time. This means that you can understand everything said in class, but will remember very little if you don't take notes. You know you need to take notes, but you're not sure how to record the important information. Examine the illustration titled "Notes That Save Time." The **Question in the Margin system** is a great way to take notes and will be explained in detail in Chapter 6 of this book; meanwhile, know that your notes will be more useful if you set your paper up as in the illustration. The left margin should be about two and a half inches wide.
- Take your notes on the wide right-hand side.
- Don't write in full sentences. Write only the few words you need to help you remember what was said in class. Use the same techniques you use when you text-message.
- Use the left margin to identify what each section of notes is about by writing a question or label in the margin as soon as you can after class.
- Use the bottoms of pages for reminders such as assignments you need to check.

Begin the semester taking notes like this, and when you get to the Question in the Margin system in a few weeks, you will be well on your way to learning how to process important information from lectures into your long-term memory.

Yes, I know that you already have reading assignments, too. You probably remember reading entire chapters and understanding the material as you read it; however, when you finished, you had no idea what you read. Again, the reason is probably that short-term memory holds only five to seven bits of information. This is the amount of information in a well-written paragraph. You read and understand one paragraph. When you begin the next paragraph, short-term memory dumps that information to make room for new information. Begin using the same system that you used for your class notes. Chapter 7 will explain in more detail how to get the most from this system. Meanwhile, as you finish each paragraph, write a question in the left margin that identifies the main ideas and underline the answer in the paragraph before you go to the next paragraph. You will get more out of the assignment if you preview it first. Study the title, headings, bold print, summary, charts, graphs, and tables before you begin reading. Again, *keep up to date with your reading.*

Exercise 1.5

Evaluating Your Classroom Savvy

You have been on the job several class periods by now. Just as when on the job or on the road, you need to meet certain expectations if you are to be successful. At the beginning of your journey, you should be aware of what is expected of you as a college student. How well are you doing? In the following list, put a plus (+) sign beside the behaviors that you already do well and a minus (–) sign beside the ones you need to improve. As you evaluate the behaviors you exhibit, analyze *why* each behavior is important.

_____ **1.** Attend every class.

_____ **2.** Come to class prepared.

_____ **3.** Be alert and attentive in class.

_____ **4.** Participate in class discussions.

_____ **5.** Show an interest in the subject.

_____ **6.** Ask questions when you don't fully understand.

_____ **7.** Seek outside sources if you need clarification.

_____ **8.** Take advantage of all labs, study sessions, and outside help.

_____ **9.** Set up meetings with your professors to discuss your progress.

_____ **10.** Go the extra mile with all papers and assignments.

_____ **11.** Always be on time for class.

_____ **12.** Take notes.

_____ **13.** When you must miss a class, make sure you find out exactly what you missed, make up the work, and come prepared for the next class.

_____ **14.** Comment on lecture material.

_____ **15.** Get to know your professors.

_____ **16.** Set goals and objectives for your classes.

_____ **17.** Evaluate yourself.

_____ **18.** Be supportive of your classmates.

_____ **19.** Have a positive attitude toward the professor and the class.

Exercise 1.6

Nonsavvy Behavior

Now let's have a little fun. Your task is to come up with a list of *nonsavvy* behaviors you have noticed in the classroom. See if you can list 10 nonsavvy things that you have seen happen this semester. You may also want to ask your professors to add to your list. Let me start you off with some obvious ones.

1. Coming in late for class

2. Copying homework or cheating on a test or other assignments

3. Leaving cell phone on or texting during class.

4. dress _____

5. _____

6. _____

7. _____

8. _____

9. _____

10. _____

Your Grade Point Average

Your college requires you to have a certain number of credit hours in certain areas in order to graduate. Each course you take is assigned the appropriate number of credit hours. Your college or university also requires that you maintain a certain grade point average (GPA) to stay in school or to qualify for certain programs. Thus, it is important that you know how to calculate your grade point average. The following chart shows how to perform this calculation using a four-point system. Check your college catalog to see by which system your grades are calculated. If a plus or minus system is used, your catalog will explain how to use it to calculate your GPA.

How to Calculate Your GPA

The following is an explanation of how to calculate a GPA. You may want to use the chart to help you calculate the examples on the following pages.

1. List each graded course.
2. Enter the letter grade received.
3. Enter the grade point value (A = 4, B = 3, C = 2, D = 1, F = 0).
4. Enter course credit hours.
5. Multiply line items from column 3 by line items in column 4, and put the product in column 5.
6. Add column 4 to get total credit hours.
7. Add column 5 to get total quality points.
8. Divide the quality points by the number of credit hours to get your grade point average.

$$\frac{quality\ points}{credit\ hours} = GPA$$

Consult your college catalog to find out how your university figures grade point averages.

1	2	3	4	5
Name of Course	**Letter Grade**	**Letter Grade Value**	**Credit Hours for Course**	**Quality Points**
			×	=
			×	=
			×	=
			×	=
			×	=
			×	=
		Total		

VIRTUAL FIELD TRIP

Check Your GPA

Visit the College Success CourseMate at www.cengagebrain.com.

Exercise 1.7

Grade Point Average Practice

Calculate John's grade point averages for the fall and spring terms. Carry the averages to hundredths; do not round.

Grade point average for spring term: _____

   Now calculate what John's *cumulative* (fall plus spring) grade point average is. The formula is the same:

$$\frac{total\ quality\ points}{total\ credit\ hours}$$

Cumulative grade point average: _____

Fall Term Course	Hours Credit	Grade
Math 1410	3	C
Hper 1070	1	A
Math 1700	3	B
Spee 2200	3	B
UVIV 1010	3	B
Psyc 1110	3	D

Grade point average for fall term: _____

Spring Term Course	Hours Credit	Grade
Art 1010	3	A
Math 1000	3	B
Biog 1010	4	D
ROTC	1	C
Eng 1010	3	C

Grade point average for spring term: _____

Now calculate what John's *cumulative* (fall plus spring) grade point average is. The formula is the same:

$$\frac{total\ quality\ points}{total\ credit\ hours}$$

Cumulative grade point average: _____

Add the following courses for the summer term, and compute John's cumulative GPA—his average for all three terms, not just his summer GPA.

Course	Hours Credit	Grade
Phy sci 2000	3	B
Eng 1120	3	C

Cumulative grade point average: _____

E-mail Etiquette

Because the first impression you make on your professors may be by e-mail and because we are in the habit of being very casual with our e-mails, it is important that you are careful to follow proper e-mail etiquette. Remember that your professor is not one of your casual friends; show proper respect in the salutation and in the body of your e-mail. Here are some minimum guidelines:

1. **Use the Subject line to summarize** the text of your message. With so much spam (junk e-mail), your message will likely be deleted without being read if you don't include a subject.

2. **Don't write anything you wouldn't say in public.** Anyone can easily forward your message, even accidentally. This could leave you in an embarrassing position if you divulge personal or confidential information. If you don't want to share something you write, consider using the telephone.

3. **Use a spell checker before you send.** This is an option on most e-mail programs. E-mail, like conversation, tends to be sloppier than communication on paper. That's OK; but even with e-mail, you don't want to appear excessively careless. *Read* the e-mail before you send it.

4. **Identify yourself.** The message contains your e-mail address (in the header); but many times the header the system uses puts only the e-mail address, and the recipient will not know who the message is from unless you include your name in your e-mail. If you are sending it to your instructor, it's a good idea to identify the class you are in as well. Be sure to address your professor as a professional.

5. **Keep your message short and focused.**

6. **Don't overuse Upper Case.** This is viewed as SHOUTING.

7. **Check your e-mail at least once a day.** Answer pertinent e-mails as soon as possible.

8. **Delete spam.** Even with filters, you will get an excessive amount of junk e-mail. You don't have to open or read it. You can check messages you want to delete and delete without reading.

9. **Don't overuse Reply All.** Use Reply All if you really need your message to be seen by each person who received the original message.

10. **Don't forward chain letters, jokes, and so on.**

Note the differences in the two e-mails below. Why would you want your e-mail to resemble the first one?

From: jones3st@mtsu.edu
To: Chopper@mtsu.edu
Subject: Question about homework assignment page 17

Dr. Hopper,
My name is Sam Jones. I am a student in your Student Success 1010 class, Section 11. I am confused about the College Life Virtual Field Trip assignment on page 17. Could I meet with you during your office hours today or tomorrow? I could come before 10 am on either day if you are available.

Thanks,
Sam Jones

From: jones3st@mtsu.edu
To: Chopper@mtsu.edu
Subject:

Hey,
Don't know wht 2 do with homework. where's ur office?

Tips for Online Courses

Familiarize yourself with the course design. Study the syllabus. Make sure you understand not only what is required but also when it is required and how to complete each requirement.

1. **Read the entire course syllabus.** The distance learning course syllabus contains all of the information you need to progress through a distance learning course. This includes information about the course description, objectives, and requirements; course meetings, assignments, and testing; media and technology used; a course calendar or assignment schedule; and support contact information.

2. **Be realistic.** You will not have to keep a class attendance schedule, but you will have to do regular academic work. Remember you should be spending at least three study hours each week for every credit hour you are taking. So if there is insufficient time in your personal schedule to do the work of the course, you will be frustrated.

3. **Set interim goals and deadlines for yourself, and stick to them.** Keep a calendar showing the number of weeks in the semester and mark it off with the amount of work you need to do each week. Mark in the days when you expect to take tests, submit projects, or talk with the instructor. Don't fall behind in your work! Keep reminding yourself that you will always have more to do near the end of a course than you do at the beginning.

4. **Organize your goals in a study schedule.** Identify study times when you are fresh and attentive, and stick to those times every week. Think of the study times as reserved times. If you miss too many study times, revise your schedule.

5. **Avoid interruptions.** Avoid all interruptions and distractions while you are viewing a video program, listening to music, reading the textbook, working on the computer, or studying. Turn your cell phone off.

6. **Know where to study.** Find a place that is free from distractions. You might consider your workplace—before or after hours and on your lunch hour—a public library, or a separate room in your home.

7. **Stay in touch with your instructor.** Contact your instructor regularly, especially when you have questions about course content materials. Instructors are usually available by telephone or e-mail, or you may make an appointment for an on-campus meeting.

8. **Prepare for assignments and tests.** In distance learning, course assignments could involve the use of different media: print, videos, audios, and the Internet. Remember, you are not just watching or listening. You are learning from the information on those various media. Take notes. In using your study guide or textbook or from videos or audiotapes or Internet course assignments, imagine questions that might be on a test.

The BREATHE System: A Tool to Help You Focus

Let's conclude this chapter with one last tool you may find helpful when dealing with the stress of the first few weeks of college.

Dr. Ralph Hillman has developed a technique he calls the BREATHE System, designed to help classroom teachers train their students to reduce anger, control potential violence, and raise test scores. The program has some benefits for college students as well. The BREATHE System is a way to deal with low self-esteem, test anxiety, feelings of being overwhelmed, anger, and stress. Like much of what you will learn in this text, the system is relatively simple, but requires discipline. It is probably not something you would automatically think of as a learning strategy; however, you will find that it promotes concentration and clear thinking, as well as routinely relieving stress. The BREATHE System involves knowing and consciously forming the habit of using what Dr. Hillman calls the Big 3.[3]

The Big 3: Posture, Neck and Shoulder Muscles, and Breath Support

1. **Straighten Your Posture.** Good posture allows the organs of your body to operate efficiently and has a positive mental effect on your self-esteem. Moreover, good posture makes you look confident and competent, as well as supplying your brain with a better supply of oxygen. The six essential components of good posture are listed below:

   A. **Unlock your knees** while standing; if you "snap," or force, the knees back, making your legs rigid, blood flow to your brain is diminished, and the natural curves in your spine are exaggerated.

   B. **Level your pelvis** so that the gentle arch of your lower spine is encouraged. If the pelvis is pulled too far back, the arch is exaggerated, and too much tension is placed on the muscles necessary for efficient breathing.

   C. **Tuck your tummy.** Make a conscious effort to pull your belly button back toward your spine. Leveling your pelvis and elevating your rib cage will make this process easier. Most of us want tight abs, but we are not willing to maintain the constant postural pressure on those muscles to allow them to be in position all the time.

   D. **Elevate your rib cage.** Keeping your ribs slightly elevated frees the thoracic cavity (rib cage) to move freely during inhalation and exhalation.

   E. **Push your shoulders back and down.** If the previous four steps are in place, positioning the shoulders is a lot easier. If you are having trouble getting a "feel" for where the shoulders should be, try this: Put your back up against a wall. For most of us, our buttocks hit the wall first, then the shoulders, and finally the head. Put your hands up at shoulder level with the backs of your hands against the wall or as close to the wall as you can get them. Notice the pull in the muscles of your upper chest. As you are standing against the wall, with your hands by your sides, your thumbs should fall easily along the seams in your slacks or trousers. As your shoulders roll forward, your hands will hang in front of your body and not along the sides.

[3]From *Delivering Dynamic Presentations: Using Your Voice and Body for Impact* by Ralph E. Hillman (Boston: Allyn and Bacon, 1999). Copyright © 1999. Reprinted by permission of the author.

F. **Hold your head up** so that there is a straight line from the bottom of your ear to the top of your shoulder, to the top of your hip, and to the center of your foot. Keep your head level, eyes forward. If your body shape is deep through the thoracic cavity, putting your head against the wall may be too far back for you. The goal here is to have your body line up, whether standing or sitting. If the angle of the back of your chair is too far back, then don't lean all the way back. Push your lower back against it, then sit erect. Use good posture as your home position. Use it often, be consistent, and soon it will become your habit.

2. **Relax Your Neck and Shoulder Muscles.** The second part of the Big 3 is to relax your neck and shoulder muscles, shoulders back and down. Most of us are unaware that these muscles are inappropriately tensed much of the time. So relaxing these tensed muscles may be as easy as realizing they are tense. By checking with a mirror, placing your hands on your neck, or using a buddy to check for your visible tension, you can learn to feel when those muscles are tight and tense. Like the home position with posture, this relaxation position should be practiced until it becomes a habit. Once good posture is achieved and awareness of the start of any tension is maintained, we are ready to work on breathing.

3. **Breathe** by taking cleansing breaths. The third part of the Big 3 is **breath support.** For proper breath support, you need to breathe using the muscles of your diaphragm, which "attach at the base of the rib cage and hump up into the chest cavity." Dr. Hillman describes breathing as most efficient when the muscle activity and movement are around the torso, between the navel and the base of the sternum. The ribs should rise slightly and move sideways. You should keep the tummy firm from the navel down, expanding the rib cage sideways.

    Dr. Hillman reminds us "to use the upper abdominal muscles without raising the shoulders or puffing out the lower abdominal cavity (our lungs are not down there)." To obtain the most value from diaphragmatic breathing, use a deep, cleansing breath: keep your posture erect and neck and shoulders relaxed (steps one and two of the Big 3).

    A. Now, **completely fill your lungs,** allowing the air to enter through your nose, freely and easily expanding the rib cage sideways.

    B. Then, **pursing your lips, completely empty your lungs** by blowing the air out, keeping the exhaled air under pressure by using your diaphragm. To determine that you are getting the full benefit of a cleansing breath, place your hands around your abdominal area at the base of the ribs. You should feel this area moving in and out, and expanding sideways.

    C. **Concentrate on slowing down your inhales and exhales.** Practice by starting with 5-second inhales and 5-second exhales. Progress to 10-second inhales and 10-second exhales. A cleansing breath will make you both more relaxed and alert.

To help form the breathing habit in the classroom, begin class by taking a few minutes to breathe. You will find that the BREATHE System gives you an edge in practicing other learning strategies. For this reason, it will be suggested as a strategy in several chapters. An overview of Dr. Hillman's BREATHE System is presented in Chapter 7 of this text. If you want to know more, read Chapter 7 of his book, *Delivering Dynamic Presentations*. You can also log on to http://thebreathesystem.com for more information.

Assignment Log

Name _____

You may find it helpful to keep up with your daily grade in this study skills class by making a chart like this. Record the quiz or assignment requested to be turned in, along with the due date. Check (✓) whether you turned it in or not. When it is returned, record points earned divided by total points possible for your daily average.

Assignment	Due Date	✓	Points Possible	Points Earned

Make sure you know how the grade for each assignment or test is derived. Check your syllabus to see how your final grade is determined.

Higher Education Vocabulary Words

At the beginning of the chapter, you were asked to list bold print words that might need clarification. List five of these words and define them as they are used on your campus.

Vocabulary Word	Definition
1.	
2.	
3.	
4.	
5.	

SUMMARY

To see if you grasped the major points of the chapter and to make a useful study guide, answer the following questions found in your reading. When you have written your answers, cover them and see if you can say the answer to each question in your own words. If you prefer to type your answers, you will find a Microsoft Word download for each summary on the College Success CourseMate for Practicing College Learning Strategies at www.cengagebrain.com.

We used three analogies at the beginning of this chapter. Explain how each could relate to your college experience.

1. Student must be the driver. _____

2. You have landed in a foreign country. _____

3. You are here to begin a new job. _____

List some skills this course should help you maximize.

_____

_____

_____

List at least three essential resources found in the college catalog.

_____

_____

_____

What are core curriculum or general education courses? Why are they required?

_____

_____

_____

List what you consider as three important reasons for consulting with an academic advisor.

1. _____

2. _____

3. _____

Explain what is found in your institution's student handbook.

_____

_____

_____

What are some important things to consider when choosing classes?

_____

_____

_____

Explain what essentials are found in the schedule book for each semester.

_____

What is a syllabus? Explain why it is important.

_____

_____

Name four student services you will use.

1. _____

2. _____

3. _____

4. _____

Name the four steps of the learning process.

1. _____

2. _____

3. _____

4. _____

List some responsibilities that professors say are necessary for student success.

_____

_____

_____

Describe the power you have as student to make your class better or worse.

_____

_____

After reviewing the general survival tips to make your journey easier, choose the four tips you consider the most important for you.

1. _____

2. _____

3. _____

4. _____

Briefly explain how to take notes using the Question in the Margin system.

_____

_____

Briefly explain how to read your textbook using the Question in the Margin system.

_____

_____

What is a GPA?

_____

Explain how to calculate your GPA.

_____

_____

Examine the list of suggestions for e-mail etiquette. Which three suggestions do you think are most important? Explain why.

1. _____

2. _____

3. _____

_____

_____

Explain how you might use the BREATHE System.

_____

_____

_____

Parallel Parking

We seem to understand concepts and remember them better when we compare them with something familiar. The running analogy in this text is comparing various strategies you may need to develop to be successful in college with strategies you may need when you are the driver on a road trip. At the end of each chapter, you will be asked to think about what we have discussed so far and compare these discoveries with driving ideas. Let's begin by reflecting on your first few days of college life.

Compare the following driving situations to something you experienced the first few days of college.

  The first few days of college were like a **Traffic Jam** because
  The first few days of college were like **Getting Lost in a new city** because
  The first few days of college were like a **Making a U** turn because

Evaluating Learning Outcomes

How successful were you in making it to your destination in this chapter?

Analyze what you learned in this chapter. Put a check beside each task you are now able to do. Now think of strategies that you learned that will help you save time and study more effectively. List them in the appropriate place on the back inside cover.

- ☐ **Use analogies to explain** what adjustments you will need to make to ensure your transition runs smoother.
- ☐ **Explain** what is found in basic resources such as the college catalog, student handbook, schedule book, and student services website.
- ☐ **Describe** the steps of the learning process.
- ☐ **Explain** the responsibilities of a college student, and identify behavior that is not acceptable.
- ☐ **Calculate** a grade point average.
- ☐ **Evaluate** your performance as a student.
- ☐ **Demonstrate** how to e-mail your instructor.
- ☐ **Demonstrate** the BREATHE System.

Listed below are a few additional Virtual Field Trips that may help you navigate campus more smoothly.

Your Student Tip for This Chapter

Use the space below to write a tip you would give to other students about what you have learned in this chapter.

_____

_____

_____

VIRTUAL FIELD TRIP

Campus Safety

College Budget

College Health Issues

Visit the College Success CourseMate at www.cengagebrain.com.

2 Applying the Principles of Time Management

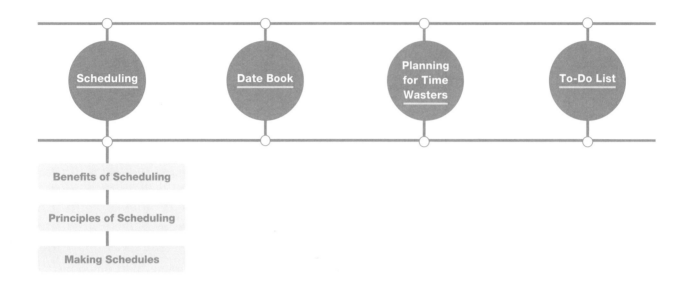

Scheduling
- Benefits of Scheduling
- Principles of Scheduling
- Making Schedules

Date Book

Planning for Time Wasters

To-Do List

The Importance of Managing Your Time

Now that you have started college, do you feel as though you have been caught in rush-hour traffic or in an extreme traffic jam? Do you wonder where you will find the time to get everything done? Don't professors know you have a life? Time management is a critical issue for college students; how smart students are is less important to their success than how well they manage their time. The demands on your time may be entirely different from anything you have previously experienced, and these demands will force you to make difficult decisions. In the margin, list some specific things you are willing to give up or spend less time on now that you are in college. Most professors agree that you can count on at least two hours of outside work for every hour you are in class. Many add that those two hours of work may earn you only a C; some classes require even more time.

How many course hours are you taking? What other responsibilities do you have? What are you willing to give up in order to be a successful college student? There is just so much time. You can't continue to do all the things you used to do and add the job of being a college student without giving up something. Obviously, you will never have more than 24 hours in a day. *You can, however, make extra time in two ways: by doing the same task in less time and by making use of time that you previously wasted.* Throughout this course, you will be seeking ways to

30

Learning Outcomes
for Chapter 2 Applying the Principles of Time Management

Here's your destination for Chapter 2. When you complete Chapter 2, you are expected not only to understand the material presented, but also to be able to:

List ways you can make use of time previously wasted and do the same task in less time.

Create an organized to-do list, and show evidence of using a planner.

Explain the learning process modeled in the chapter.

Demonstrate time-management strategies, including constructing a master schedule for the semester.

Analyze a case study, and construct advice for student having difficulty with time management.

do things not only faster, but also more efficiently. However, few of the learning strategies will work for you if you don't have time to use them. The cardinal rule of time management is to *always carry pocket* work. Always have something that you can do while waiting. Make flash cards of what you need to study for an upcoming test. Make copies of homework assignments, or just be sure to have a book with you. Those wasted ten, fifteen, or twenty minutes add up. And you will discover later that you usually learn more in short sessions than in longer ones. Program your mind; make it a habit to use waiting time. Use you mobile devices for pocket work. There are apps for flashcards. You can download review sheets, summaries, or exercises. What other apps can you find that would be helpful?

BRAIN BYTE

John Medina in his book *Brain Rules* says that "multitasking, when is comes to paying attention is a myth. The brain naturally focuses on concepts sequentially, one at a time." In fact, he says, the brain's "attentional ability is not capable of multitasking."

Exercise 2.1

Beginning Steps in Time Management

Let's examine what making extra time could mean for you. In the blocks below, list some examples of how you personally could make use of wasted time and ways you can do things in less time. Be as specific as possible. The first thing you will probably want to add are examples of wasted time you could fill with doing pocket work. Fill in things you can think of now, and revisit the chart as you find other ways.

Student Tip

"When I put my notes, vocabulary, or review lists on note cards, I punch a hole in the cards and put them on a key ring. That makes them easier to use and add to."

Two Ways to Make More Time

Make use of wasted time			Do things in less time		

 Making It Concrete

Quarterback Peyton Manning uses a good analogy with money and time that's worth thinking about. Imagine, he says, that someone puts $1,400 into your bank account each day with these stipulations:

1. There can be nothing left at the end of the day.
2. You lose what you fail to invest in worthwhile work.

You have, in fact, been presented with this situation coming to college, except that instead of dollars, you have been given 1,440 minutes each day (24 hours times 60 minutes), and those same stipulations apply. You have no minutes left at the end of the day, and those not spent on worthwhile pursuits are pretty much lost.

What will you do?

Why is this a good analogy?

How do you determine what is worthwhile?

Scheduling: The Road Map or GPS for Time Management

Scheduling is like using a GPS to make sure you don't get lost on each leg of your road trip. Because many of you may never have been in a situation that required scheduling, you may be skeptical about the necessity for doing it. But the truth is, college students are too busy to leave things to chance. There may be other times in your life when you can get by without having a schedule of some sort, but the balancing act most college students are forced to perform makes it difficult to survive without a schedule. Things probably won't ever go exactly as planned, but you have a basic plan you can adjust. You may have to take detours or adjust for road conditions, but your schedule is your guide. It will make your journey easier and help you stay on track. In fact, once you get used to being in control of your time, you'll probably never go back to random day-to-day living. For those who are still skeptical about the usefulness of a schedule, what follows is a list of the benefits of scheduling you may not have considered.

Benefits of Scheduling

1. Scheduling helps you avoid one of the great time wasters, procrastination, because it gives you a set time to do each task. It gets you started and helps you avoid putting off doing things that you dislike.

2. Scheduling keeps you up to date and helps you avoid last-minute cramming. By keeping up to date and studying things as you come to them, you will learn much more efficiently.

3. Scheduling things that you need to do creates time to do things that you want to do. As a college student, you must be careful to keep a balance in your life. You need to have time for things other than studying. Scheduling takes away the guilt because it allows you to know you have a time for play, as well as a time for study.

4. Scheduling keeps you in control. You are the creator of your schedule. You set your priorities and times to do things.

5. Having a schedule saves time. Yes, it takes time to devise a schedule, but that time is repaid many times over. Your schedule is a guide, telling you what to do next and assuring you that everything will get done. Studying the same subject at the same time and in the same place programs your mind to concentrate on that subject, and you complete your studying more quickly and more efficiently. That's what learning strategies are all about. You are seeking ways to study faster and better.

Despite these benefits, many students are still reluctant to use scheduling. Remember, however, that the job of being a college student is like no other job you've ever had. Scheduling may be your only means of surviving. At least try scheduling, and choose the aspects of it that help you the most. Let's now examine some basic principles of scheduling so you get the full benefit of this procedure. You may not be able to use all of these this semester. They represent the ideal and will help you save time. If your work schedule leaves you no daylight hours to study or you already have back-to-back classes scheduled, then you may need to add extra study time to the master schedule you will create later in the chapter.

Principles of Scheduling

1. **Make use of daylight hours.** Several studies show that each hour used for study during the day is equal to one and a half hours at night. This means you should try to make use of free hours during the school day. These are the most effective yet most often wasted hours.

2. **Study before a class in which discussion is required or pop quizzes are frequently given.** The material will be fresh in your mind.

3. **Study immediately after lecture classes.** You can enhance your retention and understanding by studying right after class. Use this time to fill in gaps in your notes and to review information you have just learned. When you become more familiar with the Question in the Margin system for taking notes and processing lecture material, you will find that the hours immediately after class are perfect for writing questions in the margin of your notes and that reviewing your notes right after class will save you valuable time as compared to studying later. You will be able to complete your assignments faster and more efficiently because you won't have to refocus your concentration. (Do you see why scheduling back-to-back classes is a mistake?)

4. **Study at the same time every day.** You should have certain hours set aside for study that you treat the same as class. Having the same study time five days a week will soon become a habit and therefore easier to follow. Because the mind is programmed by routine, it will be easier to get started and to concentrate on the task at hand. Studying in the same place also aids concentration. If you have family responsibilities, it's best to schedule your study time while you are on campus if at all possible. There are just too many things at home that could interfere. If you have school-aged children, setting a time for everyone to study is a good idea, but you will accomplish even more if you can schedule study time on campus as if it were a class.

5. **Plan enough time to study.** The rule of thumb that you should study two hours for every hour you are in class is only a guide. Depending on your background or experience or on the difficulty of the class, you may need to allow more. Start out by studying for two hours, but adjust according to your need.

6. **Space your study periods.** A study period of 50 to 90 minutes at a time for each subject is probably most efficient. You should then take a break for 10 to 15 minutes. Studying for longer periods of time often becomes counterproductive.

7. **List activities according to priorities.** By putting first things first, you will get the most important things done on time.

8. **Study during your prime time.** We all have daily cycles of alertness and sluggishness. If your work, classes, and circumstances permit, make use of this knowledge: Schedule your hardest subject at your most alert time, and schedule less demanding tasks during the day when you are less productive than you'd like to be.

9. **Leave unscheduled time for flexibility.** Packing your schedule with too many details will almost ensure its failure. Lack of flexibility is the major reason why students don't follow schedules.

10. **Analyze your use of time.** One cause of getting behind in college is failure to make use of short periods of time. By keeping a time log, you can see where you are currently wasting time. As noted previously, the time between classes and during the school day is the time most often wasted, even though it is the most efficient time to use for studying. Your time log may reveal a waste as simple as not responding to your alarm clock the first time it rings or napping in the afternoon after classes.

Exercise 2.2

Time Log

To use your time most effectively, it is necessary to analyze honestly how you normally use your time. Monitoring your time for a typical week should give you a basis for this analysis.

Carefully fill in the chart on the following page each day to account for what you did each hour. You do not have to stop each hour to fill it in, but you will probably want to do it several times a day. Don't depend on your memory at the end of the day. In addition to noting what you did, indicate your alertness by using a plus sign (+) for "I really feel sharp," a zero (0) for "I am functioning normally," or a minus sign (–) for "I am sluggish."

At the end of five days, you can take what you discover to help make a schedule that reflects the most efficient use of your time.

Exercise 2.3

Time Log Analysis

After keeping the time log (on the next page) for at least five days, answer or do the following:

1. At what times were you really sharp? _____

2. At what times were you the most sluggish? _____

3. What times were virtually wasted? _____

4. Analyze your time log as if you were a stranger. On another sheet of paper, write a short paragraph giving yourself advice.

Time Log

Name _____

Time	Day 1 Day ___ Date ___			Day 2 Day ___ Date ___			Day 3 Day ___ Date ___			Day 4 Day ___ Date ___			Day 5 Day ___ Date ___		
	+	0	−	+	0	−	+	0	−	+	0	−	+	0	−
6–7 A.M.															
7–8 A.M.															
8–9 A.M.															
9–10 A.M.															
10–11 A.M.															
11–noon															
Noon–1 P.M.															
1–2 P.M.															
2–3 P.M.															
3–4 P.M.															
4–5 P.M.															
5–6 P.M.															
6–7 P.M.															
7–8 P.M.															
8–9 P.M.															
9–10 P.M.															
10–11 P.M.															
11–midnight															

Planning a Master Schedule

A master schedule should be made every time you have a major change in your use of time; for example, at the beginning of each semester or when you get a new job. *Use the list below and the master schedule worksheet on the next page to plan for this semester.*

1. **First and foremost, note those activities for which *you have no choice about when to do them:* classes, labs, job, picking up children at school, commuting, weekly meetings.**

2. **Count the number of blank spaces. Yes, include Saturday and Sunday. Write this number at the bottom of the master schedule. These are the hours in which *you can choose what you do.*** Note that the master schedule accounts for only the hours between 7 a.m. and midnight. You can create more choices by getting up earlier or accounting for hours after midnight.

3. **Now, note in those blank spaces the activities that *you need to do but have a choice about when to do them.* Assuming that your first priority is school, begin there. For each three-hour class that you are taking, fill in three spaces with study time for that particular course. Don't just write *Study*. Write *Study math*. Make sure that you use what you already know about scheduling to make wise choices.** Use daylight hours. Study right after a lecture class or right before a recitation-type class. Schedule one hour of study for every hour you are in class. *Treat these times as if they were classes,* as a part of your job! Miss them only for the same reason you might miss class or work. Even if you don't have homework to do, use these times to review or work ahead. But for most classes, you will probably need at least two hours of study time; however, by scheduling one hour and making it routine, you will find your study time more efficient. After several weeks of class, you may need to schedule additional hours of study time, depending on the class. Scheduling one hour that is treated as a class for a specific subject and one hour at another time allows you to be more flexible and still establish routine study times.

4. **Note the other things that you need to do: recreation, shopping, meeting with friends, time with family, laundry, cooking, eating, and so on.**

5. **Any remaining blanks are for use in whatever comes up without guilt!**

Student Tip

" *I took my instructor's advice and treated my set study time as a class. When my boss asked for my schedule, I included those as times I could not work.* "

" *I treated my scheduled study time as class time and scheduled day care for the children at those times. When I picked them up, my studying was done and I could be Mom.* "

BRAIN BYTE

Not managing your time can affect not only what you have time to learn, but also the types of learning that can take place. When a person is relaxed and in control, the parts of the brain that allow creativity, analysis, synthesis, planning, and problem solving are active. However, when a person feels that he or she is not in control, these parts of the brain shut down and the only learning possible is rote memorization or simple learning based on habit or instinct.

Master Schedule Worksheet

	Sun	Mon	Tue	Wed	Thu	Fri	Sat
7–8							
8–9							
9–10							
10–11							
11–12							
12–1							
1–2							
2–3							
3–4							
4–5							
5–6							
6–7							
7–8							
8–9							
9–10							
10–11							
11–12							

Putting Your Master Schedule into Practice

Now you are ready to make a master schedule for the semester. You will probably need to continue to make a weekly and daily checklist also. Study your master schedule. Did you consider the following things in your planning?

_____ Have you used daylight hours for studying? (For most people, these are more effective than nighttime hours.)

_____ Have you scheduled study time immediately before classes in which there is discussion or a possible pop quiz?

_____ Have you scheduled study time immediately after lecture classes?

_____ Have you scheduled either your most difficult class or your most difficult studying when you are the sharpest?

_____ Have you scheduled either relaxation or exercise when you are the most sluggish?

_____ Have you scheduled enough sleep?

_____ Have you scheduled time for eating well-balanced meals?

_____ Have you considered your work schedule?

_____ Have you considered travel time?

_____ Do you have a regularly scheduled study time for each class (even if you have nothing due for the next class)?

What will you do differently when you schedule your classes next semester?

_____

_____

Now it's time to try what you planned to see if it will work. Use your planned master schedule to fill in the time-management log on the following pages. There is a column for what you planned to do and one for what you actually did. Keep the log for a week. Then make adjustments to your master schedule as needed. There is a clean master schedule following the exercise if you need to make adjustments. You may also want to put your revised Master Schedule on any electronic devise you usually have with you and use often such as your laptop, your iPad, or your smart phone. Many researchers say that it takes 21 days for something to become habit. Be sure that you purposefully practice your master schedule for that long. Don't abandon it after only a few days.

Master Schedule Follow-up

Time Management

	Monday		Tuesday		Wednesday		Thursday	
	Planned	Reality	Planned	Reality	Planned	Reality	Planned	Reality
7 A.M.								
8 A.M.								
9 A.M.								
10 A.M.								
11 A.M.								
12 noon								
1 P.M.								
2 P.M.								
3 P.M.								
4 P.M.								
5 P.M.								
6 P.M.								
7 P.M.								
8 P.M.								
9 P.M.								
10 P.M.								
11 P.M.								
12 midnight								

Notes:

Time Management (cont.)

	Friday		Saturday		Sunday	
	Planned	**Reality**	**Planned**	**Reality**	**Planned**	**Reality**
7 A.M.						
8 A.M.						
9 A.M.						
10 A.M.						
11 A.M.						
12 noon						
1 P.M.						
2 P.M.						
3 P.M.						
4 P.M.						
5 P.M.						
6 P.M.						
7 P.M.						
8 P.M.						
9 P.M.						
10 P.M.						
11 P.M.						
12 midnight						

Notes: _____

41

Master Schedule

Now you are ready to make out a master schedule for the semester. You will need to continue to make a weekly and daily checklist also.

Master Schedule

	Sun	Mon	Tue	Wed	Thu	Fri	Sat
7–8							
8–9							
9–10							
10–11							
11–12							
12–1							
1–2							
2–3							
3–4							
4–5							
5–6							
6–7							
7–8							
8–9							
9–10							
10–11							
11–12							

Date Book

Your master schedule is your guide in planning, but you will need at least two other time-management scheduling tools. The first is your date book (also called an appointment book, assignment book, plan book, or agenda). You should keep it with you at all times and write your assignments in it for each class each day. Consult it before you make any commitments of your time. Remember, this is your job. You are the manager of your time. (The manager of any efficiently run business would also schedule appointments.)

Even though you may have a syllabus for each class, you need to keep your assignments for all your classes together in one place so that you can see all that you have to do and set priorities. Early in the semester you should examine the syllabus for each class and record the dates for major tests and assignments. This way, you know if you have two or three major tests or assignments due on the same day and can do some planning. Your date book will help you stay organized. In addition to assignments and appointments, you can keep track of phone numbers, addresses, and other important information all in one place. You will also want to use the calendar or datebook apps for your Blackberry or smart phone to record due dates for assignments and test dates. Most college bookstores will have several types of date books. Choose one that is easy to keep updated. You should not be without your date book any more than you should be without your wallet, watch, or ID card.

To-Do List

The second managing tool is your daily schedule, or to-do list. The easiest way to construct a daily to-do list is, before you go to bed at night or as soon as you get up, make a list on an index card of everything you want to accomplish during the day. That's the easy part! You also want to prioritize the things you need to do. Look over your list and decide which items *absolutely must* be done. These are your first priority. The second order of importance might be those things that *should* be done. The third order might be those things that you *would like to do* but that could be put off. You can also have a category for routine things.

You can use any system you want to label your priorities. Some students color code with highlighters; others use a 1, 2, 3 or A, B, C system to indicate importance. Because you will seldom make your list in order of importance, marking priorities is a must. Develop the habit of making the same type of list each day, and it will become easy and routine. When you have your to-do list organized, it is also a good idea to put it on your cell phone, laptop, or iPad if you have an app for that. I also e-mail myself my to-do list.

Student Tip

❝ My first semester, I was sure I didn't need anything as complicated as a master schedule. I refused to use it. I was also always behind, late with assignments, and in general not very successful. Second semester, I adjusted my master schedule a bit and used it successfully. What a difference! Don't waste a semester. Make yourself stick to a master schedule. ❞

Making Connections

Managing time is not a skill that is limited to college students. Think of one or two people you admire because they are successful in what they do. Choose one person and list what you know about how he or she manages time.

Person ————————————————

Some time-management skills this person uses:

_____

_____

_____

_____

_____

Which of these could you use as a student?

_____

_____

_____

_____

_____

_____

Side Trips, Road Blocks, and Detours

Time Wasters: Plan Your Attack

Because you are so busy as a college student, it is important that you stay in control. This does not mean you can't be flexible, but it does mean you need to have a plan. By analyzing your master schedule and time log, you will get some idea of just how flexible you can be. If you have a job, a family, or other responsibilities, you will have less time with which to be flexible. If something unexpected comes up at a time you already have scheduled, try to trade off hours and plan when you can accomplish your originally scheduled task. You want to be careful not to waste time doing something you really don't want or need to do.

On page 45 is a list of frequent time wasters for college students. There is a difference between allowing time to do these things and having them interfere with things you need to accomplish. Plan how you will avoid such time wasters should they occur. Probably the most frequent time waster is visitors dropping in unexpectedly, especially if you study in your dorm room, apartment, or home. One logical solution is to study elsewhere. Can you think of other solutions?

Afternoon naps are another real hazard for college students. Remember, what takes you an hour to do in the daytime may take you an hour and a half at night. Many students use naps as a form of procrastination. Getting enough sleep at night is one solution.

Exercise 2.7

My Plan for Time Wasters

Study the list in the first column. Give at least two possible plans in the second column to combat each time waster.

Time Waster	Plan A and Plan B What to Do When This Occurs
Drop-in visitors	Plan A
	Plan B
Phone interruptions	Plan A
	Plan B
TV	Plan A
	Plan B
Afternoon naps	Plan A
	Plan B
Family or friends making demands	Plan A
	Plan B
Checking Facebook	Plan A
	Plan B
Your biggest time waster not mentioned	Plan A
	Plan B

You may have discovered something in this exercise that you want to add to your chart in Exercise 2.1 Ways to Save Time.

VIRTUAL FIELD TRIP

Procrastination and Time Management

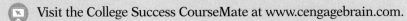

Visit the College Success CourseMate at www.cengagebrain.com.

Critical Thinking About Prioritizing Exercise

Choose *either* John *or* Mary. It is not uncommon to find yourselves in a situation similar to John's or Mary's. Study the things John or Mary needs to do. Prioritize and rank each item in the order you think it should be accomplished. Number the items from 1 to 10. One is the item that should be done first. When you get to class, you may want to compare your rankings with those of your classmates.

John's To-Do List

_____ John's roommate just broke up with his girlfriend—needs comforting.

_____ 500-word English paper due tomorrow afternoon.

_____ Psychology exam tomorrow morning is on the syllabus.

_____ Book report for history due tomorrow. He's read part of the book, but he's not really sure what it's about.

_____ It's his mom's birthday. He promised to go to dinner.

_____ Biology test announced as he left class today.

_____ No clean shirts. He hasn't done laundry in two weeks.

_____ History paper due in two days, but he has tickets to the big basketball game tomorrow and

_____ A date with that someone he's been wanting to date all term.

_____ It's not his day to work, but his boss wants him to come in for a couple of hours (probably means all night).

_____ Party tonight with a live band and free food.

Mary's To-Do List

_7_ 500-word English paper due tomorrow afternoon.

_6_ Psychology exam tomorrow morning is on the syllabus.

_3_ Book report for history due tomorrow. She's read part of the book, but she's not really sure what it's about.

_4_ Son is having trouble with his math homework.

_2_ Tomorrow is gym day, and daughter's gym clothes are dirty.

_10_ Biology test announced as she left class today.

_1_ Out of milk and stuff for school lunches.

_8_ Promised to help desperate friend study for algebra test.

_5_ Daughter has spelling test.

_9_ Message on voice mail to come in for part-time job interview.

1. What is your rationalization for the order you selected?

2. What are some ways John or Mary could have avoided letting so many things pile up?

3. Suggest a plan for managing upcoming commitments and assignments.

Modeling the Learning Process

As we discussed in Chapter 1, learning is more than memorizing facts. You have modeled the learning cycle in this chapter. There were facts about saving time and helping you be more in control of your time, but you went further than gathering facts. You *analyzed* your use of time. You took your personal information and predicted ways for you to save time by creating a master schedule. You then put your plan into action and tried to use your master schedule. For many of you, adjustments were necessary so you started the cycle over again. Your plan for dealing with time wasters also fits this model.

Gathering. You learned the benefits and principles of scheduling, how much time to allow for each class, and ways to save time.

Analyzing. You analyzed the use of your time with a log.

Creating New Ideas. You created a master schedule.

Acting. You followed the master schedule.

If adjustments were necessary, you started the cycle over again and made changes to the master schedule.

SUMMARY

To see if you grasped the major points of the chapter and to make a useful study guide, answer the following questions found in your reading. When you have written your answers, cover them and see if you can say the answer to each question in your own words. If you prefer to type your answers, you will find a Microsoft Word download for each summary on the College Success CourseMate for Practicing College Learning Strategies at **www.cengagebrain.com.**

1. pg30

According to most professors, how much work outside class will be required?

_____

_____

_____

2. pg 30

What are two ways to make extra time?

1. _____

2. _____

3. pg 31

What is the cardinal rule of time management? Give some examples.

_____

_____

_____

4. Explain the significance of the number 1,440 when dealing with time management.

_____

_____

_____

What is your road map or GPS for time management?

_____

_____

_____

What are five benefits of scheduling?

1. _____

2. _____

3. _____

4. _____

5. _____

What are 10 principles of good scheduling?

1. _____

2. _____

3. _____

4. _____

5. _____

6. _____

7. _____

8. _____

9. _____

10. _____

Explain how to create a master schedule.

_____

_____

_____

What are two tools, in addition to your master schedule, that are necessary in managing your time?

1. _____

2. _____

Name your three biggest time wasters and briefly explain your plan to combat each.

1. _____

2. _____

3. _____

Case Study: What's Your Advice?

Philip is a junior at a major university. He is 24 years old, not married, and he lives in an apartment near campus with three other students. He does most of his studying there. This semester he is taking 15 credit hours, and he works 20 hours a week. Philip has flexible work hours, and he chose to work on Monday, Wednesday, and Friday and schedule his classes on Tuesday and Thursday. Although he really wants to do well in school, Philip has struggled to make Cs in his classes. He says he reads extremely slowly and simply doesn't have time to read everything his instructors assign. What advice would you give Philip?

Write your answer in paragraph form. Address it to Philip, and be specific in your advice.

Parallel Parking

We seem to understand concepts and remember them better when we compare them with something familiar. The running analogy in this text is comparing various strategies you may need to develop to be successful in college with strategies you may need when you are the driver on a road trip. At the end of each chapter, you will be asked to think about what we have discussed so far and compare these discoveries with driving ideas.

When you fill in your answers, make sure you complete both sides of the analogy by comparing the driving term with a term for being a successful college student. I have given you one example. There are no correct or incorrect answers. The exercise is to get you critically thinking about things you are learning.

Driving

A driver is in charge of where he is going. He chooses the route. He must keep his eyes on the road, know when to fuel up, and know when to ask for directions. He will likely remember where he has been. As a student, I must be in charge of what classes I take, when I must study, when I need a break, and when I need extra help. I must keep my eyes on why I am in college. It's hard work. I can't just sit in class and listen; I must take notes and ask questions.

Defensive Driving

Driving defensively involves _____

As a student, if I want to be successful, I need to:_____

_____

_____

_____

_____

Being a Passenger

_____

_____

_____

_____

Rush-Hour Traffic

_____

_____

_____

_____

License

_____

_____

_____

_____

An additional one you think of

_____

_____

_____

_____

Evaluating Learning Outcomes

How successful were you in making it to your destination in this chapter?

Analyze what you learned in this chapter. Put a check beside each task you are now able to do. Now think of strategies that you learned that will help you save time and study more effectively. List them in the appropriate place on the back inside cover.

☐ **List** ways you can make use of time previously wasted and do the same task in less time.
☐ **Demonstrate** time-management strategies, including constructing a master schedule for the semester.
☐ **Create** an organized to-do list, and show evidence of using a planner.
☐ **Analyze** a case study, and construct advice for students having difficulty with time management.
☐ **Explain** the learning process modeled in this chapter.

Your Student Tip for This Chapter

Use the space below to write a tip you would give to other students about what you have learned in this chapter.

_____

_____

_____

3 Critical Thinking

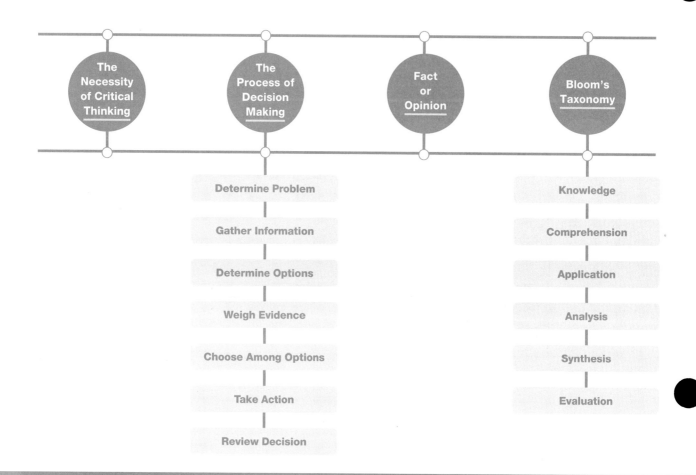

The Necessity of Critical Thinking	The Process of Decision Making	Fact or Opinion	Bloom's Taxonomy
	Determine Problem		Knowledge
	Gather Information		Comprehension
	Determine Options		Application
	Weigh Evidence		Analysis
	Choose Among Options		Synthesis
	Take Action		Evaluation
	Review Decision		

In Chapter 1, you began your adjustment to college. Chapter 2 covered the first steps in managing your time. Your primary job as a college student, as the driver of your vehicle, is to process information. In order to do your job well, you need to understand how your brain processes information. It will be necessary for you to take control by gathering information from lectures and making that information yours. You want to grasp what you read and process it so that you own it.

A good place to begin learning how to do this is with a brief discussion of *critical thinking*. The thinking demanded of college students goes far beyond the memorization of facts. You will meet some concepts of critical thinking here and then encounter them again throughout the text. While you are developing basic skills in taking notes, reading textbooks, and taking tests, you will be simultaneously developing critical-thinking skills that form the core of higher education and educated thinking.

Learning Outcomes
for Chapter 3 Critical Thinking

Here's your destination for Chapter 3. When you complete Chapter 3, you are expected not only to understand the material presented, but also to be able to:

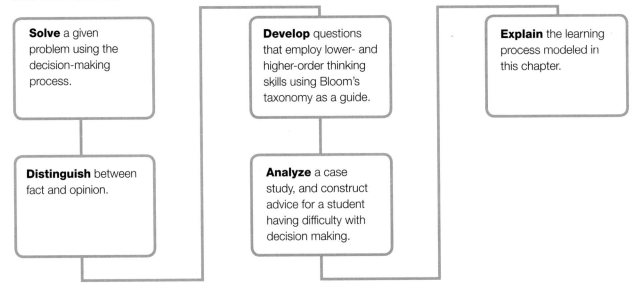

Solve a given problem using the decision-making process.

Develop questions that employ lower- and higher-order thinking skills using Bloom's taxonomy as a guide.

Explain the learning process modeled in this chapter.

Distinguish between fact and opinion.

Analyze a case study, and construct advice for a student having difficulty with decision making.

The Necessity of Critical Thinking

There is a great deal of difference between learning the answer to a question and analyzing the implications of the answer, synthesizing and evaluating what you have learned, and applying what you have learned. Problem solving—critically analyzing a situation for the best solution and creatively finding an answer to the problem—is a skill that involves *thinking*. Thinking is a skill and, like other skills, can be learned and improved with practice. In thinking, the focus is not on the final answer, but on the process of getting the answer and going beyond facts.

In a previous history class you may have learned the dates of the Spanish-American War and the causes of that war. A *thinking* problem might require you to analyze how our country might be different if the war had not occurred. Most of the courses you will take in college involve not just learning facts, but also developing thinking skills. A critical thinker is constantly asking questions, trying to distinguish between fact and opinion. A critical thinker analyzes all sides of an issue to find more in the situation than the obvious. And a critical thinker makes assertions built on sound logic and solid evidence.

It is important to use critical thinking when learning and processing new information, but it is also necessary to use critical thinking in making decisions about when, where, and how to study; managing your time; and setting goals. You will use critical thinking when you take notes in class, read textbooks, and take tests. You will also use critical thinking in determining the validity of an Internet or library source, the best way to complete an assignment, or even how to get along with your professor or classmates. Moreover, you will need to use critical thinking to determine what you believe and what's important to you. And although not a part of this learning strategies text, decisions about partying, drinking, taking drugs, and entering and maintaining relationships are certainly a major factor in your success at college and will benefit from critical thinking.

Students seldom fail because they aren't smart enough; they more often fail because they make poor decisions or fail to seek solutions to problems. The critical-thinking skills you develop will not only make you a better student, but they will also make you a better employee or employer, a better spouse, or a better parent. Critical thinking is a life skill. The important decisions you make in your life will not be based on memorizing the "right answer." Each new situation demands defensive driving: questioning, analyzing, and evaluating. You can use the opportunities this course provides to practice and fine-tune your critical-thinking skills.

The Process of Decision Making

By thinking critically, you will find that your decisions are not made randomly. Rather, they follow a pattern. You will first determine exactly what the problem is. Second, you will gather any information necessary for you to make an informed decision. The third step is to determine what your options are. A major decision seldom has one solution. There's always another way. Fourth, you will weigh the evidence. Ask all the what-ifs. You will then—fifth step—make a choice among your options. The sixth step is to take action. Your action will be based on informed critical thinking. After you have taken action, you will review your decision and examine the consequences. Many times you may begin the process all over when your decision results in a consequence that requires a decision!

Your critical thinking about a decision may look something like this.

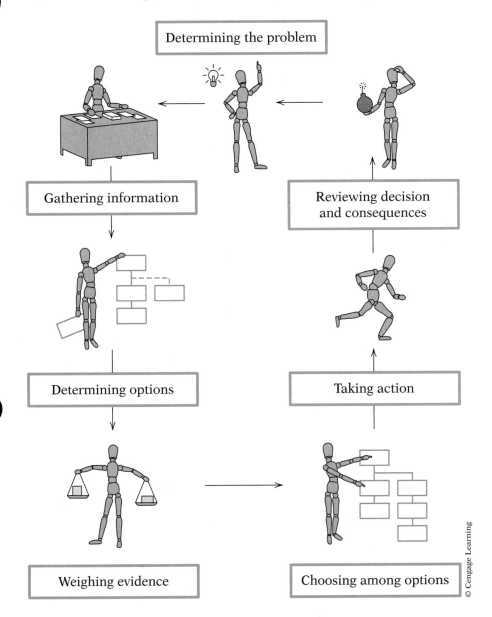

© Cengage Learning

Exercise 3.1

The Decision-Making Process

Walk yourself through the decision-making process by examining Antwuan's situation. His car has become unreliable. He has missed class twice and several appointments in the past two weeks because of various mechanical problems.

Clearly state what you think Antwuan's problem is.

Where can he gather useful information? What types of information does he need to gather?

What options become apparent?

What is some of the evidence he should weigh?

What are some of his options?

What specific action do you advise he take?

What might be the consequences of that action?

So now, what is the problem?

Student Tip

Exercise 3.2

Decisions About Grades

You may not have thought about the grade you make in each class as a decision. However, you can use the decision-making process to choose the grade you want.

You may want to earn an A in this class.

Gather the information. List specific things you must do to earn an A.

What are your options?

What evidence is there that they will earn an A?

What options do you choose?

Set goals for those options and take action.

Exercise 3.3

Thinking About Thinking

1. Describe the process of your thinking in both choosing to come to college and choosing this college over other colleges. You may want to include, among other things: What facts did you gather? What opinions did you weigh? What issues were important to you?

2. What is the difference in trying to make an A in a course and trying to determine a way you might learn and use the content of a course?

3. Ben missed the first day of class because he registered late, and then he missed the next two days because he had the flu. Ben didn't notify the instructor. Explain to Ben what critical thinking skills he should have used and why.

4. Name three specific decisions you will have to make in the next several years that will require the use of critical-thinking skills.

5. Write a short paragraph in which you describe a past situation in which you wish your thinking skills had been better.

BRAIN BYTE

In *Human Brain and Human Learning*, Leslie Hart suggests that if we want to expand our knowledge, we should seek alternative methods, multiple answers, critical thinking, and creative insights. The process is often more important than the end result.

Fact and Opinion

A crucial part of critical thinking is distinguishing between fact and opinion. A fact is something that is true no matter what we think about it. A fact can be verified. Opinions, on the other hand, are personal prejudices. Our opinions should be based on fact and supported by fact, but should not be confused with fact.

Fact	18,000 students attend this university.
Opinion	The campus is too crowded.
Fact	Teenage pregnancies are at an all-time high.
Opinion	Sex education should begin in elementary school.

Exercise 3.4

Fact or Opinion?

Read the following statements. Are they fact or opinion? In the blank to the left mark *F* for fact and *O* for opinion. If the statement is opinion, decide what kinds of facts are needed to support that opinion.

_____ O **1.** Mickey Mantle was the strongest switch hitter in baseball history.

_____ F **2.** During his career, Mantle hit 536 home runs.

_____ O **3.** Grades do not encourage learning.

_____ O **4.** Human life is not valued in a technological society.

_____ F **5.** The average car traveling at 57 miles per hour gets only two-thirds the gas mileage of a car moving at 50 miles per hour.

_____ O **6.** The society in the United States is violent.

_____ F **7.** A giraffe can go without water longer than a camel can.

O _____ F **8.** The attention that the news media gives to criminals contributes to crime.

_____ O **9.** We should drink less cola.

_____ F **10.** Eighteen ounces of an average cola drink contain as much caffeine as a cup of coffee.

_____ O **11.** We should ban smoking in public places.

_____ F **12.** The amount of nicotine the average pack-a-day smoker inhales a week—400 milligrams—would kill a person instantly if it were taken all at once.

_____ O **13.** The need to develop alternative energy sources is critical.

_____ F **14.** If the current rate of inflation continues, a worker making $7 an hour in the year 2000 will make $4,799 an hour in 2090.

_____ O **15.** There is an overemphasis on sports on college campuses.

A critical thinker, when trying to determine whether something is fact or opinion, asks questions. What was the source of information? Was the source of information an authority? Was the information accurate? Can it be substantiated? Where? Is the information current? Look back over the previous 15 statements. Do any statements that you marked as facts need more evidence? Place a question mark beside any that you think should be verified further. Be sure to explain what verification each needs.

Levels of Learning: Bloom's Taxonomy

When discussing critical thinking, learning experts usually categorize levels of thinking. One of the most influential models for such categorizing is *Bloom's taxonomy of higher thinking*.[1] The level, or depth, of your learning will probably depend on several factors. Your interest in learning the material and the urgency of your need to use or master it are two important factors. Bloom asserts that you must master one level before you can move on to the next. You can use Bloom's taxonomy as a road map of sorts to see where you are going with your thinking. We learn best by asking questions. Understanding the levels of Bloom's taxonomy will be helpful in formulating questions to ask in class and in determining what questions might be asked on tests and exams. The first three levels of this system deal with lower-order thinking skills that are essential in laying the foundation for deeper understanding. The last three employ higher-order thinking skills.

1. The first level of learning is **knowledge.** You can remember something without fully understanding it. The knowledge level is demonstrated when you can make a list of something or recognize the correct answer on a multiple-choice test, knowing it as fact. Test questions that ask you to list, define, identify, or name who, when, or where usually require only the knowledge level. Students often fall into the trap of studying for a test at this level and thinking they are prepared, when in fact they will need a higher level of preparation. An example of a knowledge-level question is "Where were the first Olympic games held?"

2. The second level of learning is **comprehension.** You understand the information to the degree that you can explain it in your own words, or you can translate or interpret it. Test questions that ask you to summarize, discuss, or compare are likely to be at the comprehension level. An example of a comprehension-level instruction is "Name and explain the steps necessary for a bill to become law."

3. The third level of learning is **application.** Application means that you can determine some practical use for the information and use it to solve problems. Most of what goes on in a math class is at the application level. You may know a law or understand a formula, but in order to "do your homework," you must apply them. Test instructions might ask you to apply, demonstrate, calculate, or modify. An example of an application-level instruction is "Demonstrate that you know how to take notes using the Question in the Margin system."

The next three levels demand a deeper level of thinking. They are sometimes referred to as *higher-order thinking skills (HOTS)*.

4. The fourth level of learning is **analysis.** When you analyze, you break complex ideas into parts and see how the parts work together. You recognize patterns, organize parts, and recognize hidden

---

[1]B. S. Bloom et al., eds., *Taxonomy of Educational Objectives: The Classification of Educational Goals. Handbook 1: Cognitive Domain* (New York: David McKay Company, 1956).

BRAIN BYTE

D. C. Berliner says the better the quality of question asked, the more the brain is challenged to learn. Performance scores of learners improve when they improve the depth of their questioning.

Lots

meanings. An example of an analysis-level question is "What evidence can you present to support the statement that the Confederate Army was unprepared in the Battle of Shiloh?"

5. The fifth level of learning is **synthesis.** When you synthesize, you make connections with things you already know. You are able to draw conclusions and make predictions. You use old ideas to create new ones, or you relate knowledge from several areas. An example of a synthesis-level question is "What would happen if you combined sulfur and iodine?"

6. The sixth level of learning is **evaluation.** When you evaluate, you judge something's worth. Did the note-taking system work for you in history class, or do you need to make adjustments? This step involves making choices based on reasoned argument, checking, and critiquing. An example of an evaluation-level question is "What were the merits of Hannibal's plan to take Rome?"

In 2001, Anderson and Krathwohl revised Bloom's taxonomy.[2] In the higher-order thinking skills, they list *evaluate* as level 5 and *create* (instead of synthesis) as level 6. For our purposes, learning to ask questions at different levels and preparing for test questions at different levels, the revision is interesting, but the result is really the same. You may want to search the Internet for more about the revised taxonomy and decide which makes more sense for you.

 Making It Concrete

When trying to learn something new, we get a better understanding if we compare it to something we already know. For example, if I play or watch football, I may know the name of a play; that's *knowledge*. If I can explain that play to someone else, I have moved to the *comprehension* level. When I actually run the play in practice or in a game, that's application. If the play isn't successful, I would want to *analyze* it to see why not. The *synthesis* level would be using what I found out in my analysis to determine how I should change the play to make it successful. This would be creating a solution. *Evaluation* would involve determining if it is a good play to run in certain situations or against certain teams.

Now it's your turn to make it concrete. Choose one of the following and explain each level in terms of your selection: (1) making an apple pie, (2) buying a car, (3) planning and taking a vacation, or (4) studying for a test.

Knowledge

Comprehension

[2] L. W. Anderson and D. R. Krathwohl, eds., *A Taxonomy for Learning, Teaching, and Assessing: A Revision of Bloom's Taxonomy of Educational Objectives* (New York: Longman, 2001).

Application

Analysis

Synthesis

Evaluation

Copyright © 2013 Wadsworth, Cengage Learning. All rights reserved.

Exercise 3.5

Levels of Learning

For a quick check of your understanding of levels of learning, list the level of learning that you think each of the following tasks involves: *knowledge, comprehension, application, analysis, synthesis,* or *evaluation:*

_____ Changing a flat tire

_____ Finding the main idea of a paragraph

_____ Explaining a class lecture to a friend who was absent

_____ Summarizing an article

_____ Finding the lowest common denominator for fractions

_____ Finding the correct answer in a multiple-choice question

_____ Creating a webpage

_____ Appraising the damage on your wrecked car

_____ Listing the states and capitals

_____ Making an apple pie

_____ Comparison shopping for the best buy

_____ Writing an essay for English class

_____ Computing your grade point average

Student Tip

❝ I studied four hours for my first history test. I knew all the facts. However, I made an F on the test. When I examined the test questions, most of them required higher-order thinking skills. I hadn't studied with that in mind. Now when I study, I try to predict questions that include analysis, synthesis, and evaluation. ❞

VIRTUAL FIELD TRIP

Bloom's Taxonomy

 Visit the College Success CourseMate.

Exercise 3.6

Asking and Predicting Questions

We learn best by using the material or asking questions. Bloom's taxonomy provides a framework for identifying things to do or asking questions and for predicting test items. Let's have some fun. Assume you are having a test on "Goldilocks and the Three Bears." Remember the story? Goldilocks goes into the bears' house, eats their porridge, sits in their chairs, and sleeps in their beds. Take a minute to tell the story to students in your group to make sure you all heard the same version and to make sure those who haven't heard the story know what happened. Now let's practice using the material to ask questions at each level. I have provided you with one instruction or question from each level. **Your job is not to do the task or answer that question but to think of another task or question at that level.** Before you begin, you may want to take the preceding Virtual Field Trip to find more about Bloom's taxonomy and the types of tasks or questions to use for each level.

Knowledge (recall specific details)

What are some of the things that Goldilocks did in the bears' house?
Your question: _____

Comprehension (understanding what was read)

Why did Goldilocks like the little bear's chair best?
Your question: _____

Application (converting abstract content to concrete situations)

Draw a picture of what the bears' house looked like.
Your question: _____

Analysis (looking for patterns in the story, maybe even comparing the context to a personal experience)

What parts of the story could not have actually happened?
Your question: _____

Synthesis (making a hypothesis from your analysis)

How might the story have been different if Goldilocks had visited the three fish?
Your question: _____

Evaluation (making judgments)

Do you think Goldilocks was good or bad? Why do you think so?
Your question: _____

Follow-up

Now select a section from one of your textbooks that you will probably discuss in class and be tested on. Give an instruction or ask a question at each level.

Look over a returned test, and label the level of each instruction or question.

When you first learn something, you can't be expected to jump to the sixth level. In order to master it, first you have to know it, understand it, and apply it. This is why when you wait until the last minute to study for a test, you can do little more than memorize the information, and then you are often caught short when the answer requires more depth.

You will continue to look at other aspects of critical thinking when you learn about taking notes, reading textbooks, studying for and taking tests, and doing research both in the library and on the Internet.

VIRTUAL FIELD TRIP

Learning More About Asking Questions

Visit the College Success CourseMate.

Modeling the Learning Process

You have modeled the learning cycle in several ways in this chapter. Let's look at a couple of ways you completed the learning cycle.

Gathering. You got information about the steps of the decision-making process and the levels of Bloom's taxonomy.

Analyzing. You analyzed options in the decision you needed to make. You analyzed and found examples for each level of Bloom's taxonomy to make sure you understood it.

Creating New Ideas. You created a plan for making a decision. You predicted test questions at each level of Bloom's taxonomy.

Acting. You followed your plan for solving your problem. You practiced giving instruction and answering questions you predicted and found actual instructions and questions in tests you had taken.

 Making Connections

Did you notice that *gathering* is like the first level of Bloom's taxonomy, knowledge? *Analyzing,* making meaning of the new information, combines comprehension and analysis? *Creating* and *acting* are really a combination of synthesis and evaluation?

SUMMARY

To see if you grasped the major points of the chapter and to make a useful study guide, answer the following questions found in your reading. When you have written your answers, cover them and see if you can say the answer to each question in your own words. If you prefer to type your answers, you will find a Microsoft Word download for each summary on the College Success CourseMate for Practicing College Learning Strategies at **www.cengagebrain.com.**

List three characteristics of a critical thinker.

1. _____

2. _____

3. _____

List the six steps of the decision-making process.

1. _____

2. _____

3. _____

4. _____

5. _____

6. _____

What is the difference between fact and opinion?

_____

_____

What are some important questions you should ask in trying to determine fact or opinion?

_____

_____

List and explain the six levels of Bloom's taxonomy.

1. _____

_____

_____

_____

_____

_____

2. _____

_____

_____

_____

3. _____

4. _____

5. _____

6. _____

Case Study: What's Your Advice?

Nina is taking her first required history course at her university. She did very well in her history courses in high school and therefore was not worried about the first test. As she read each chapter, she made flash cards of dates, people, terms, and places. She even drew a time line so that she knew the sequence of events. She prepared a study plan and studied for several days before the test, including studying the night before. However, when Nina began her test, she found that she didn't know what to do. Instead of asking for dates, people, terms, and places, the test instructions and questions were as follows:

- Compare the ways in which the market revolution affected middle-class white women and slave women.
- Describe the role that railroads played in sectional conflicts between 1850 and 1870.
- Trace the changes in Americans' expectations of government that occurred during the Age of Anxiety, and explain what caused those changes.
- Compare the responses of Eisenhower, Kennedy, and Johnson to the civil rights movement.
- In your opinion, what was the true birthday of the United States: 1776, 1789, or 1812? Justify your answer.

What advice can you give to Nina to prepare for her next test?

Parallel Parking

We seem to understand concepts and remember them better when we compare them with something familiar. The running analogy in this text is comparing various strategies you may need to be successful in college with strategies you may need when you are the driver on a road trip. As in the parallel parking exercise at the end of Chapter 2, think about what we have discussed so far or you have discovered about college in your first few weeks and compare these discoveries with driving ideas.

When you fill in your answers make sure you complete both sides of the analogy by comparing the driving term with a term for being a successful college student.

Side Trips

_____

_____

_____

_____

Refueling

_____

_____

_____

_____

Defensive Driving

_____

_____

_____

_____

Fender Bender

_____

_____

_____

_____

Evaluating Learning Outcomes

How successful were you in making it to your destination in this chapter?

Analyze what you learned in this chapter. Put a check beside each task you are now able to do. Now think of strategies that you learned that will help you save time and study more effectively. List them in the appropriate place on the back inside cover.

☐ **Solve** a given problem using the decision-making process.
☐ **Distinguish** between fact and opinion.
☐ **Develop** questions that user lower- and higher-order thinking skills using Bloom's taxonomy as a guide.
☐ **Analyze** a case study, and construct advice for a student having difficulty with decision making.
☐ **Explain** the learning process modeled in the chapter.

Your Student Tip for This Chapter

Use the space below to write a tip you would give to other students about what you have learned in this chapter.

_____

_____

_____

4 Setting Goals

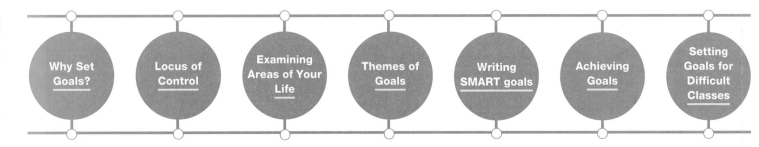

Why Set Goals? • Locus of Control • Examining Areas of Your Life • Themes of Goals • Writing SMART goals • Achieving Goals • Setting Goals for Difficult Classes

When you think about the skills you need to be successful in college, you probably think of skills in test taking, note taking, getting the main idea from textbooks, doing research, writing, enhancing memory, concentrating, managing time, or thinking. However, the driving force behind achieving all these skills is one we seldom think of as a skill at all. It is the skill used to set goals and priorities. We need to know where we want to go and what we need to do to get there. If we are to become proficient at goal setting, we need to look at why we set goals, when we should set goals, and some ways to set useful goals.

Few of us really know specifically what we want out of life. And most of us don't spend time setting goals. We are too busy. We go with the flow and just let things happen to us. The truth is, however, we *can* make things happen. We have choices. The things that we spend our time, money, and emotional energy on are the things we make happen.

Learning Outcomes
for Chapter 4 Setting Goals

Here is your destination for Chapter 4. When you complete Chapter 4, you are expected not only to understand the material presented, but also to be able to:

Identify your locus of control, and develop a plan for improvement if necessary.

Develop an action plan for a personal goal.

Explain the learning process modeled in this chapter.

Write goals for various areas of your life that are specific, measurable, have an action plan, are realistic, and have a target time.

Analyze a case study, and *construct* advice for a student having difficulty coping with goal setting.

Why Set Goals?

Setting goals may be compared to planning a trip. There is a great deal of difference between going for a drive and just ending up somewhere and planning details to reach a certain destination. There is a great deal of difference between driving a car and being a passenger. You will always arrive at some destination whether you plan for it or not. However, if you carefully plan with a specific destination in mind, if you are in charge of where you are going, you might not get there, but you significantly increase your chances for getting where you want to be. Like planning a trip, when you set goals, you are essentially organizing a plan to reach a certain destination. Few good things just *happen*; rather, they come with planning and hard work. Not planning leaves us drifting through life and maybe even stalled in a place we'd rather not be.

BRAIN BYTE

Brain research shows that students achieve more when they feel they are in control and have set specific goals for learning. There is a definite connection between being in control and setting goals.

Exercise 4.1

What Does It Take to Make You Happy?

List 20 things you love to do.

1. _____
2. _____
3. _____
4. _____
5. _____
6. _____
7. _____
8. _____
9. _____
10. _____
11. _____
12. _____
13. _____
14. _____
15. _____
16. _____
17. _____
18. _____
19. _____
20. _____

Go back down your list and use the following codes for each item:

$ If it costs more than $10

A   For an activity that you prefer to do alone

P   For an activity that you prefer to do with people

AP   For an activity that can be done alone or with people

2   If this would not have been on your list two years ago

10   If you think this will make you happy 10 years from now

M   If you think this might have been on your mother's list when she was your age

F   If you think this might have been on your father's list when he was your age

Personal analysis. Use another sheet of paper and write down what you have discovered about yourself.

Critical analysis. Explain why this exercise is relevant in a chapter on goal setting.

Locus of Control

The way you feel about being able to make changes in your life affects your ability to change. John Roueche and Oscar Mink in *Improving Student Motivation* say that students who feel powerless to change the direction of their lives are unlikely to try.[1] They say a person's locus of control is of paramount importance for change and therefore for setting goals. The locus of control represents an individual's feelings of personal control over the events in his or her life, specifically the ability to derive positive reinforcement from the environment.

People who have an internal locus of control believe their actions, abilities, characteristics, and so on, are effective in controlling reinforcements received from the environment. In other words, people with an internal locus of control believe in setting goals because they believe they have the power to reach them. People who have an external locus of control believe that such factors as fate, chance, luck, or powerful others are more important than personal efforts in controlling what they can achieve. People with an external locus respond as *victims*. And while things beyond their control may affect people with an internal locus of control, they respond as *creators*; they can create a solution. People with an internal locus of control are the drivers; they make adjustments for the road conditions. In contrast, people with the external locus of control are the passengers; they believe they have no control over where the vehicle is going or where it will stop.

Exercise 4.2

Locus of Control

Examine the following statements made by students with either a strong internal or external locus of control. Supply an example for each blank. Your answer for internal locus of control should create a solution.

External (victim)	They made me take this learning strategies class.
Internal (creator)	I should be able to gain skills in this class to use in other classes.
External (victim)	That teacher hates me; he'll never give me a good grade.
Internal (creator)	I can meet with my instructor to see how I can do better.
External (victim)	What's the answer to number 5?
Internal (creator)	How do I find the answer to number 5?
External (victim)	The instructor assigns too much reading in history class.
Internal (creator)	_____

[1]John Roueche and Oscar Mink, *Improving Student Motivation* (Austin, TX: College Associates, 1976).

BRAIN BYTE

Dr. Hillman, whose BREATHE System was described in the Chapter 1 asserts that one benefit of using the BREATHE System is that it helps you feel the confidence you need to be a creator rather than a victim.

External (victim) Internal (creator)	My children won't let me study. _____
External (victim) Internal (creator)	My boss makes me work too many hours. _____
External (victim) Internal (creator)	I have never been good in math. _____
External (victim) Internal (creator)	Other people in my class are smarter. _____
External (victim) Internal (creator)	I always get the hard questions. _____
External (victim) Internal (creator)	Just my luck to be externally motivated. There's nothing I can do. _____

VIRTUAL FIELD TRIP

Locus of Control

 Visit the College Success CourseMate.

Students who are internally motivated are better adjusted, more independent, more realistic in aspirations, more creative, more flexible, more self-reliant, more open to new learning, more interested in intellectual achievement, and less anxious. They make higher grades than those who are externally motivated. It's your choice. However, when beginning to set goals later on in this chapter, if you measured a high degree of external motivation in your locus of control, you may want to begin with very specific short-term goals before venturing too far into your future. Mastering short-term goals is a sure-fire way of beginning to change your locus of control to internal.

Exercise 4.3

Why Are You Here?

You have chosen to be a college student, but not everyone in college is here for the same reason. Why are you here? What are your goals? Stop for a minute and examine your reasons for going to college. Rate the following reasons from 1 (most influential in your decision to go to college) to 16 (least influential in your decision). Please use a different number for each item.

_____ To be exposed to new ideas or experiences

_____ To prepare for a job or profession

_____ To gain problem-solving skills

_____ To gain prestige or status

_____ To prepare for good citizenship

_____ To raise economic status

_____ To gain maturity

_____ To become a productive member of society

_____ To get a degree

_____ To please parents or family members

_____ To assimilate knowledge

_____ To have something to do

_____ To learn how to learn

_____ To find a spouse or mate

_____ To make friends

_____ To have fun

Exercise 4.4

Dreaming

If you already had all the time and money you needed, what would you be doing?

What would you drive?

Where would you live?

What kind of vacations or hobbies would you enjoy?

What kind of education would you provide for your children?

What type of charities or volunteer work would you be involved in?

What would your purpose in life be?

When Should You Set Goals?

You are constantly setting and reaching small or short-term goals. You probably should not begin any day without setting some goal to accomplish. This is a relatively simple task; and with a little discipline, it can become a habit. However, any time there is a major change in your life, you should take time to reevaluate what you want out of life. Some of these times are graduating, starting college, beginning a new job, moving to a new place, getting married, or getting divorced. A birth, a death, a promotion, an illness, or an accident, or other major change may have altered previous goals. Most of us dream of things we would like to do. The difference between dreams and goals is that goals are written down. You need to do more than simply scribble some ideas on a piece of paper. Your goals need to be complete and focused, but first you need to brainstorm. To guide you in a brainstorming activity, let's examine different areas of your life.

Examining Areas of Your Life

Beginning college is a major change for you. It's time to do some goal setting. However, just as it might have been difficult to think of 20 things that make you happy, it could be even more difficult to just sit down and make a list of things you want to do in your life. Some of you clearly know what your goals are, but you may not have examined all areas of your life. Most of us just go from day to day without a great deal of thought about what we ultimately want. Let's direct your focus by examining different areas of your life. To help you think about goals that you might want to set, let's divide your life into different **areas** and think about what you want for that area. (You could just as easily examine your goals by the roles you play: student, son or daughter, father or mother, friend, and so on).

35-Minute Brainstorming Activity

On page 75 is a think sheet containing seven areas of your life: (1) *Family/Home,* (2) *Mental/Educational,* (3) *Financial/Career,* (4) *Social/Cultural,* (5) *Spiritual/Ethical,* (6) *Physical/Health,* and (7) *Fun/Recreational.* Use this sheet to brainstorm.

Spend 5 minutes on each area, listing anything you would like to have happen or do in that particular area for the rest of your life. Be as specific as possible. In some areas you will write nonstop for the full 5 minutes and perhaps need more time. Other areas may be more difficult for you to develop ideas in. You will probably need more room for some areas. Needing more room to write for an area is usually an indication that the area is important to you.

BRAIN BYTE

Professor Martin Ford of George Mason University says the goal-pursuing process will be effective only if learners have (1) enough feedback to make corrections, (2) enough belief in their capabilities to continue in the face of negative feedback, (3) enough actual skill to complete the task, and (4) an environment conducive to success.

Time Management

Family/Home	Mental/Educational	Financial/Career	Social/Cultural	Spiritual/Ethical	Physical/Health	Fun/Recreational

Themes of Goals

Look back over your brainstorming think sheet. Could you add more to each area with a little more guidance? In order to help you think further about the areas of your life, consider some common themes in each area. You may want to cut back on something, such as eating sweets, or you may want to expand something, such as the amount of time spent on studying. You may want to improve a situation in an area of your life or solve a problem. Sometimes your goals involve maintaining your present situation. And sometimes you want to dream and become innovative.

To help you focus your thinking further, you may want to consider themes that goals might have. At the bottom of each area, list the following themes: (1) *Expansion or Cutting Back,* (2) *Improvement,* (3) *Problem Solving,* (4) *Maintenance,* and (5) *Innovation.*

Continue your brainstorming by thinking of things you need to expand or cut back on having or doing in your family and home. Then think of things that you could improve in your family and home. Is there a problem in your family that you would like to solve? Are there good things about your family or home that you would like to maintain? Or are there things in your family or home you would like to try that are totally different from anything you've ever done? Continue this procedure with each area of your life. When you finish, you will have a wealth of information to help you begin to set some concrete goals. You will probably want to develop goals in all areas of your life; however, you cannot be an expert in all areas. Again, it is a matter of what you value. If you aren't sure what you value most, look at what you spend your time, money, and effort on. The areas that were easiest for you to brainstorm are probably the most important to you.

Exercise 4.5

Brainstorm Follow-Up

At different times in our lives, one or more of these areas will take priority over the others. After you have completed the brainstorming activity on page XX, list the seven areas in order of importance to you at this time.

1. _____

2. _____

3. _____

4. _____

5. _____

6. _____

7. _____

Some Guidelines for Writing Goals

Make sure that the goal you are working for is something that you really want, not just something that sounds good. Be certain it is indeed your goal and not someone else's. Be sure that your goal is positive instead of negative. And be sure that it is something within your control.

Making Dreams Come True

The dreaming exercise and the brainstorming should have helped you begin to think about things that important for you to accomplish in your life. **Long-term goals** are detailed descriptions of what you want for yourself in the future. Your long-term goals may include graduating from college, getting a job you enjoy, owning your home, or being able to travel. Review your brainstorming for specific things that are important to you. What are some things you want to accomplish in your life?

The way to make your long-term dreams come true is to set a series of short-term goals that lead to the accomplishment of what you want. The more specific you can make your long-term goals, the easier it will be to set short-term goals that will help you achieve your dream. You have it in your power to reach your dreams. The first step in making your dreams concrete is to analyze what you must do in order to reach your goal.

Short-term goals are the steps you take to reach your long-term goals. Short-terms goals are plans of action. They are your to-do list for today and tomorrow and the next day. A well-written short-term goal will give you directions for exactly what you need to do and set a deadline for its completion. The first step in your long-term goal to graduate may be completing your math assignment for class today.

BRAIN BYTE

Researchers Edwin Locke and Gary Latham surveyed nearly 400 studies on goals, and the results were definitive. They found that specific, difficult goals lead to better performance than easy, vague ones.

Critical Thinking About Setting Goals

When setting goals, we can use the same critical thinking process we used in the decision-making process we discussed earlier in the text. After all, developing a plan is really a decision you make to achieve your goal. This puts you in control of what you accomplish.

With your goal in mind, you first want to gather as much information as you can to help you to determine what your options are for getting closer to your goal.

- What skills do I need to achieve this?
- What information and knowledge do I need?
- What assistance or collaboration do I need?
- What resources do I need?
- What can block my progress?
- Am I making any assumptions?
- Is there a better way of doing things?

If your goal is you want to declare your major (part of your goal to graduate from college), you want to gather as much information as you can.

What are your options?

- You could visit you academic advisor.
- You could study the college catalog to see what majors are offered.
- You could talk to professors teaching in a field you think you might be interested in.
- You could take a career decision-making inventory.
- You could study references such as *Occupational Outlook Handbook*.
- You could shadow someone in a career that interests you.
- You may, in fact, want to do all of these.

In the decision-making process, we next weighed the evidence—*Do I need to do more than one thing? What needs to be done first?*

Next, you must take some kind of action. Goals are never achieved by just thinking about them. You have to do something. You want to clearly define the plan of action you choose to take.

Your action plan should give you specific directions such as who, what, when, where, why, and how.

"I will schedule an appointment with Dr. Hatfield for February 3 at 3 o'clock to discuss setting career options."

Writing SMART Goals

Many coaches and consultants use the **SMART** acronym as a guide to writing useful goals. Read the guide below and then explain how the goal to meet with your advisor meets all of the elements.

With long-term goals, the more of these elements you include, the more likely you are to reach your goal. Short-term goals **should** have all five of the elements with the emphasis on plan (or plans) of action.

Specific	Describe what you want to accomplish with as much detail as possible.
Measurable	Describe your goal in terms that can be evaluated clearly.
Action Plan	Your goal should explain what action you will take.
Realistic	You know you are capable of doing or achieving this goal.
Time Framed	Clearly specify target-completion time—with longer goals broken into shorter pieces.

Exercise 4.6

SMART Goal Setting: Let's Think This Through

You did poorly on a test and so you say **that your goal is to study more.** (*Not a SMART goal!*)

Study what? *History*

Exactly what will I do? *Read Chapter 5 and make flash cards for possible test questions as I read it.*

How much? *1 hour 3 times a week*

When? From 3 p.m.-4p.m. Monday, Wednesday, and Friday

Where? *In the library*

With whom? *By myself*

Why? *I really want to make an A in history.*

What else?

Instead of "I will study more," your goal now reads: **"From 3-4 on this MWF, I will go the library and read Chapter 5 of my history book and make flash cards of possible test questions as I read."**

A separate goal might be **"On Friday at 6 o'clock, I will meet Bob in the library and we will practice flash cards until 7."**

Now, are you going to continue doing this next week with Chapter 6? 7? 8?

How would you rewrite your goal to include that you are setting this study routine as a pattern for the rest of the semester?

Exercise 4.7

Practice Writing an Action Plan

Let's say you think that you are overweight. Your long-term goal is to lose weight. You realize that this goal doesn't meet the SMART goal requirements. How much? When and how often will I check my weight loss? What do I need to do to lose weight? Is my goal realistic? What is my deadline? So you revise you goal: **I want to lose 10 pounds in the next three months**. This is specific, measurable, probably realistic, and there is a time frame. However, there is no plan of action—nothing to tell you specifically what to do. You gather your information and determine that you could probably lose 10 pounds in three months by cutting you calories by 300–500 calories a day. Now you are ready to set short-term goals. How can you change your food intake or what exercise could you do to burn 300–500 calories a day?

Let me start the list for you.

1. Each day I can replace drinking one Coke (150 calories) with a bottle of water (0 calories).

Continue to list things you might do daily to cut 300-500 calories.

2. _____

3. _____

4. _____

Have you given yourself directions that are specific, measurable, and have an action to complete? Is your goal realistic? Have you given a time frame?

Looking at these examples, you can see that breaking a goal down to specific steps will help you focus daily on your goal. Remember your goal needs to be realistic so you may need to make adjustments to it—not just abandon it.

Setting a long-term goal that you want to be successful or you want a happy life may sound good, but you really have no directions for how to reach your goal. Let's look back at Exercise 4.1, What Does It Take to Make You Happy? You listed 20 things that make you happy now. You could develop a plan of actions to do some of those things on a regular basis.

List one SMART goal for this week from your What Does It Take to Make You Happy list.

My goal: _____

_____

Your reaction to spending this much effort to develop an action plan may be frustration. You say you don't have time to think through everything. However, it becomes a matter of setting priorities. If your goal is important to you, you owe it to yourself to make the time. No one else can do it for you.

Exercise 4.8

Writing SMART Goals

Look over your brainstorming list. Choose one thing that is important for you to accomplish. List it as your long-term goal. Try to use the SMART guidelines to state your goal.

Next, break it down to three or four short-term goals that you might do to accomplish that goal. Be sure you have included all the SMART elements. Pay particular attention to the action plan.

Long-term goal:

Short-term goal:

Short-term goal:

Short-term goal:

Short-term goal

Tips for Achieving Goals

1. Make sure the goal you have written is specific, measurable, has a clear plan of action, is realistic, and has a target time for completion.

2. Find someone who has accomplished a similar goal. Ask how this person reached the goal and what obstacles to look for.

3. Don't drive around aimlessly. Determine what skills, what knowledge, and what information you need to reach your goal.

4. Break your goal into smaller goals that you can readily accomplish.

5. Share your goal with others. They may have valuable information you need, or they may offer the encouragement you need when you get off track.

Exercise 4.9

Making Your Goals Visible

Educator Skip Downing suggests that it is useful to draw your goals so you can see them. He suggests framing your picture and putting it where you see it often. Choose three goals that are important to you. Draw or cut and paste a picture you can fame, depicting at least three of your goals.

   Making It Concrete

One of my dad's favorite expressions was, "If you don't have directions for where you are going, you may end up somewhere you don't want to be." Write a short paragraph in which you describe a time in your life where setting a specific goal would have resulted in you being in a "different place."

Setting Goals for Difficult Classes

As an example of what you can do, examine Gina's most difficult class, American History 221. Here is her brainstorm of what is specifically wrong: "There is too much to read. I am behind three chapters and an outside reading book. The professor goes so fast I can't take notes. I study, but his questions ask more than I know."

You should look at these problems one at a time.

"There is too much to read. I am behind." If Gina is to be successful in the class, she must read all the material. Is there really too much to read so that there is no possible way to read it all within her current time schedule? If so, what can she *give up* in order to make time to read it? Does she need to drop the course until she is able to make time? What elements of time management does Gina need in order to reach her goal? If she chooses to stick with it, here are a couple of smaller goals that will help her.

Student Tip

" I found making specific goals for each class a real motivation to keep up-to-date. Saying I want to make an A in history is not enough. My goals needed to be what I specifically need to do in a course to make the A on a test or make an A in the course. They involved things like taking notes in each class, making summary sheets when I completed an assignment, and setting aside a specific time to study that course. "

Gina's Goals I

1. Gina needs to immediately find and set a time to catch up, and set a time for keeping up with her reading—a specific time of day and amount of time—and a place to do it.

2. Gina needs to take notes while reading so that she won't have to reread. ("I will read and take notes on Chapter 3 today at 3 o'clock, Chapters 4 and 5 tomorrow at 10 o'clock.")

"The professor goes so fast, I can't take notes." Of course, you know that if Gina had kept up with her reading, it would be easier to take notes. Where do the notes come from? Do they supplement or follow the reading assignments? Gina needs to analyze her note-taking system. (Taking good notes takes practice.) She needs to check her listening attitude and where she sits in class. She needs to discuss her problem with her professor. Probably, most of all, she needs a partner or group from the class. Immediately after class, her partner or group needs to meet with her and compare notes or non-notes, as the case may be, and maybe even check with the professor to fill in spots.

Gina's Goals II

1. Gina needs to analyze her note-taking system. Is she trying to write too much? Does she give up too easily? What specifically can she do to get more out of the lecture?

2. Gina needs to find a partner or group willing to meet consistently after class and make the effort to get notes. She needs to do it now, not wait until just before a test.

3. Gina needs to make an appointment with the professor. She needs to plan the conference before she goes, tell the professor what efforts she has made, and ask for help with problems she has not yet solved. She needs to be specific in what she asks for. (Just complaining or talking to the professor is not going to take the place of reading assignments and taking notes.) If the professor offers a suggestion, she needs to try it.

"I study, but his questions ask more than I know." One reason Gina has had trouble is that she wasn't keeping up with the assignments. When test time came, she had time to learn only on the first level of Bloom's taxonomy. She recalled facts only. Setting a daily time to study and process information improves the possibility of mastery at deeper levels. When Gina begins to synthesize the information, she can begin to predict what the test questions will be.

Gina's Goals III

1. Gina needs to take time after each class to understand the information presented and to prepare for the next class as if there is going to be a pop quiz on that material.

2. Gina needs to read the assignment and try to predict what questions will come from each section. She needs to write down the questions in the margin.

3. Gina should analyze old tests from the professor.

4. In a study group, she should try to predict what the questions on the test will be.

5. Gina needs to meet with the professor and test the predicted exam questions by asking if she is on the right track with the kinds of questions that will be on the exam.

There is a real difference between saying you want to do well in class and actually giving your best effort. Often students fool themselves into thinking that they can treat the courses they are taking in college like those in high school. You have learned that you can count on at least two hours of outside work for every hour you are in class maybe just to earn a C, depending on the class, and that study involves much more than just doing homework. If you have been out of school for a time, it will take more time in the beginning. It takes time to become a good note taker and an efficient reader. Now, what is your goal? Do you want to master the material in each class or just get through the class? If you are serious about learning, reevaluate your master schedule. Are you sticking with your plan? Practicing time management will help you accomplish your goals.

● Critical Thinking About a Difficult Class?

Brainstorm about your specific problems. Then write at least two goals that address these problems that you will tackle today. (Remember to make your goals SMART—be specific, be measurable, include an action plan, be realistic, and have a target date for completion.)

Class _____

Brainstorm Goal 1

_____

_____

_____

_____

Brainstorm Goal 2

_____

_____

_____

_____

Much of the time in a study session, students fail to have specific goals; they feel they just get homework. Having specific goals for each study session helps you get more from your time.

Modeling the Learning Process

Again in this chapter, you were modeling the learning process. Remember the cycle includes gathering, analyzing or finding meaning, creating, and acting.

Gathering. You got information about setting goals: why set goals, elements of a useful goal, and guidelines for setting goals.

Analyzing. You analyzed areas of your life with goal setting in mind. You tried to determine where you really want to be.

Creating New Ideas. You tried to determine what you must do to reach your destination.

Acting. You wrote goals useful for several areas of your life and created a plan by breaking large goals into smaller ones.

You took the first steps in achieving your goals.
You also found that you needed to begin the cycle over by gathering information you need to reach your goals.

SUMMARY

To see if you grasped the major points of the chapter and to make a useful study guide, answer the following questions found in your reading. When you have written your answers, cover them and see if you can say the answer to each question in your own words. If you prefer to type your answers, you will find a Microsoft Word download for each summary on the College Success CourseMate for Practicing College Learning Strategies at **www.cengagebrain.com.**

Why have goals? pg 69

_____

_____

_____

Explain the locus of control. pg 71

_____

_____

_____

When is the best time to reevaluate goals? pg 74

_____

_____

_____

What are seven areas of your life described in the goal-setting exercise? pg 74

1. _____

2. _____

3. _____

4. _____

5. _____

6. _____

7. _____

5 **What are five themes of goals examined in the goal-setting exercise?** pg 76

1. _____

2. _____

3. _____

4. _____

5. _____

6 **What are the five elements of a SMART goal?** pg 78

1. _____

2. _____

3. _____

4. _____

5. _____

7 **What are two specific goals you have set for your difficult class? (Be sure that your goals contain all elements of a SMART goal.)** pg 81

1. _____

2. _____

Case Study: What's Your Advice?

Bob has just graduated from high school. He has decided to go to a community college in his hometown because he can continue to work for his dad, live at home, and still take classes. College is not something he's really excited about because he doesn't know what he wants to do. Bob knows his parents want him to continue his education, so he is really going to college to please them. There is plenty of time to see what comes up. Bob is working on his time management, and most of the time he is able to get everything done at work and at school without having too much free time left. He thinks that it's just his luck that he has instructors who give so much homework and that his boss is always changing his schedule. Given what you have learned about goal setting, what advice would you give Bob?

Parallel Parking

Remember in college you are successful only when you are driving, not just going along for the ride. Like the parallel parking exercise at the end of the previous chapters, think about what we have discussed so far and compare these ideas to driving concepts. When you fill in your answers, make sure you complete both sides of the analogy by comparing the driving term to a term for being a successful college student.

Knowing Your Destination

_____
_____
_____
_____

Changing Direction

_____
_____
_____
_____

Planning the Trip of a Lifetime

_____
_____
_____
_____

Evaluating Learning Outcomes

How successful were you in making it to your destination in this chapter?

Analyze what you learned in this chapter. Put a check beside each task you are now able to do. Now think of strategies that you learned that will help you save time and study more effectively. List them in the appropriate place on the back inside cover.

☐ **Identify** your locus of control, and develop a plan for improvement if necessary.
☐ **Write** goals for various areas of your life that are specific, measurable, have an action plan, are realistic, and have a target time.
☐ **Develop** an action plan for a personal goal.
☐ **Analyze** a case study, and construct advice for a student having difficulty coping with goal setting.
☐ **Explain** the learning process modeled in this chapter.

Your Student Tip For This Chapter

Use the space below to write a tip you would give to other students about what you learned in this chapter.

_____
_____
_____
_____

Use this page to set some specific goal for this week

5 Learning Principles

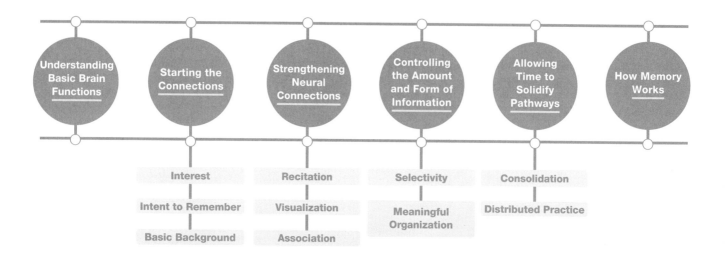

Understanding Basic Brain Functions

Starting the Connections
- Interest
- Intent to Remember
- Basic Background

Strengthening Neural Connections
- Recitation
- Visualization
- Association

Controlling the Amount and Form of Information
- Selectivity
- Meaningful Organization

Allowing Time to Solidify Pathways
- Consolidation
- Distributed Practice

How Memory Works

The core of academic success is knowing enough about how your brain processes information to successfully develop strategies for learning. This chapter is divided into three sections. The first section deals with some very basic information about how your brain processes information. Yes, you can drive a car without knowing how the engine works, but you are better equipped to troubleshoot if you know the basics. Knowing how your brain works gives you the ability to develop strategies based on how the brain naturally learns best. It gives you the information you need to critically think about your learning strategies. The second section introduces you to 10 learning principles based on what we know about the brain. The third section demonstrates how the learning principles work together. To remember what you are studying (that is, to make it your own), you first have to understand the material. You must also have

Learning Outcomes
for Chapter 5 Learning Principles

Here's your destination for Chapter 5. When you complete Chapter 5, you are expected not only to understand the material presented, but also to be able to:

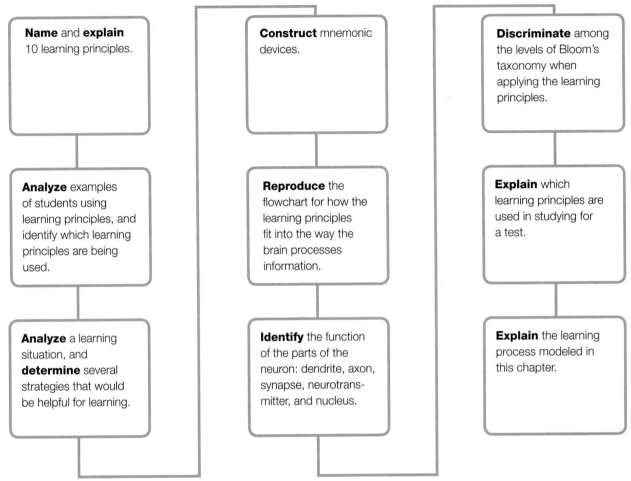

Name and **explain** 10 learning principles.

Analyze examples of students using learning principles, and identify which learning principles are being used.

Analyze a learning situation, and **determine** several strategies that would be helpful for learning.

Construct mnemonic devices.

Reproduce the flowchart for how the learning principles fit into the way the brain processes information.

Identify the function of the parts of the neuron: dendrite, axon, synapse, neurotransmitter, and nucleus.

Discriminate among the levels of Bloom's taxonomy when applying the learning principles.

Explain which learning principles are used in studying for a test.

Explain the learning process modeled in this chapter.

a desire to learn it. Sometimes you understand the material and truly want to learn it, but just don't know how to process the information in such a way that you are likely to remember it and use it.

Your short-term memory holds only five to seven bits of information. When you receive more than that load of information, you must either push it out of your memory to make room for more or transfer it to long-term memory. This is why you sometimes understand everything while it is being presented in class but do not remember it later: Your short-term memory has dumped that information in order to make room for more.

Although the learning principles do deal with your memory, the principles explained in this chapter are not ways to memorize. Memory and learning are literally biological changes in the brain. Memory is evidence that learning has taken place. Memory is learning that can be retrieved from your brain, not from your notes or your text. The learning principles are ways to process or transfer information into long-term memory and strengthen connections that allow for learning. To continue with the driving analogy, the more familiar you are with where you are driving, the easier it is to manipulate in traffic, to find alternative routes and short cuts, to avoid traffic jams and speed traps, and to reach your destination safely. Likewise, the more familiar you are with the learning principles and with how your brain processes information, the better you are able to manipulate information so as to learn it.

Basic Information About the Brain: Providing Background for Learning Principles

It is only in the last decade that scholars from separate disciplines like biology, chemistry, psychology, information science, philosophy, anthropology, and linguistics have come together to discover the information contained in this text. Neuroscientists have learned more about the brain in the last decade than in the entire preceding century. Research by neuroscientists has given us the reasons why many strategies used by successful students are so efficient. They are able to see how the brain processes information using positron emission tomography (PET) scans and other neuroimaging devices. With this equipment, neuroscientists are able to determine the chemical and electric reactions taking place in the brain and have mapped exactly what part of the brain is used in various functions. The benefit for you is that the more you understand how your brain processes information, the more empowered you are to develop techniques to remember relevant material.

In analyzing what neuroscience is discovering about the brain and memory, Eric Jensen suggests that there are many pieces of the puzzle that make for efficient and long-term learning.[1] Each piece of the puzzle is necessary for optimal learning. Too often, you concentrate on the content of what you need to learn and not on what you need to do to learn it. Each component plays a role in your learning. Jensen states that (1) your personal history, (2) present circumstances, (3) what meaning you bring, (4) how information is input (sensory modes), (5) how information is processed (learning preferences), and (6) how you respond (multiple intelligences) must be meshed for you to learn best. This is often referred to as brain-based or brain-compatible learning, using what you know about the brain to develop strategies for learning that work for you.

The six components Jensen says must be considered for optimal learning are all incorporated in the 10 learning principles. In the learning styles lessons in Chapter 6, you will examine the components of sensory modes (input), hemispheric dominance (processing preferences), and multiple intelligence (responses) in more detail.

Let's begin with a quick look at some basic biology of your brain. Your brain works on electrochemical energy and weighs approximately three pounds. If you make fists with your hands and put your fists together at

[1]Eric Jensen, *Super Teaching* (San Diego: The Brain Store, Inc., 1998).

the knuckles, the two fists give you a fairly accurate picture of the brain's size. Your brain has more than 100 billion brain cells, called **neurons**. However, *it is not the number of neurons that is significant; it is the connections they make with each other that determine learning.*

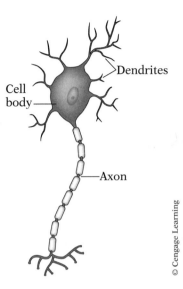

Cell body

Dendrites

Axon

Every neuron is made up of three major regions: (1) a cell body (sometimes called a **soma**), containing a nucleus and other organelles where information is integrated, (2) an **axon**, a long, single fiber that sends information, and (3) **dendrites**, minute twigs, or web-like branches, that receive information. The action inside the cell is electric, and the action between cells is chemical. Both the axon and dendrites have many connector points, so a neuron receives and sends many messages at a time. The electric activity within cells results in the growth of new dendrites stretching from the neuron. As learning takes place, the branches spread and thicken, making more connections possible. No actual contact is made between axons and dendrites; rather, communication occurs through the release of neurotransmitters, chemical molecules, into the space between the axon and dendrite called the **synapse**. There are many types of chemicals that act as neurotransmitter substances. The type of neurotransmitter affects the strength of the connection.

In his article, "A Computer in Your Head?" Dr. Eric Chudler says:

When information is transferred from one neuron to another, molecules of chemicals ("neurotransmitters") are released from the end of one neuron. The neurotransmitters travel across the gap to reach a receiving neuron where they attach to special structures called receptors. This results in a small electrical response within the receiving neuron. However, this small response does not mean that the message will continue. Remember, the receiving neuron may be getting thousands of small signals at many synapses. Only when the total signal from all of these synapses exceeds a certain level will a large signal (an "action potential") be generated and the message continue.[2]

[2]From "A Computer in Your Head?" by Eric Chudler, as appeared in *Odyssey Magazine*, March 2001. Reprinted by permission of the author.

In *The Great Memory Book*, Karen Markowitz and Eric Jensen summarize other important brain facts:[3]

- A stimulus enters the brain through the senses.
- This information is promptly processed by a complex network of neurons, protein, and electric impulses.
- The information is prioritized by value, meaning, and usefulness, as well as how it relates to prior learning.
- Memory is not stored in one place in the brain like a snapshot; bits and pieces of memory are stored in various functional areas. Neuroscientists are beginning to map the different parts of the brain where memory resides.
- When information is recalled, it is instantaneously retrieved from storage areas in many parts of the brain to form an integrated composition.
- Memory is continually changing and evolving as new information is added to it. (We speak of this as the brain's *plasticity*.)

Memory and learning, then, are a biological process. For learning to occur, there is a physical change in the brain when these new neural pathways are formed. The stronger the connection, the more concrete the learning. However, developing a strong connection requires repeated effort.

Making It Concrete

When trying to learn something new, you get a better understanding if you compare it to something you already know. Now that you have read a description of how learning occurs in the brain, try making comparisons of new terms you have learned to some familiar things. I have begun the exercise with analogies about a car and driving; you may continue along this line or completely switch to another analogy.

Neurons	are like cars	in that cars are the bodies containing the parts that provide transportation just as neurons are the bodies that contain the parts to transport information.
The nucleus	is like the driver of a car	in that it
Dendrites	are like	in that they
Axons	are like	in that they
Synapses	are like	in that they
Neurotransmitters	are like	in that they
The connections made	are like	in that they
Learning	is like	in that it

---

[3]Karen Markowitz and Eric Jensen, *The Great Memory Book* (San Diego, CA: The Brain Store, Inc., 1999.)

I own a computer and can make it do all sorts of amazing things. I use it to word process, create PowerPoint presentations, use Facebook, Twitter, send e-mail, surf the Internet, and develop web pages. However, it is capable of doing much more than I personally make it do. I could learn how to do more by reading and studying the owner's manual. Your brain, like my computer, will do much more than you make it do. You need to read your owner's manual!

Owner's manuals begin with a quick look at features. They have a use-and-care guide and chapters detailing specific functions. At the back there is usually a troubleshooting section. I like it best when there is a chart or card that contains a quick reference guide. The learning principles in this chapter are your quick reference guide. As a college student, you have a limited amount of time to learn volumes of information in your classes. The learning-principle reference guide will help you get the most out of the time you have to study. The strategies you develop to use the principles become your troubleshooting section. The Brain Bytes scattered throughout the text margins are excerpts from the detailed chapters to help you understand why certain strategies work or act as tips for use and care of your brain.

I know you don't have time to read the entire manual. In fact, you've used your brain for a long time without ever owning a manual. In the margin here, list how you remember things that are important to you. Try to list at least five ways.

On the next page is a list of 10 learning principles with a short explanation of each. After you have read these principles, create some pocket work so that you can begin to learn them. *Make a flash card for each principle* by writing the name of the principle on the front of an index card and the explanation of the principle on the back of the card. You might further your understanding of each principle by drawing an illustration of the principle beside the definition. Then carry the cards around with you so that you can study the principles while waiting in line or waiting for class to start or when in between classes, and so on. What are some times in your day that you could use flash cards?

Starting Connections
INTEREST

FRONT OF CARD

Your brain prioritizes by meaning, value, and relevance.

To remember something, you not only have to understand it, you also have to be interested in it.

BACK OF CARD

Learning Principles: Quick Reference Guide

Starting the Connections

1. **Interest.** The brain prioritizes by meaning, value, and relevance. For something to have meaning, you must understand it. In order to remember it thoroughly, you must be interested in it and think that it has value and relevance in your life.

2. **Intent to remember.** Your attitude has much to do with whether you remember something or not. A key factor in remembering is having a positive attitude, believing that you will get it right the first time. Attention is not the same as learning, but little learning takes place without attention.

3. **Basic background.** Your understanding of new material will depend on how much of it can be connected to knowledge you already have. The more you increase your basic knowledge, the easier it is to build new knowledge on this background.

Controlling the Amount and Form

4. **Selectivity.** You must determine what is most important, and select the main idea before you add the supporting details.

5. **Meaningful organization.** You can learn and remember better if you group ideas into meaningful categories or groups.

Strengthening Neural Connections

6. **Recitation.** Saying ideas aloud in your own words strengthens synaptic connections and gives you immediate feedback. The more feedback you get, the faster and more accurate your learning is.

7. **Visualization.** Visualization is the brain's quickest and probably longest-lasting response to images. By making a mental picture, you use an entirely different part of the brain than you do by reading or listening.

8. **Association.** Memory is increased when facts to be learned are consciously associated with something familiar to you. Memory is formed by making neural connections. Begin by asking, "What is this like that I already know?"

Allowing Time to Solidify Pathways

9. **Consolidation.** Your brain must have time for new information to establish a neuronal pathway. When you make a list or review your notes right after class, you are using the principle of consolidation.

10. **Distributed practice.** A series of shorter study sessions distributed over several days is preferable to fewer but longer study sessions.

Applying the Learning Principles

In the classroom, the most difficult part of your job is not to understand new concepts, but rather *to make those concepts your own* so that you *don't forget them*. An understanding of some things your brain does will help you devise techniques to avoid forgetting what you have learned. Remember you are the driver on your journey as a college student. You are in control. The driving analogy works well with each of the learning principles. The first three principles involve Starting the Connections to remember.

Starting the Connections

For us to learn something new, we must make a connection to something that is already in our brain. The first three learning principles assure that this initial connection is made.

Interest

The first learning principle is called **interest.** The plain and simple truth is that in order to remember something thoroughly, you must be interested in it. Brain research has discovered that the brain is really poorly designed for textbook memory. Obviously, you can't just say, "My brain isn't designed this way." You need to find ways to make information relevant.

The brain prioritizes by value, meaning, and usefulness. Because of your college's requirements for graduation, it's almost a sure thing that you will have to take some courses that you don't think you are interested in. So, in these classes you must devise some way to get interested. You must go beyond "textbook memory." You may create interest by having a study partner, getting to know the professor better, or doing some extra practice or research. (We tend to be uninterested in things we are not good at.) You might try teaching an assignment to someone else, seeking a way to make the information personal, or finding a way to make it kinesthetic (make something) and do something with it.

We tend to be interested in things that we are good at, know a great deal about, are affected by personally, or enjoy doing; so sometimes developing an interest may be as simple as doing a bit of extra research or practice, trying to make the information personal, or approaching the material in a fun way. In addition, finding a study partner who is interested in the subject or getting to know the professor better often provides interest. You can't just jump into a car and take off. You must be aware of your surroundings. If you are not interested in where you are going, you may get from one point to another but you miss the journey itself.

Intent to Remember

In addition to interest, attitude has much to do with whether you remember something. When you are positive that the speaker has nothing to say or that the lecture will be boring, you are ensuring that you will not remember it, if it even enters your brain at all. Being positive that you

Student Tip

" *Although I didn't know anyone in the class, I reluctantly joined a study group after my first history test. That may be the best thing I ever did. Going to class started being fun, and I had a group I could depend on.* "

BRAIN BYTE

Any time our emotions are engaged, we are more likely to form a deeper imprint of the event. Excitement, humor, celebration, suspense, fear, surprise, or other strong emotions stimulate the production of adrenaline while also activating the amygdala (the part of the brain that controls emotions).

will remember is a key factor in remembering. We call this attitude the principle of **intent to remember.** Suppose that before you come into class today, your instructor pulls you aside and says, "I'm going to cover ten major points in my lecture today. Don't tell anyone, but at the end of class, I'll give you $20 for every major idea you can explain to the class." Would this make a difference in how well you listen? Would it make a difference in how many questions you ask or how many notes you take?

It's this attitude of getting it right the first time and making sure you understand, this turning on of the *intent-to-remember switch,* that you should begin each class with. You are seeking ways to learn faster and better, so this principle is one that needs constant practice. Remember, you are not the passenger. A passenger can daydream, catch a catnap, read a book, text-message a friend. You are the driver. You must keep your eyes on the road. You must pay close attention to what you are learning. You must constantly look for road signs and landmarks to help you understand where the class or reading assignment is going. The passenger can reach the end of the class or the end of a reading assignment and not know where he has been, but not the driver.

Attention is not the same as learning, but little learning takes place without attention. Moreover, John Medina in his book *Brain Rules* reminds us that "multitasking when it comes to paying attention is a myth. The brain naturally focuses on concepts sequentially one at a time.[4] According to Jensen, brain research shows that as stimuli enter your brain through your senses, if the information does not get enough attention or if it is "not deemed necessary for long-term memory, it will be encoded in short-term memory only and ultimately discarded and reclassified."[5] He further suggests that although you can probably retrieve almost all of what you pay close attention to, the accuracy of the memory is very dependent on state, time, and context.[6]

Let's go back to our driving analogy. If you are going to reach your destination safely, you need to keep both hands on the wheel. Too many accidents happen when you let passengers distract you, try to take in too much scenery, or drive while text-messaging or talking on your cell phone. You can increase the probability that you get it right the first time by getting enough sleep, eating a high-protein breakfast, limiting your caffeine intake, and eliminating as many distractions as possible. You can increase the oxygen supply to your brain by paying attention to your posture and breathing. Remember the BREATHE System we discussed in Chapter 1? The Big 3—paying attention to posture, relaxing shoulder and neck muscles, and taking deep, cleansing breaths—help to realign your focus and get more oxygen to the brain. When you become restless and inattentive, practicing the BREATHE System may be the conscious switch you need to turn on the *intent to remember*. Physical activity can also increase the blood flow and the brain's oxygen supply.

BRAIN BYTE

Researchers Markowitz and Jensen have found that positive attitude (optimism, that is, believing you can do something, in this case learn something) relaxes the body and directs its full energy to the task at hand. A positive attitude can change the brain in at least three ways: (1) It alters the chemistry of the brain with the production of dopamine, the feel-good transmitter. (2) It increases noradrenaline flow, which provides physical energy. (3) It produces constructive thinking, which activates the frontal lobes, which are most responsible for long-term planning and judgment.

[4]John Medina. *Brain Rules: 12 Principles for Surviving and Thriving at Work, Home, and School* (Seattle, WA: Pear, 2008).
[5]From *Where Memory Resides* by Karen Markowitz and Eric Jensen. Copyright © 1999, p. 9.
[6]Ibid., p. 52.

Basic Background

Your understanding of new material depends to a great degree on how much you already know about the subject. Remember, it is cellular connections building on one another that activate learning, consciousness, intelligence, and memory. The more learning, the more connections you make. The greater the number of connections in the brain, the greater the meaning derived from learning. If there is not a neural network for something, it simply doesn't exist in our brain. That is why totally new concepts are so difficult to grasp at first.

Researchers have discovered that when you activate what you already know about a subject before learning something new, the brain makes more connections. Reviewing notes from the day before or surveying a chapter before you read it will increase your learning and comprehension. That's why taking basic courses that give you knowledge to build on is so important. The principle of **basic background** is at work here. If you find you do not have the background, you must make the effort to get it. The more you know about where you are going, the easier it is to drive with confidence. It is very difficult to drive in an unfamiliar place. You make wrong turns; you get confused. The more you can find out about your destination before you begin, the easier your drive will be. This might be as easy as reading and doing the assignments before you go to class.

The Making It Concrete exercises in each chapter help you to connect with the background or synaptic connections you already have. When something is totally new to you, a good way to begin is by asking, "What is this like that I already know?" The brain processes new information by looking for connections. The similes and metaphors you talked about in your literature classes were not just an academic exercise. The brain processes information by relating whole concepts to one another, looking for similarities and differences or relationships among them.

Exercise 5.1

Starting the Connection

Interest. Think about courses you have taken from which you remember almost all the material and courses from which you remember almost nothing. Then list one course you are taking now that you are having difficulty developing an interest in. What are two specific strategies you can try to promote interest?

Class:

_____

Strategies for interest: 1. _____

2. _____

Intent to remember. We know that some professors are not entertaining and engaging in class, and there are always things going on in your life that are probably more important to you than what is going on in class. What are two specific strategies that you can try in class this week that might improve your attitude and keep you involved in class?

Strategies for intent to remember: 1. _____

2. _____

Basic background. Classes are easier when you have a background to build on. Retracing established neural connections is comfortable for students, and you really only learn new material by making connections to those well-established connections. Building new connections in your brain takes the same hard work and repetition that you need to build new muscle in your body. Think of a class where you lack a lot of background. Name two specific strategies that you might try to make sure you have something to connect new material to.

Class:

_____

Strategies for basic background: 1. _____

2. _____

BRAIN BYTE

In essence, the pattern of learning is as important as what is learned. The brain theorist Leslie Hart notes that what you perceive as a pattern depends on your prior knowledge, the existing neural networking of the brain used to process the input, and the context in which the learning takes place.[7]

Controlling the Amount and Form of Information

Given the nature of short-term memory, you need to find ways to control the amount and form of the information you are trying to learn. Just as a driver does, you have control over the speed you go and the route you take. When learning something new, you can learn it more efficiently if you control the amount of information you take in at one time and how you process it. These next two learning principles help you do just that.

Selectivity

Brain researcher Eric Jensen notes that "most students are drowning in information and starved for meaning." I am sure you can relate to this. There is so much material covered in your classes that it would be impossible to remember everything. You should therefore carefully determine what is most important and select this material to study and learn. In doing so, you are using the principle of **selectivity.**

As you read a textbook, notice that the author has provided clues and guides as to what is important by dividing the chapter with major headings, using bold print and italics, and providing summaries and questions. Follow these road signs. Finding the important points in a lecture may be more difficult. But there are also road signs here. You can learn to

[7]Leslie Hart, *Human Brain and Human Learning* (White Plains, NY: Longman, 1983).

concentrate on both verbal and nonverbal clues such as the numbering of items, the repetition of an idea, or things an instructor writes on the board.

Meaningful Organization

Some scientists estimate that the average brain can hold as many as 1 quadrillion bits (that's a 1 followed by fifteen 0s) in long-term memory. Neuroscientists assure us that our brains, however, are designed to retain meaningful rather than random bits of information. Because memory is stored in web-like fashion throughout the brain, depending on how you process it, it follows that you can improve your memory by learning to encode in a conscious and organized way.

How you organize your memory, much like how you organize your road trips, your office, or your notebooks, will determine how efficient your memory system is. Even though you may know where you are going, you need the names of the highways and interstates in the correct order to get there. Even though information is filed in your memory filing cabinet, your file needs a name to retrieve it. Because the conscious brain can process only five to seven bits of information at a time, you are able to learn and remember better if you group ideas into meaningful categories of fewer than seven items. This is the principle of **meaningful organization.** Note that it combines the principles of interest (making the group meaningful to *you*) and selectivity (cutting the job down to a manageable size) and that it also involves organization. For example, you might break down a list of 25 items into five groups of five (no more than seven) that have some organizational principle in common.

Mnemonic devices are one way of organizing new information. A **mnemonic device** is a means for enhancing memory. Most people think of it as a trick that you use to help memorize something. When you can't find an obvious way to remember something difficult, you can organize it by using a mnemonic device, called a *mnemonic*, for short. In other words, mnemonic devices are a way of using meaningful organization. Although they do not replace other techniques for learning, mnemonics are sometimes the only way to remember something difficult for a short period of time. Mnemonic devices can be rhymes, phrases, or words arranged in a special way to help us remember. Here are some examples.

BRAIN BYTE

Because of the tremendous volume of information you encounter (millions of bits of random information per minute), it is crucial that you consciously cue into your memory system.

BRAIN BYTE

For you to form a sharp memory of something, the original information must be encoded accurately, maintained and strengthened over time, and triggered by association or cue. When information is poorly encoded, there is no hope for data recovery.

Type of Mnemonic Device	Explanation	Example
Acronym (word mnemonic)	An invented combination of letters, with each letter acting as a cue to an idea you need to remember	**HOMES** to remember the names of the Great Lakes: *Huron, Ontario, Michigan, Erie,* and *Superior*
Acrostic (sentence mnemonic)	An invented sentence in which the first letter of each word is a cue to an idea you need to remember	**K**ing **C**harles **A**dded **A**nd **S**ubtracted **E**quations to remember Bloom's taxonomy: *Knowledge, Comprehension, Application, Analysis, Synthesis,* and *Evaluation*
Poems or jingles	Organizing the information in a catchy rhyme or jingle	*i* before *e* except after *c* or when sounded like *a* as in *neighbor* or *weigh*

Exercise 5.2

Controlling the Amount and Form of Information

Selectivity

You have been assigned four chapters to read in your psychology course. How will you decide what is important to remember?

_____

_____

Listen to a lecture, and list the verbal and nonverbal clues the lecturer gives to indicate which ideas being conveyed are important.

_____

_____

Meaningful Organization

1. First look at the following list of items and try to remember them: _car keys, a ribbon, a paper clip, a piece of peppermint, a pair of sunglasses, a birthday card, a stapler, a tea bag, a cookie, a windshield wiper blade, a pencil, a flower, a spoon, a pair of scissors, a stamp, a scarf, a ballpoint pen, a computer disk, a Kleenex, a calculator, a pack of gum, an iPod, a dollar bill, a notebook, and flash cards._

2. Study the list for one minute; then cover it and see if you can list all the items.

   _____

   _____

   _____

3. Now group the items into meaningful categories in the space below. Then cover them and see how many you can remember.

Category	**Category**	**Category**	**Category**
_____	_____	_____	_____
List:	List:	List:	List:
_____	_____	_____	_____
_____	_____	_____	_____
_____	_____	_____	_____

4. You are going to the grocery store and have forgotten your list. What are some ways to organize items you need to buy that are meaningful so that you won't forget what you need?

   _____

   _____

   _____

5. Here's a mnemonic for remembering the seven continents: Eat An Aspirin After A Nighttime Snack. Can you list the continents below?

   _____

   _____

   _____

6. List some mnemonic devices you know and use.

_____

_____

_____

Now devise some mnemonic devices of your own.

7. Devise a mnemonic to help you remember the five elements necessary for a useful goal.

_____

_____

8. Make a mnemonic device for a biology class in which you need to learn the seven major taxonomic categories, or taxa, used in classification: (1) kingdom, (2) phylum, (3) class, (4) order, (5) family, (6) genus, and (7) species. Remember order is important here.

_____

_____

9. Devise a mnemonic (maybe two) to remember the 10 learning principles just discussed.

_____

_____

_____

Strengthening Neural Connections

Once you have manipulated what you wish to learn by selectivity or meaningful organization and have established connections, you need to seek ways to strengthen and maintain those connections. Connections that are not strengthened disappear. Learning depends on the *strength of the connection combined with the neurotransmitters*. The more times you have traveled the same road, the more confident you are in your driving and direction.

The next three principles deal with this process. After all, what good is having something in your long-term memory if you can't get it back out or make connections to it?

Recitation

Recitation is probably the most powerful tool you have for transferring information from short-term to long-term memory. (Recitation involves saying something out loud in your own words.) It is not the same as rereading, just as reading the steps on MapQuest or your GPS is not the same as knowing each turn to take. Recitation works because it triggers the intent-to-remember switch. If you know you're going to recite something, you tend to concentrate and pay more attention.

BRAIN BYTE

Seeking feedback is a natural and essential learning tool that helps you minimize false impressions before inaccurate memories are formed.

Student Tip

"I love to draw. So when I go over my notes, I try to illustrate them. It helps me stop and think about the material, as well as giving me a visual prompt to think of on a test. **"**

BRAIN BYTE

The brain has an attentional bias for high contrast and novelty. The brain has an immediate and primitive response to symbols, icons, and strong, simple images.

Recitation gets you involved in the material. It makes you a participant (a driver), not an onlooker (a passenger). Further, recitation gives you immediate feedback. You discover whether you know something well enough to say it in your own words or you need to go back and study it more. Remember, in addition to making an effort to understand, you are also giving synaptic or neural connections the repetition they need to become strong. You are trying to *own* the material you are learning. This is one reason why flash cards or study index cards are so effective.

You now know that the more senses you use, the stronger the neural trace is. You need repetition and review; and, particularly, the brain needs feedback in order to judge and correct its course. The more feedback you get, the faster and more accurate your learning is. The neuroscientist Richard Bandler says that you really need to "know that you know" something before learning takes place. Recitation is where the difference in understanding something and knowing something becomes most apparent.

Visualization

Another very powerful learning principle is **visualization,** which involves making a mental picture of what needs to be remembered. By visualizing, you use an entirely different part of the brain than you use for reading or listening. In addition, you remember pictures much longer than words. In fact, 90 percent of the brain's sensory input is visual. Researchers have found the brain's quickest response is to color, motion, form, and depth. You have probably found driving directions easier to follow if you have visual landmarks as checkpoints.

Visualization can be a powerful part of preparing for a test. Experiments using new brain-imaging equipment show that the same brain patterns occur when people visualize themselves doing something as when they actually engage in the task. Most memory experts say that short-term memory will hold more pictures than words. (Later, when learning styles are discussed, you will see that if you are a visual learner, making a mental video of things you want to remember is a must.) The visualization portion of Exercise 5.3 illustrates how powerful the principle of visualization can be for you.

Association

Another way to strengthen your neural network is to tie new information in with something you already have stored in your long-term memory. This is called the principle of **association.** By recalling something you already know about a subject and placing new information in the same brain file as the old information, you will find that the new information is easier to retrieve, easier to remember. For example, there are certain dates that you are sure of, such as the year Columbus discovered America, the year the Declaration of Independence was signed, your mother's birthday, and the year you graduated from high school.

So, when you need to learn a new date, think of the new date as being, say, 5 years after or 10 years before the one you already know. As you observe a PET scan or other neuroimaging technique, it becomes

Exercise 5.3

Strengthening Neural Connections

Recitation. List the eight learning principles we have discussed. Then cover them up and recite them until you can name and explain them without looking.

1. _____   5. _____

2. _____   6. _____

3. _____   7. _____

4. _____   8. _____

Visualization. Try the following exercise to illustrate how powerful visualization may be for you. It is important that you follow the directions carefully.

Memorize the following pairs of words by repeating the members of each pair several times to yourself. For example, if the pair is CAT–WINDOW, say over and over, "cat–window," "cat–window." Do not use any other memory method.

CUSTARD–LUMBER	MOTHER–IVY
JAIL–CLOWN	LIZARD–PAPER
HAMMER–STAR	BEAR–SCISSORS
APPLE–FRECKLES	CANDLE–SHEEPSKIN
SLIPPER–ENVELOPE	CANDY–MOUNTAIN
BOOK–PAINT	TREE–OCEAN

Now cover the list and try to remember as many pairs of words as you can.

ENVELOPE– _____   JAIL– _____

FRECKLES– _____   IVY– _____

TREE– _____   CANDLE– _____

CANDY– _____   BOOK– _____

SCISSORS– _____   LIZARD– _____

CUSTARD– _____   HAMMER– _____

Now memorize these pairs of words by visualizing a mental picture in which the two objects in each pair are in some kind of vivid interaction. For example, if the pair is CAT–WINDOW, you might picture a cat jumping through a closed window with glass shattering all about. Just make up a picture, and do not use any other

[8]David A. Sousa, *How the Brain Learns: A Classroom Teacher's Guide* (National Association of Secondary School Principals, 1995).

memory technique. The more color and action your picture holds, the easier it will be to recall.

SOAP–MERMAID	MIRROR–RABBIT
LAKE–FOOTBALL	HOUSE–DIAMOND
PENCIL–LETTUCE	LAMB–MOON
CAR–HONEY	BREAD–GLASS
CANDLE–DANCER	LIPS–DONKEY
FLEA–DANDELION	DOLLAR–ELEPHANT

Now cover the list and try to remember as many pairs of words as you can.

CANDLE– _____   DOLLAR– _____

FLEA– _____   CAR– _____

BREAD– _____   LIPS– _____

MIRROR– _____   PENCIL– _____

LAMB– _____   SOAP– _____

LAKE– _____   HOUSE– _____

Find something you need to learn for one of your classes. First list or explain exactly what you need to learn. Then explain *specifically* what you could do with the material visually to help yourself remember it.

Association. The Making It Concrete exercise at the beginning of this chapter is a good illustration of association. What metaphor did you use for learning?

Learning is like _____ in that _____.

abundantly apparent that association is central to the process of encoding and retrieval. It is extremely important when you encode new information that you do so consciously. Association is consciously making a connection to the basic background you have established. Using similes, metaphors, or analogies helps to begin the process of association.

Allowing Time to Solidify Pathways

As you are probably beginning to discover, the learning principles can be used in combination and, in fact, are more powerful that way. For example, as you associate something new with something you already know, you will want to use visualization and perhaps recitation to strengthen your memory. The last two learning principles are important because, as you learned in regard to short-term memory, the brain can

BRAIN BYTE

Researcher Eric Jensen reminds us that "optimal learning occurs when the brain's multiple maps work in synchronization or network with each other. The more connected these neural networks are, the greater the meaning derived from learning."

absorb only a certain amount of *new* information and that information needs time for a pathway to solidify—that is, time to soak in.]

Consolidation

An important factor to consider in terms of how your brain processes new material is that you are making a biological change in your brain by establishing new neuronal pathways. This is not an easily accomplished task. It takes time for the pathway or connection to become established. Think about the sidewalks on your campus. They are established ways to get from one place to another. However, I'll bet your campus is like mine in that there are paths students' feet have worn where there are no sidewalks. The first time a student cut through that way, the footsteps didn't leave a path; but the more students used that way, the more apparent the new path became. On my campus, eventually the worn paths are made into sidewalks! Compare this to the pathways you are establishing in your brain. (This example is the kind of analogy, simile, or metaphor that you are encouraged to use to connect to your own experience when you process new information.)

Researchers Markowitz and Jensen remind us that the brain is not designed for nonstop learning. As the brain learns new information, new connections are formed. Because learning is a biological process that literally changes the configuration of the brain, "processing time is necessary to build the inner wiring necessary for connectivity and recall."[9] Repetition of information strengthens these new connections. We call this principle **consolidation.** *Consolidation is taking ownership of new information by allowing time for neuronal pathways to be established.*

You are usually bombarded with much more new information than you can remember. You must, therefore, allow time to sort through it, to reflect on it, and to integrate it with old information. As discussed, the more ways new information is processed into the brain, the faster and deeper the connections will become. (See the Brain Byte in the margin that suggests that it may take many ways and many times of receiving new information for your brain to know that it knows.) Encoding that is random is at best difficult to retrieve. The brain needs feedback and repetition. John Medina, who you will meet him in some Virtual Field Trips, reminds us, "The brain acts like a muscle: the more activity you do, the larger and more complex it can become."[10] You wire and rewire yourself with every activity you choose.

Here are a few ways to consolidate: taking notes in class, asking questions in class, reviewing notes, stopping after each paragraph you read and writing a JEOPARDY question, visualizing, reciting, making flash cards, and designing practice tests. Check your smart phone or iPad for apps that could help you consolidate information. You will notice that many of these activities give you a hard-copy backup of new information, as well as strengthening connections in your brain.

[9]Markowitz and Jensen, p. 7.
[10]Medina, p. 58.

BRAIN BYTE

Brain research suggests that breaks are needed for at least two reasons. First, new neural connections need time to fix and strengthen without interference from other new stimuli. Second, fatigue causes more errors.

Student Tip

" *After my instructor told us flash cards use all 10 learning principles, I started making flash cards from my notes in biology class. I was shocked when I started acing pop quizzes. Using the flash cards also cut my study time for exams in half.* "

BRAIN BYTE

Richard Bandler, co-discoverer of neuro-linguistic programming, says that for you to take ownership of new information, your brain needs to "know what it knows." Three criteria necessary for this are: (1) reinforcing the information in your preferred modality (visual, auditory, or kinesthetic), (2) reinforcing it the right number of times (for some once, for others maybe 20 times), and (3) reinforcing it for a sufficient length of time (from a couple of seconds to several hours).

Distributed Practice

If you are going on a long road trip, you are better off not trying to drive it in one stretch. When you get there, you may be too tired to do anything. Similarly, you tend to remember better if you are not overly tired and are able to concentrate; therefore, a series of shorter study sessions (no longer than 50 minutes each) is usually better than hours and hours of straight studying. Using the principle of **distributed practice** is probably the most effective way to study.

Because the connections in your brain are strengthened by the number of times you use them, several short sessions are better than one or a few long ones. The structure of your brain literally changes each time you add new information. When your study sessions are frequent and spread out, there is time for branches to form on dendrites and new chemical and electric responses to occur. Each time you study, the brain will respond more quickly because there are more connections. If you wait until the last minute to cram for an exam, there are fewer dendrites and the connections are weaker. You tend to remember things at the beginning and the end, whereas things in the middle often get fuzzy or blurred.

It stands to reason, then, that the more beginnings and endings you experience, the more you will remember. If you remember the first 20 minutes and the last 20 minutes of what you study in a 50-minute study session, you are well on your way to *owning* that material. However, what happens when you study for four hours straight? You remember the first 20 minutes and the last 20 minutes. That amounts to 3 hours and 20 minutes of blur.

Exercise 5.4

Consolidation

List some learning principles that you think are most important in promoting consolidation.

_____

_____

_____

_____

List activities that work for you to promote consolidation.

_____

_____

Check your study schedule. Describe ways you will use distributed practice this week.

_____

_____

_____

Exercise 5.5

Putting Learning Principles to Use

Kelley has a history textbook assignment for her history class. She has used what she has learned about the learning principles to make sure she knows the material. Circle or highlight all of the learning principles she uses to complete the assignment. (She will probably use more than one in each example.)

1. Before she begins to read, Kelley reviews her notes from the class where the instructor introduced the material.

   Interest   Intent To Remember   Basic Background   Selectivity Meaningful Organization   Visualization   Recitation Association   Consolidation   Distributed Practice

2. Kelley reads the chapter summary, studies the review questions, and examines pictures and charts before she reads.

   Interest   Intent To Remember   Basic Background   Selectivity Meaningful Organization   Visualization   Recitation Association   Consolidation   Distributed Practice

3. When she reads, Kelley focuses on the bold print, topic sentences, and italicized words.

   Interest   Intent To Remember   Basic Background   Selectivity Meaningful Organization   Visualization   Recitation Association   Consolidation   Distributed Practice

4. At the end of each paragraph, Kelley stops and chooses the important information and writes a question in the margin of her book. Kelley then underlines as few words as possible in the text to answer the question.

   Interest   Intent To Remember   Basic Background   Selectivity Meaningful Organization   Visualization   Recitation Association   Consolidation   Distributed Practice

5. Before she goes to the next paragraph, Kelley covers the text, asks herself the questions in the margin, and says the answer out loud in her own words.

   Interest   Intent To Remember   Basic Background   Selectivity Meaningful Organization   Visualization   Recitation Association   Consolidation   Distributed Practice

6. In addition, Kelley tries to picture what the people and events she is reading about look like. As Kelley reads, she tries to make connections with things she has already studied.

   Interest   Intent To Remember   Basic Background   Selectivity Meaningful Organization   Visualization   Recitation Association   Consolidation   Distributed Practice

7. This chapter is about World War II, and Kelley remembers hearing stories about her grandfather being in the war. Kelley asks her parents exactly what her grandfather did and where he was at that time.

**Interest   Intent To Remember   Basic Background   Selectivity
Meaningful Organization   Visualization   Recitation
Association   Consolidation   Distributed Practice**

8. Kelley reads and marks a few pages right after history class, a few more when she has a break between classes, and additional pages while she is waiting for her friend Marge and finishes the chapter before she leaves school. Later that night she reviews the whole chapter.

**Interest   Intent To Remember   Basic Background   Selectivity
Meaningful Organization   Visualization   Recitation
Association   Consolidation   Distributed Practice**

9. When Kelley is finished, she makes a chart that lists the roles and major players of each country involved.

**Interest   Intent To Remember   Basic Background   Selectivity
Meaningful Organization   Visualization   Recitation
Association   Consolidation   Distributed Practice**

10. Kelley also makes flash cards of terms, people, places, and dates.

**Interest   Intent To Remember   Basic Background   Selectivity
Meaningful Organization   Visualization   Recitation
Association   Consolidation   Distributed Practice**

VIRTUAL FIELD TRIP

Learning Principles

Visit the College Success CourseMate.

VIRTUAL FIELD TRIP

Learning Principles Quiz

Visit the College Success CourseMate.

Making Connections

The learning principles are the core of learning strategies. If you are going to be a successful student, you need to master the principles. Let's review Bloom's taxonomy to show how you can master them.

Knowledge. First you memorize the 10 learning principles so that you know the name and definition of each principle. You can easily do this without having to use the principles.

Comprehension. Once you are able to list the learning principles, you then explain them to someone. You see that they are more than definitions. You see that the principles explain how you personally can use your brain more efficiently.

Application. You practice using the learning principles—you visualize, you recite, you spread your study time out, and so on. You discover that you can use the learning principles to study faster and better. You are able to process information in less time and retain the information longer.

Analysis. When you analyze, you break complex ideas into parts and see how the parts work together. With the learning principles, you discover relationships among the various principles. You see that there is a time and place to use certain principles, that some principles are best used in combination with other principles, and that some principles work better for you than others. You see that different information and learning situations call for different combinations of learning principles. You can take the learning principles and develop a note-taking system or a textbook-reading system that uses a combination of learning principles that work for you. You use analysis to determine the best time, place, and way for you to study.

Synthesis. You draw conclusions and make predictions. You are able to take a specific learning situation and use the learning principles to make a plan for learning that is best suited for you and for the information you need to learn. Summarizing a unit or predicting test questions is a form of synthesis. Using a note-taking system built on the learning principles in all of your classes is a way of using synthesis.

Evaluation. When you evaluate, you judge something's worth. Did the note-taking system work for you in history class, or do you need to make adjustments? Did you use the right combination of learning principles to study for your psychology test, or do you need to try a different combination?

How Memory Works: Putting Principles in Perspective

If you use Bloom's taxonomy to measure the depth of learning, you should be competent through three levels in your thinking about the 10 learning principles. You have learned the names of the principles (knowledge), you understand how they help you learn new material (comprehension), and you have begun to use them in developing strategies for learning (application). The deeper the level of your thinking, the stronger the neural traces or connections will become.

Keeping the analogy of the brain owner's manual, let's dig deeper. You need to understand the relationships among the principles, to see how the principles fit into the overall pattern of information processing and learning, and to determine which combinations of principles work best for you in specific learning situations. When you analyze, synthesize, and evaluate, you have progressed from simply learning something for an exam to using it to become a better student. Neuroscientists may not know exactly how the brain processes information, but they and now you know enough to see how the 10 learning principles fit into the overall scheme for learning new material. You know that memory is not an object or file stored in one place in the brain; rather, it is a "collection of complex electrochemical responses activated through multiple sensory channels and stored in unique and elaborate neuronal networks throughout the brain."[11]

We began this chapter by giving a simplistic overview of what happens physically to the brain when learning occurs. We next examined 10 learning principles as a quick reference to brain-compatible learning. Now, let's put the two together in a visual representation of where the learning principles fit into the learning process. Again, we are well aware that memory and learning are not linear processes; however, the following flowchart should help you visualize how the pieces fit together.

Learning can be described as an interactive process that takes place in three stages. First is **reception,** or **encoding,** the gathering of information from your senses. This information enters your short-term memory. In **short-term memory,** information fades away, is intentionally tossed away, or is processed for storage in **long-term memory** as synaptic connections or neuronal pathways, stage two. Stage three is the tricky one. Once information enters long-term memory, there must be a way to retrieve, or activate, the information so that you can use this information when you need it. Without a way to retrieve information from long-term memory, it may as well be lost. Information retrieved from long-term memory is temporarily placed in what we call **active memory.**

[11]Markowitz and Jensen, p. 1.

The process will look something like this.

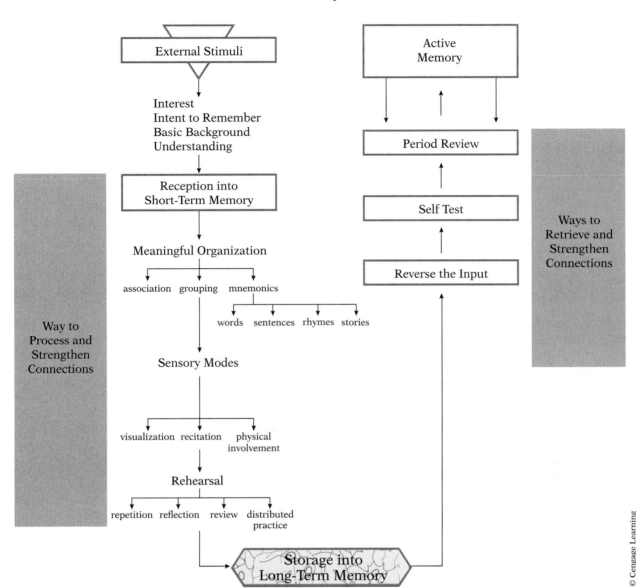

How Memory Works

Stage One: Getting Information into the Brain—Reception into Short-Term Memory

The first stage of the learning process involves information entering the brain. We call this gathering of information, this acquisition of knowledge, **reception**. The brain uses sensory receptors to gather information from things that you see, hear, smell, touch, or taste. Some of these simply pass on through—in one ear and out the other, so to speak—whereas others become part of short-term memory.

BRAIN BYTE

For you to form a sharp memory of something, the original information must be encoded accurately, maintained or strengthened over time, and triggered by an association or cue.

Obviously, everything around you is not important; thus, you do not receive everything. In a classroom lecture, there is more happening in the room than just the lecture. There are other people in the room, each doing his or her own thing. Or there may be something going on outside the window, in the hall, or in your mind. You are feeling, smelling, seeing more than you can take in, but basically you are in control of what you select to receive. Some of the time you may choose to receive nothing at all.

Factors That Influence Reception

As explained earlier in this chapter, when information is received from sensory input, it is encoded in various parts of the brain to form synaptic connections with cell bodies called *neurons*. The axon of the cell reaches out and connects to the newly formed dendrites on other cells, making a network of neuronal pathways. Sometimes, however, you discover that no connections are formed at all or the connections are very weak. There are four factors that influence whether the information you need to learn is even received by your brain or whether new connections are formed. Three factors are the learning principles categorized earlier as "Starting the Connection."

The first has to do with your attitude—your **intention to remember**. If you are not listening or reading as if there will be a pop quiz on the material, the information may not even get into your short-term memory. If there is no intent on your part to get it right the first time, you may hear or see the information, but no synaptic connections are made, and no dendrites are grown.

The second is the learning principle of **interest**. If you are not interested, the information never makes it into short-term memory to even begin to make connections. Remember that an essential part of the interest learning principle is that you both value and *understand* the new concept. Most of you have heard or seen something in a foreign language that you do not understand. That information simply does not enter the brain as meaningful information to be processed. This is also true of material presented either in lecture or in print that you do not understand. If you do not understand it, it has little chance of being received into short-term memory. So understanding, although not one of the three learning principles, also determines if the new information is processed. If the intent and interest are there, information must still be understood in order to be processed. You can probably think of times when you memorized terms for a test without understanding them. In such situations, no real learning or remembering took place.

A third learning principle that influences what you allow to go into short-term memory is **basic background**. Everything you see, hear, smell, touch, or taste is affected by that which you already know. If there is no prior knowledge, there is nothing to which new information can be connected. This is why the more you know about something, the easier it is to learn more about it. Your lack of knowledge may make some concepts difficult for you to understand; whereas for some of your classmates, the same concepts seem simple. For example, suppose a classmate

BRAIN BYTE

Learning is different from attention. But if you are not attending, you are not learning.

builds model airplanes. History lessons about World War II may be easier for her because she has built models of planes used in that war. They may also be easier for the classmate who has heard war stories from his grandfather. You may have noticed that when you learn a new vocabulary word, you begin to see or hear it everywhere.

If you are going to encode something in your brain, you must employ the strategies you developed for using the principles of intent to remember, interest, and basic background, in addition to making sure that you understand the information.

● Critical Thinking About Reception

From the three learning principles and the fourth factor that influence reception, you can create strategies to ensure that what you want to remember is at least on its way to your memory.

- Make a conscious decision that you intend to remember. Concentrate, and try to eliminate both internal and external distractions.
- Create interest in the information being transmitted; personalize it. Try to make it mean something to you.
- If you don't understand what is being transmitted, ask for a translation or explanation. Never just memorize it.
- If you lack basic background about the information, try to acquire it.

Assume that your assignment for psychology class is to read Chapter 3 in your text. You read it; but the next day on the quiz, you find you can't remember anything you read. Using some of the strategies that have been described, make a plan for studying your psychology assignment for tomorrow.

1. _____

2. _____

3. _____

Short-Term Memory

The hippocampus acts as a gatekeeper and director of what you experience when information enters the brain through your senses. If you are interested in some information, find it of value, or make a conscious effort to select it, the hippocampus lets that information into short-term memory.

Short-term memory is limited; usually it can hold only five to seven bits of information at a time. When you are presented with more than seven bits, one of two things must happen. The hippocampus gets rid of what's in the short-term bank by letting it escape, that is, forgetting it, or it directs the information to an appropriate part of your brain for long-term memory. This is the reason you can understand an entire lecture while you are listening to it but later cannot recall the major points. This becomes an important point in developing strategies for note taking and textbook reading, which are discussed in later chapters. You need to hold or record information until you can process it into long-term memory.

Yet you must be very careful when you process information for storage into long-term memory, because transferring information to long-term memory is not enough. You must be able to retrieve this information after it is filed. Just as there are several factors influencing whether sensory information gets to short-term memory, there are instructions in your brain's owner's manual for processing information into long-term memory in such a way that you can later retrieve it. Once synaptic connections are made, if they are not strengthened, they may be lost.

Stage Two: Processing from Short-Term to Long-Term Memory

There are three broad categories of ways that can aid in transferring from short-term memory to long-term memory, and each has several divisions. The first way makes use of various forms of **organization** and **association**. The second way makes use of various **sensory modes**. The third is **rehearsal**. All three ways overlap and interconnect.

Organization

Organization is one method of ensuring that information you want to remember is properly stored. If you go into my office, you will usually see my desk cluttered with stacks of papers. If I wanted my desk cleared, I could randomly stack this information and shove it into a desk drawer. However, if I want to be able to find things again, they must be sorted and organized. Your memory is similar to my desk. If you just cram information in, you may not be able to find what you need when you need it. The strategies you developed when using meaningful organization such as color coding and mnemonics help process the information into long-term memory so that retrieval is possible. The synaptic result of learning is memory.

You now understand that the brain is a web-like network of neurons that can form memory only by association. Facts are not stored in just one place in the brain; but, rather, when you need to recall something, memory is re-created by the electric and chemical actions in many parts of the brain through synaptic connections. The more associations you make when you process new information, the stronger the connections will be. If associations are not consciously made, connections may be weak and information lost.

Explain some strategies for using **meaningful organization** to sort information when the amount of information seems overwhelming.

How could you use **mnemonics** to organize information you want to move from short-term to long-term memory?

Give an example of how **association** could be important in organizing information you need to remember.

Sensory Modes

Another way to ensure that information from short-term memory is properly transferred for storage in long-term memory and that the neural traces are strengthened is to use various **sensory modes**. Most of us have a preferred mode of learning. Some of us are visual learners, others learn best by hearing, and still others learn best by doing. You will want to be sure that you process new information in your preferred mode; however, the more senses you involve, the more neurons are used in the connections and the *more likely you are to remember*.

Visualization and recitation form different connections of the same information. When you do something physically to learn new information, you process that information as procedural knowledge and connect to pathways in different parts of your brain. You may also want to include what something smells like or tastes like.

Three ways of using your sensory modes for learning are to visualize, to recite, and to do something to become physically involved in your learning. Suppose you have a long list of history terms you will need to explain on an upcoming test. Devise specific strategies for learning these terms using each of the following strategies of learning. Include an explanation of why these strategies will work for you.

Visualization

Recitation

Physical involvement

Rehearsal

A final way to transfer information from short-term memory to long-term memory is **rehearsal,** or practice. You are familiar with the rehearsal used by actors to learn their lines. Rehearsal does something similar for you. The first form of rehearsal is **repetition,** which is saying or doing things over and over until you are familiar with the information.

Repeating something over and over may temporarily transfer information to long-term memory at the knowledge level; but in order to make sure the information is permanent, you need to understand it.

The second form of rehearsal is **reflection.** This involves a deeper level of learning and takes you to at least the comprehension level of Bloom's taxonomy. You quickly lose what you don't understand. One way of promoting a deeper understanding of a concept is reflection, examining information and trying to discover how it relates to what you already know and what meaning it has for you. The more meaning something has for you, the more likely you are to remember it.

The third form of rehearsal is **review.** Once a transfer has been made from short-term memory, review is necessary to make sure you can retrieve the information later. Good times to review are right after class, right before class, and 30 minutes before you go to bed. Reviewing right after class catches material before short-term memory has time to completely dump it and while you still understand certain concepts and can identify concepts you need to ask about. Reviewing before class strengthens your basic background and enables you to more easily store what is presented in class. And reviewing just before you go to bed gets your subconscious working while you sleep.

Note the third form is *review,* not "study for the first time." Neurochemical and biochemical studies using imaging of the brain show that when something new is introduced, a sufficient review of this information *must* take place during the following 24 hours in order for long-term memory to retain the concept. This will be difficult for many students who are extremely pressed for time as it is. However, reviewing within 24 hours will save time later. The master schedule becomes an essential tool.

A fourth important principle of rehearsal is that you tend to remember better with several spaced practices than with one long session. We called this principle **distributed practice**. Forty-five- to 50-minute sessions with a 5- to 10-minute break seems to be about right for most students. Don't fool yourself into thinking you can do it all at once. You tend to remember things at the beginning and end of the presentation or study time better than those things in the middle. If there are more beginnings and more ends and less middle, then you remember more! Cramming creates one big middle! Instead of cramming, start studying several days before a test with spaced study periods. This is the hardest thing for most students to do, but it is the most effective way of learning material; and it will save you from having to pull an all-nighter. The more combinations of organization, sensory modes, and rehearsal you use, the more **consolidation** takes place. And the more powerful the transfer to long-term memory, the more likely you will be able to retrieve the information you need when you need it.

Long-Term Memory

Although short-term memory can hold only a limited amount of information for a very short time, long-term memory acts as storage for larger amounts of information for longer periods of time. Notice that the term is not *permanent* but *long-term*. In actuality long-term memory is the neural pathways and synaptic connections that have stabilized through repeated use.

Some things do become part of permanent memory through rehearsal, but more things decay with time and interference. It appears that the more frequently we take things in and out of our long-term memory, the more interest we have in the information, and the more understanding we have of the concepts involved, the more stable the connections will be and the longer the information will stay in our long-term memory. Again, long-term memory is not a *place* but a *process* that takes place in many parts of the brain to make connections and reconstruct memory.

Stage Three: Retrieving from Long-Term Memory

You have cleared your cluttered desk, and your information is either in the trash or in the file cabinet we call long-term memory. Now comes the real challenge, getting the information back out. When test time comes, do you know which drawer to open and how you filed the information? Obviously, the storage and retrieval processes are interactive. The more you use the information—activate connections—the more likely you are to remember where you filed it. There are several things to consider in retrieving information. They involve **reversing the input process, self-testing,** and **periodic review.**

If you were systematic in your filing, to retrieve the information you **reverse the input process**. For example, if you grouped information in categories to remember it, recall those categories to retrieve it. If you used a mnemonic device to file the information, use the same mnemonic device to take the information out of the file. You can use meaningful grouping, association, and mnemonic devices to retrieve information as well as store it. If you stored information using sensory modes, you can use visualization, recitation, or physical involvement to retrieve that information. If you used the rehearsal process to ensure depth of storage, a similar rehearsal can be used to bring the material out of storage.

Long-term memory is not necessarily permanent memory. How long-lasting long-term memory is depends on such things as your understanding, your interest, how you stored it, and how often you retrieve it.

One of the best ways to retrieve information is by **self-testing**. Asking yourself questions about the information is important for several reasons. First of all, it simulates test conditions; that is, it gives you practice in taking tests. Self-testing also gives you feedback so that you know whether you remember what you need to know. Brain research shows that an essential part of learning is knowing that you know something. And self-testing is, after all, a form of rehearsal and will strengthen the retrieval process and add to the depth of storage in your memory.

In addition, **periodic review** is necessary because information in long-term memory seems to decay or fade without review. You should review at least once a week for each class you have. All the time you spend reading and studying is wasted if you can't remember what you have read or studied; therefore, the investment of a little extra time spent retrieving and reviewing filed material is worth it. The bottom line is that connections must be strengthened, or they fade.

What Happens When You Retrieve Information from Long-Term Memory?

When you retrieve information from long-term memory, you activate it, or transfer it to **active,** or working, memory. You can compare active memory to your actual desktop or your computer desktop. This is the space where you gather the information you need to solve a problem, answer a question, or draw a conclusion. There is a limited amount of work space in active memory; and when it becomes cluttered, you must refile the information in long-term memory or trash what information you no longer need.

The more you activate information, take it out of long-term memory and refile it, the more permanent it becomes. Systematically retrieving and refiling material saves hours and hours of time in the long run. In fact, your aim is to make this filing and refiling a habit. The owner's manual presented here is certainly a simplification of how your brain operates; however, you can now begin to use what you know about the learning principles and how they are used in your brain to devise strategies for processing information.

Exercise 5.6

Applying Learning Principles in Retrieval

You studied five hours for your geology test. You remembered most of what you needed to know on the test. On the next test, there are many of the same questions; but you do not remember the answers.

Explain what you think happened.

What could you have done to prevent this from happening?

BRAIN BYTE

Making associations forms new connections between neurons and encodes new insights similar to a tree growing new branches (Sousa, 1995).

VIRTUAL FIELD TRIP

Learning More About the Brain

Visit the College Success CourseMate.

Can you re-create the flowchart describing how memory works?

How Memory Works

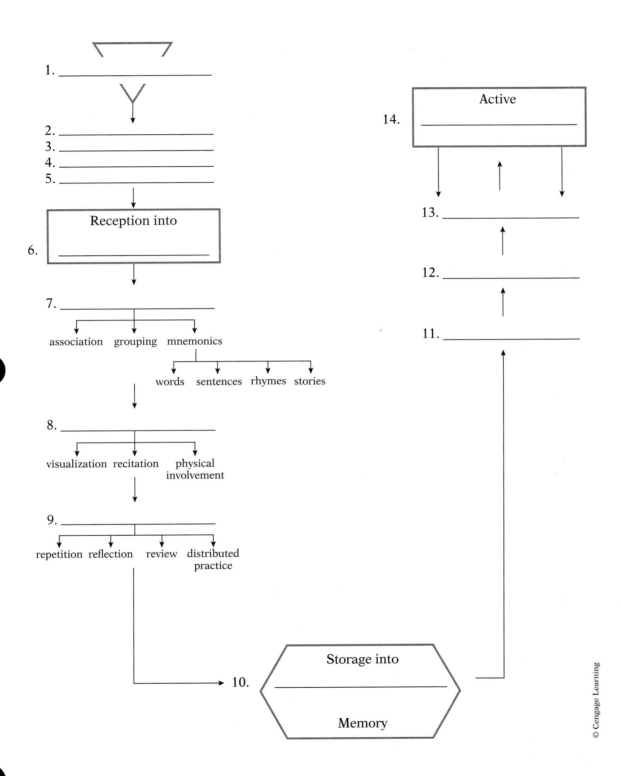

1. _____

2. _____
3. _____
4. _____
5. _____

Reception into

6. _____

7. _____

association   grouping   mnemonics

words   sentences   rhymes   stories

8. _____

visualization   recitation   physical involvement

9. _____

repetition   reflection   review   distributed practice

10. _____

Storage into

Memory

14. _____

Active

13. _____

12. _____

11. _____

Modeling the Learning Process

Although we have also looked at the brain in various ways in this chapter, we have again modeled the learning cycle when we processed the information in each section of the chapter. Let's look at the learning principle section.

Gathering. You gathered information about 10 learning principles.

Analyzing. You made sure you understood each learning principle. You could identify which principle was being used.

Creating New Ideas. You created a plan for using learning principles; you predicted which principle might work for a particular learning task.

Acting. You followed your plan by using each of the principles in appropriate ways.

SUMMARY

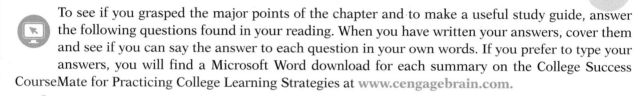

To see if you grasped the major points of the chapter and to make a useful study guide, answer the following questions found in your reading. When you have written your answers, cover them and see if you can say the answer to each question in your own words. If you prefer to type your answers, you will find a Microsoft Word download for each summary on the College Success CourseMate for Practicing College Learning Strategies at **www.cengagebrain.com.**

What disciplines came together to discover more about the brain?

_____

Name the six components Jensen says makes up optimal learning.

_____

_____

What is brain-compatible, or brain-based, learning?

_____

Define the following:

• Neuron

_____

• Dendrite

_____

• Axon

_____

• Synapse

_____

• Neurotransmitters

_____

5 Memory is not a snapshot stored in one place in the brain. Explain this statement.

_____

6 Which three learning principles require that you make an effort to remember? Explain each principle.

1. _____

2. _____

3. _____

7 What two learning principles control the amount and form of information to be remembered? Explain and give an example of each.

1. _____

2. _____

8 What is a mnemonic?

_____

_____

9 Name three kinds of mnemonic devices.

1. _____

2. _____

3. _____

10 Which three learning principles strengthen the memory? Explain and give an example of each.

1. _____

2. _____

3. _____

11 Which two learning principles allow time for information to soak in? Explain and give an example of each.

1. _____

2. _____

12 What are four factors that influence reception into short-term memory?

1. _____

2. _____

3. _____

4. _____

13 Organizing is one way to process information into long-term memory. Name three ways of organizing information for transfer to long-term memory.

1. _____

2. _____

3. _____

14 Name the three sensory modes used to transfer to long-term memory.

1. _____

2. _____

3. _____

15 What are three ways to rehearse?

1. _____

2. _____

3. _____

Once information is in long-term memory, what are three ways to retrieve it?

16 1. _____

2. _____

3. _____

Case Study: What's Your Advice?

Marlene is a very conscientious and capable 30-year-old student who has quit her job as a receptionist in a doctor's office to work on her degree in nursing. She attends class every day. Marlene keeps up with her reading assignments and homework and listens carefully in class. She uses a planner to make sure she has plenty of time set aside for studying for tests. The night before a test, Marlene rereads the chapters in the text and looks over any review sheet the professor may have given. She repeats definitions and facts she thinks will be on the test over and over. However, Marlene is very frustrated after failing her first history and psychology tests and barely passing her biology test. She is beginning to think she may have made a mistake in her decision to attend college. Using what you know about how memory works, what advice can you give Marlene?

Parallel Parking

Remember in college you are successful only when you are driving, not just going along for the ride. Like the parallel parking exercise at the end of the previous chapters, you are asked to think about what has been discussed so far and compare these ideas to driving terms.

When you fill in your answers, make sure you complete both sides of the analogy by comparing the driving term to a term for being a successful college student using brain-compatible learning and learning principles. Be sure to use a phrase that says both what the driving phrase is like and why it is like it. For example: *Neural pathways and synaptic connections in the brain are similar to the interstate network in that one allows information to flow and the other allows traffic to flow.* You may choose the interstate network as one of the three driving terms to compare if you add other similarities. Choose at least three of the following.

Stopping for Fuel	I've Driven Here Before
Rest Stops	Getting Insurance
Parallel Parking	Finding a Place to Park
Asking for Directions	Finding the Right Exit
Getting Your License	The Interstate Network
Knowing Your Destination	Following the Road Signs

1. _____

2. _____

3. _____

Evaluating Learning Outcomes

How successful were you in making it to your destination in this chapter?

Analyze what you learned in this chapter. Put a check beside each task you are now able to do. Now think of strategies that you learned that will help you save time and study more effectively. List them in the appropriate place on the back inside cover.

☐ **Name** and **explain** 10 learning principles.
☐ **Analyze** examples of students using learning principles, and identify which learning principles are being used.
☐ **Analyze** a learning situation, and determine several strategies that would be helpful.
☐ **Construct** mnemonic devices.
☐ **Reproduce** the flowchart for how the learning principles fit into the way the brain processes information.
☐ **Identify** the function of parts of the neuron: dendrite, axon, synapse, neurotransmitter, and nucleus.
☐ **Discriminate** among the levels of Bloom's taxonomy when applying the learning principles.
☐ **Explain** which learning principles are used in studying for a test.
☐ **Explain** the learning process modeled in this chapter.

Your Student Tip For This Chapter

In the space below, write a tip you would give to other students about what you have learned in this chapter.

_____

_____

_____

_____

6 Processing Information from Lectures

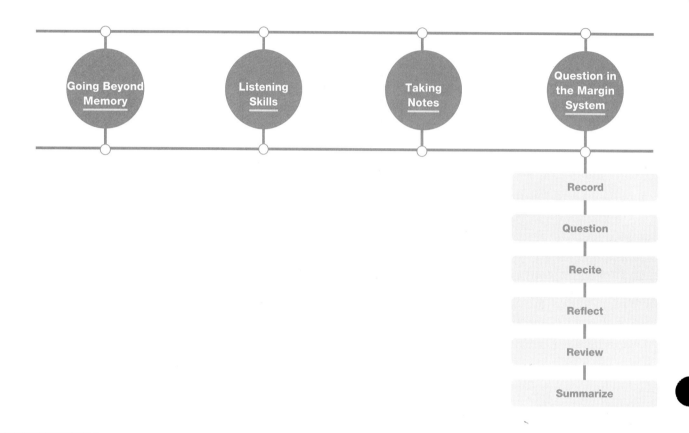

Going Beyond Memory

Listening Skills

Taking Notes

Question in the Margin System

- Record
- Question
- Recite
- Reflect
- Review
- Summarize

Processing Information: Going Beyond Memory

The learning principles are the foundation of memory and learning. However, if you analyze them in light of Bloom's taxonomy, you may conclude that they primarily address lower-level thinking skills. For higher learning to occur, you must go beyond them to *own* the information. In other words, the information needs to become your *personal knowledge*, an integral part of your neural network. This process usually involves using the information to make it personal and meaningful and then creating ideas of your own from this information. The latter involves analysis, synthesis, and evaluation. The proof of your higher learning comes in testing your ideas about what you have learned and finding out that they work. In other words, your goal is to shift your role from passenger to driver—from receiver of knowledge to producer of knowledge. It should become apparent that taking responsibility is necessary. Higher-order learning must be active and personal.

Learning Outcomes
for Chapter 6 Processing Information from Lectures

Here's your destination for Chapter 6. When you complete Chapter 6, you are expected not only to understand the material presented, but also to be able to:

Use the 10 learning principles to **develop** strategies for processing information from classroom lectures.

Give several reasons for taking notes in class.

Explain how to use the Question in the Margin system to someone who has never used it.

Appraise your listening habits, and **construct** strategies for improving them.

Demonstrate the six steps of the Question in the Margin system for taking notes: record, question, recite, reflect, review, and summarize.

Explain the learning process modeled in this chapter.

Dr. James Zull, author of *The Art of Changing the Brain*, says:

Although the human brain is immensely complicated, we have known for some time that it carries out four basic functions: getting information (sensory cortex), making meaning of information (back integrative cortex), creating new ideas from these meanings (front integrative cortex), and acting on those ideas (motor cortex). From this I propose that there are four pillars of human learning: gathering, analyzing, creating, and acting. This isn't new, but its match with the structure of the brain seems not to have been noticed in the past. So I suggest that if we ask our students to do these four things, they will have a chance to use their whole brain.[1]

The flowchart in Chapter 5 on learning principles helped us put into perspective how those principles work. Zull's model represents what really happens in the brain. The importance of his model is that it takes us beyond memory to higher-level learning.

[1] James Zull, *The Art of Changing the Brain* (Sterling, VA: Stylus Publishing, 2002). Reprinted by permission of Dr. James Zull.

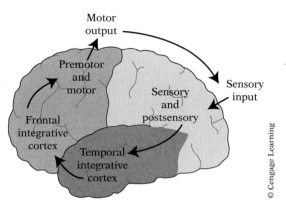

Zull's Model of the Brain

Four Essential Functions for Learning

The four functions Zull outlines become our guidelines for going beyond memory and using what we have discussed. The four functions are gathering, analyzing, creating, and acting. They should sound familiar. We have applied (modeled) the four functions of higher learning in the previous chapters. Now that we have accumulated more basic background about these functions, let's go into a bit more detail.

Gathering. Data enter the brain through the senses. Gathering involves getting information by using many of the learning principles, particularly those that involve "Starting the Connections." Zull says that prior knowledge is the beginning of new knowledge. Prior knowledge is always where all learners start. We have no choice. Part of the learner's job is to find ways to combine the established network with new neural networks—to build new concepts using a mix of the old and the new. Gathering parallels the lower-order thinking skills. In our driving analogy, gathering might include reading the road signs and writing down directions.

Analyzing. Analyzing involves discovering meaning in information by reflection. Zull explains that the back cortex gets information in small bits and reassembles it. In terms of the learning cycle, this integration process is reflective. We examine new information. We try to make it personal. We try to determine where it fits in with our experiences and if it has relevance or meaning for us. We look for connections, and as we find these connections, we make new ones. All this takes time. This process of analyzing also involves most of the learning principles. In terms of Bloom's taxonomy, this is analysis. In our driving analogy, analyzing might involve things like considering alternative routes to adjust for possible traffic and road conditions and investigating what stops we might want to make.

Creating New Ideas. Data enters the brain through concrete experience. The brain organizes and rearranges data through reflection. But it is still just data until the learner begins to work with it. Understanding is not ownership. When we as learners convert comprehension into ideas, hypotheses, plans, and actions, we take control of the information. We have created a meaningful neural network and are free to test our own knowledge. In terms of Bloom's taxonomy, this is synthesis. In our driving analogy, creating new ideas or synthesis is putting together the knowledge we have to predict that if we take a certain route, we may avoid a traffic jam or accident or hypothesize that although the interstate might be quicker, we would enjoy the scenic route more.

Acting. The testing of the knowledge requires action for the learning cycle to be complete. Writing, speaking, drawing, or other action creates a strategy that may work for us and provides a way that we can test the newly learned information. When this stage, acting, is reached, the learner becomes a producer of knowledge rather than a receiver. Let's look at the bigger picture. We can consider, for example, the choice of a vocation. People have previously come up with ideas to improve things within the vocation. Someone created better medicines from this stage of learning. Someone developed the Internet, search engines, a better accounting system, a more efficient engine, and smarter phones and apps for almost everything. Our learning goals move us from receiver to producer of knowledge. Of course, everything learned in a classroom isn't going to be earthshaking. The connections we form, however, multiply to possibilities of creating something better.

Essential Functions of Learning and the Question in the Margin System

If your goal as a learner is to be able to own and use new information, you must reflect and create something of your own beyond the information, then actively test your hypothesis. This chapter provides an opportunity to practice doing this by creating your own system for processing information using what we have discussed in previous chapters. This will become the basis for making the Question in the Margin system work more efficiently for you.

Your primary job as a college student is to process information. You want to take information from lectures and make that information yours. You want to grasp what you read and process it so that you own it. Otherwise, you would spend a great deal of time going to class and even more time reading, yet benefit little in the long run. How, then, do you process information from lectures and textbooks so that you are in control of that information? The Question in the Margin system can help.

Here's the challenge. You want to take what you know about the learning principles, time management, goal setting, and critical thinking and analyze this knowledge, then develop some strategies to help you process information from lectures. You want a way to take what you hear in lectures in the classroom and remember it, understand it, and take ownership of it by using it. Your task is to devise a system using strategies you have just learned in this text. The result should be a system that not only processes information faster and better than any you have used before, but also demonstrates that you truly own what you have already studied. Once you have devised your system, you can compare it to the Question in the Margin system explained in this chapter and combine the best features of both.

Relating Information Processing to Learning Principles

In most college classrooms, the primary mode of teaching is the lecture. However, according to Edgar Dale's research, people generally remember only 20 percent of what they hear.[2] Given that short-term memory holds only five to seven bits of information, it is possible to understand everything that the lecturer says, yet remember only a few things.

It is important, then, to use what you know about memory and the functions of the brain to process information from lectures. Try to apply the four brain functions to process information from your classroom lectures. You have already performed the gathering function for the information in the first few chapters of the text. You know strategies for managing time, thinking critically, setting goals, and remembering new information. The reflecting exercise that follows will guide you through the other three functions: analyzing, creating, and acting.

Exercise 6.1

Modeling the Learning Process (Reflecting)

Keep in mind that your ultimate task here is to come up with step-by-step strategies for taking what you hear in lectures and making it your own. Begin by brainstorming and reflecting. First make a list of what you learned in Chapter 1, Making a Smooth Transition to College, that might be useful.

Ideas About Making a Smooth Transition

Now consider what you learned about time management in Chapter 2 that would be useful in classroom lectures.

Ideas About Time Management to Keep in Mind

Are there things in Chapter 3 on critical thinking that would be useful in devising your step-by-step system?

[2]E. Dale, *Audio Visual Methods in Teaching*, 3d ed. (New York: Holt, Rinehart and Winston, 1969).

Ideas About Critical Thinking to Keep in Mind

What about things you learned in Chapter 4 about goal setting that would help you own lecture material?

Ideas About Goal Setting to Keep in Mind

Now consider the learning principles presented in Chapter 5. The four categories of learning principles are listed below to help you brainstorm.

Ideas About Learning Principles to Keep in Mind

Starting the Connections involves *interest, intent to remember,* and *basic background.*

Controlling the amount and form of information involves *selectivity* and *meaningful organization.*

Strengthening memory involves *recitation, mental visualization,* and *association.*

Allowing time for memory to soak in involves *consolidation* and *distributed practice.*

Now that you have this information where you can see it, take it and form a hypothesis—a plan for processing lectures that you think may work for you. Step 1 may involve what you need to do before you come to class. Other steps will involve what to do in class and what to do after class.

You probably won't come up with the perfect system in one try, but you will have accomplished two things in your attempt. You will have begun to take ownership of the material you have already covered in previous chapters, and you will have demonstrated that Zull's model of learning has potential for you.

For each step, explain your reasoning in enough detail that someone could read your explanation and know what to do and when to do it. The list below has fill ins for six steps. Your system may have more or fewer steps.

Step 1: _____

_____

_____

_____

Step 2: _____

_____

_____

_____

Step 3: _____

_____

_____

_____

Step 4: _____

_____

_____

_____

Step 5: _____

_____

_____

_____

Step 6: _____

_____

_____

_____

Keep your plan handy. You will use it later in this chapter.

Listening Skills

A quick inventory on college campuses reveals that as much as 80 percent of what you need to learn is delivered through lectures. Sometimes the lectures are exciting and easy to follow. Other times they may be dry, or it may be difficult to grasp the main idea. No matter how entertaining, confusing, or boring the lecture may be, you are responsible for learning and remembering the information presented.

If you are having problems with your note taking, follow the steps of critical thinking and first determine what the problem is. One cause may be bad listening habits. Use the following exercise to check your listening habits. One of the first things you probably concluded was that intent to remember and interest are triggered by listening carefully.

Exercise 6.2

Obstacles to Listening

From the following list choose the five obstacles that most often get in the way of your listening in class. In the space following the obstacle, explain in detail how you can overcome this obstacle (not just "I won't do it anymore!").

1. Talking instead of listening

2. Thinking of what you're going to say instead of listening

3. Mentally arguing with the speaker

4. Thinking about something else while the speaker is talking

5. Getting impatient with the speaker

6. Giving in to a poor environment—too noisy, too hot, too hungry

7. Dividing your attention—texting, finishing homework, writing a letter, staring at someone cute

8. Not listening actively—not taking notes, not asking questions, and so on

9. Not being motivated to listen—thinking the subject is boring

10. Being distracted by the speaker's mannerisms, voice, or appearance

Exercise 6.3

Improving Your Listening

Here are some commonsense principles that will help you become a better listener in class. Study the following list and answer the questions that follow each statement.

1. Come to class prepared. What does this involve? _____

_____

How will this make you a better listener? _____

_____

What learning principles does this involve? _____

_____

2. **Sit as close to the instructor as possible.** Why? _in order to make eye contact + to hear_

3. **Come to class as early as possible.** Why? _____

4. **Make eye contact with the instructor.** Why? _____

5. **Listen for verbal clues that something is important.** What are some examples of things the instructor might say to let you know that a point is important?

_____

_____

_____

6. **Watch for nonverbal clues that a point is important.** What are some examples?

_____

_____

_____

_____

7. **Listen with a pen or pencil in your hand.** Why?

_____

_____

8. **Think of questions as you are listening.** Mentally ask questions such as "What is the main idea?" or "What point is she trying to make?" What other questions might you ask? How will this help?

_____

_____

9. **Get rid of as many distractions as possible.** Name some things that might distract you.

_____

_____

_____

Making Connections

Good listening skills are an essential component of the **intent to remember,** one of the three principles that affect whether new material even gets into your short-term memory. As pointed out, attention is not the same as learning, but learning cannot occur without attention.

Review the BREATHE System presented in Chapter 1. Explain how using this system could affect your listening.

_____

_____

_____

_____

_____

_____

_____

VIRTUAL FIELD TRIP

Improve Your Listening

 Visit the College Success CourseMate.

Taking Notes

Taking notes in class gives you a record of what was said there so that you can study that information after class. However, taking notes does much more. It helps you learn the material as you write it. In *Brain Rules*, John Medina says that the brain can hold only five to seven bits of information for about 30 seconds. If you don't repeat it within 30 seconds, it disappears.[3] Taking notes is one way of repeating it.

Your notes are not simply a record of what was said in class; they are part of the processes of active listening, mental processing, and manual recording, which employ all 10 learning principles. Taking notes in class is the beginning of taking ownership of the lecture material. Remember, you listen better if you understand the lecture. To understand the lecture, you need to drive. You need to (1) be prepared, (2) develop a basic background of the material if you don't already have one, and (3) ask questions. In Exercise 6.4, you will study a list of reasons students give for taking notes. Now that you know the learning principles, you can probably add more.

---

[3]John Medina, *Brain Rules: 12 Principles for Surviving and Thriving at Work, Home, and School*. (Seattle, WA: Pear, 2008).

Exercise 6.4

Why Take Notes?

Below is a list of reasons for taking notes in class. Read them, decide which is the most important reason to you, and number it 1. Number all the reasons in order of importance to you, with number 1 being the most important and number 8 being the least important. If there are reasons you think of that are not listed, list and rate them.

_____ **1.** Taking notes makes me pay attention. It keeps my mind from wandering. I am more likely to stay aware of what is important.

_____ **2.** Taking notes helps me concentrate. When I am trying to take good notes, I concentrate more on what the speaker is saying.

_____ **3.** Taking notes gives me a record of what was said in class. I know what was said on which days and also what was not covered in class.

_____ **4.** Taking notes forces me to select the main ideas. I can't write down everything.

_____ **5.** The simple act of writing something down helps me remember it longer.

_____ **6.** Taking notes gives me a place to write down assignments so that I will be able to find them later.

_____ **7.** Taking notes gives me information to use to study for tests and for class assignments.

_____ **8.** Taking notes reminds me of what the teacher has emphasized.

_____ **9.** _____

_____ **10.** _____

Using the Question in the Margin System for Lectures

A simplified version of the Question in the Margin system was introduced in Chapter 1. Now that you understand the learning principles for learning, you are ready to expand the system and examine why it works. During this discussion, you will want to refer to the steps you devised in Exercise 6.1 at the beginning of the chapter. See if you came up with many of the same steps.

Controlling the Amount and Form of Information

Although you can't control the amount of information in a lecture or the form in which it is presented, you *can* control what you write down and how you write it down. The Question in the Margin system introduced in Chapter 1 is the best way I know to control both the amount and the form of your notes. This is more than a system for taking notes. It is a complete system for processing information from lectures that makes use of all the learning principles for learning.

You begin by using the principle of selectivity to choose what's most important to write down in your notes. Then you organize your notes in question-and-answer form, using the principle of meaningful organization.

The Question in the Margin system is based on the note-taking system developed at Cornell University in the 1950s. This system may take some getting used to, but in the long run you will find that it saves you energy and time. Note taking is a skill, and as with all new skills, it takes practice. The more you use it, the better you become at it!

There are six basic steps in the Question in the Margin system. We will discuss each in turn.

Before You Begin

You will need a loose-leaf notebook with wide-ruled lines. If possible, take your notes in pen rather than in pencil. (On your laptop or computer, you could create this by using a table with 2 columns.)

First, draw a line down your paper about 2 1/2 inches from the left side. Disregard the red vertical line usually used for the margin. You will use the wide section on the right to record your notes in class. The section on the left becomes your question (or label) margin, where you will write a question that identifies the main idea (or key words or phrases that will serve as labels for the main idea). The margin at the top of the page is used for indicating the date, class, and page number and for writing assignments or other important information that you don't want to forget.

Six Steps

Step 1. *Record what is said.* Use a shortened form of writing to *record* what is said. Most of you have already perfected a shortened form of writing for when you text-message. Be stingy with your words. Never write a whole sentence when a word or two will do. The whole idea behind note taking is to write no more than you need to in order to remember what was said. Use abbreviations whenever possible. Your *basic background* will determine what you write. The more you know, the less you will have to write to remind yourself what was said. One good way to determine what to write down is to pretend that you are text-messaging your friend the important things she should know about class.

| Label notes with a question here. | Put name, date, class, and page number here. Take text message–like note here. |

For example, if your instructor says:

Recitation is the most powerful way of transferring information from short-term memory to long-term memory.

You might write:

Recite most pow'ful way to get s-t-mem to l-t-mem

If your instructor says:

Four reasons recitation is so powerful are that it makes you pay more attention because you know you are going to recite. It makes you participate in your learning. You must understand in order to explain in your own words. And it gives you feedback as to how much you actually know.

You might write:

1. Makes pay attent
2. Makes participate
3. Have to understnd
4. Feedbck

Exercise 6.5

Note Taking

1. Your instructor says:

Because of Switzerland's strict neutrality, Geneva provides an impartial meeting ground for representatives of other nations.[4]

You write:

Switz neutral so Geneva impartial meeting grnd for other nations

2. Your instructor says:

The Olympic games were held in ancient times on the plain of Olympia in Greece every four years. It was a time for laying aside political and religious differences, as athletes from all Greek cities and districts competed.[5]

[4]E. D. Hirsch Jr., J. F. Kett, and J. Trefl, *The Dictionary of Cultural Literacy*, 2d ed. (Boston: Houghton Mifflin, 1993).

[5]Ibid.

Your turn to try. You write:

3. Your instructor says:

   Obsolescence is a decline in the value of equipment or of a product brought about by an introduction of new technology or by changes in demand.[6]

   You write:

Step 2. *Question.* Recording the information during the lecture is only the first step in using the Question in the Margin system. The next step is to cue yourself what each section of your notes is about by writing a question (or key word or phrase) in the 2 1/2-inch margin on the left, and as soon after class as possible. The best way to determine what question to write is to play *Jeopardy* with the notes you took. What question do they answer? If this information appears on a test, how will it be asked? This questioning makes you use your critical-thinking skills. You have gone beyond just the facts you have written down. You understand the information enough to analyze how it might be asked for on a test. As already discussed, learning is enhanced when you ask questions. For example, your questions for the notes on the preceding page might look something like this.

Now go back to the other samples you just recorded and write a question in the margin. The *Jeopardy* question for the first sample might be "Why is Geneva a good place for nations to meet?"

Put a margin question here.	Put name, date, class, and page number here. Take text message–like notes here
What principle is best form short-term to long-term memory?	Recite most pow'ful way to get s-t-mem transferring from to l-t-mem.
What are four reasons why recitation works?	1. Makes pay attent 2. Makes participate 3. Have to understnd 4. Feedbck

[6]Ibid.

Step 3. *Recite.* The third step in the Question in the Margin system is to test yourself by *reciting* the information. Remember that reciting involves saying out loud in your own words what you have learned. This is part of strengthening your memory, and it begins the process of transferring the information to your long-term memory. Cover up the wide column and use the questions (or key words or phrases) in the left margin to recite the covered material. Repeat this until you are able to recite each section.

Making Connections

Learning Principles Used in the Question in the Margin System
One of the reasons that the Question in the Margin system is so effective is that it uses all of the learning principles. To check your understanding of the first three steps of the Question in the Margin system, skip ahead and study the list of the learning principles in Exercise 6.8 (page 146) and explain which of the learning principles are used in the recording, questioning, and reciting steps. Use the examples already given to model your explanation of how the learning principle selected is used. The chart will be a good summary sheet to use for studying.

Step 4. *Reflect.* Reflection, step 4, strengthens the memory as it further processes information into long-term memory. To *reflect* is to think about the ideas and how they fit in with other things you know. Try to make them personal—make connections, make them relevant to you. Can you think of examples from your own experience to reinforce the main point? Can you make it concrete by creating an analogy ("This is like . . .")? Can you visualize the information in some way? Do you agree with the information? How could you use that information?

After reflecting, you will probably want to add comments, illustrations, and questions to your notes. Reflection may be the most important step in the system. This is not only where you process new information, but also where you begin to take ownership of it. You are analyzing new information, integrating it into your experience by relating it to what you already know, and trying to find out if it has relevance and meaning for you. Reflecting takes information that you receive from a lecture and turns it into personal knowledge. This step is, in fact, step 3 of Zull's four pillars of learning, which you worked with in modeling the learning process.

Step 5. *Review.* Whereas reflection begins the soaking-in, or consolidation, process, reviewing continues it. In step 5, you *review* your notes systematically. If your reviews are regular and routine, you can keep the level of recall high.

Tony Buzan, in *Use Both Sides of Your Brain,* makes the following suggestions for reviewing:[7]

1. Use distributed practice to review. You should stop after about an hour of learning and take a 10-minute break. Your **first review**

Student Tip

" My study partners and I found that if we took the time to compare notes after class and write the questions in the margin together, our notes were better because we knew others would see them. Besides, it was more fun and easier, and the result is we know the material better. "

[7]Tony Buzan, *Use Both Sides of Your Brain* (New York: Penguin Books, 1990)

should come after this 10-minute break and should probably last about 10 minutes. This should keep the recall high for approximately one day.

2. The **second review** should take place within one day and should probably not take longer than three or four minutes. This should help you retain the information for about one week.

3. The **third review** should come before the week is up. It should require only a few minutes, because you are reviewing, not relearning, the information.

4. A **fourth review** will probably be required if you have not used the material within a month. This should firmly place the information into long-term memory.

In the first review you should include bringing notes up to date by writing your questions, reciting, reflecting, and so on. In other words, use the Question in the Margin system on the notes you took in class to process the information into your long-term memory.

In the second, third, and fourth reviews, you should make use of any consolidating method that works for you. Do whatever is necessary for the information to soak in. You could use the reciting part of the system again, or you could write down everything you can remember about the question you wrote in the margin. Reviewing might include such things as making and using flash cards, creating mnemonics, making practice tests, and rerunning your mental videos. This activates your memory. You are strengthening synaptic connections by taking information *from* your long-term memory. The more you activate information from your long-term memory, the easier it is to find that material when you need it. Make sure you are self-testing, not just mentally mumbling.

The times you set in your master schedule for routine study of a subject should be used for these reviews. Of course, immediately before and immediately after class are good review times. Right before you go to bed is also a good time to review.

One of the most significant aspects of reviewing is the cumulative effect it has on all aspects of learning, thinking, and remembering. You are building basic background. The more you know, the easier it is to learn. People who do not review are, in effect, wasting the efforts they put forth the first time. Your time is too valuable for that.

Step 6. *Summarize.* When you summarize, you condense main points in your own words. Either at the bottom of the page or at the end of your lecture notes, write a *summary*. You will want to do this after you review. Summarizing is a form of selectivity. If you understand your notes enough to make a concise version of them, you are probably well on your way to owning them. Your summary may be just one sentence, a few sentences, a paragraph, or even a page. However, you may prefer to make your summary a list, chart, time line, or map. Mapping is a good form of summary to use if you rely heavily on visualization to remember (see the illustrations at the beginning of each chapter for examples of mapping, or look ahead at the mapping section in Chapter 7).

One of the best strategies I know for summarizing is to pretend that you have been assigned to present to your class the material you need to summarize. Make a PowerPoint presentation for your assignment. Because it is a pretend assignment, you can make pretend PowerPoint slides from index cards. Decide which points you need to include and how you will present them. You should even include the illustrations you will use. You will find that when you finish, not only do you have a great summary, but you also understand the material better and probably already remember most of it.

Making Connections, Continued

Return to Exercise 6.8 and continue your explanation of how the learning principles are used in the Question in the Margin system by including how reflecting, reviewing, and summarizing use the learning principles.

Sample Notes—Question in the Margin

Lecture notes from the information presented about the Question in the Margin system might look something like the following sample:

Why use the Question in the Margin system?	Q-M system based on mem principles Process info into long-term mem
What is step 1?	Set up w/line 2 1/2 Write important info on right—wide—telegraph **RECORD**
What is step 2?	After class asap question infor w/?? here **QUESTION**
What is step 3?	After writing ?, cover notes—ask question & say answer out loud in own wrds **RECITE**
What is step 4?	After basic understand'ng of info, try to make personal, visualize, make connections **REFLECT**
What is step 5?	B 4 put up notes, go back over all Use difrent techniques like flash cards, practice tests, etc. **REVIEW**
What is step 6?	Condense main points in own words—writ sum at bottom of page or on sep activity **SUMMARIZE**

Note: The Question in the Margin system uses most of the learning principles and consists of six steps—Record, Question, Recite, Reflect, Review, and Summarize.

Making It Concrete

Probably the most difficult part of using the Question in the Margin system for many students is breaking the habit of writing too much or writing in complete sentences. Because you will be bringing your notes up to date very soon after class, you can get by with writing less. While you may use the same form of shortened writing that you use to text-message, there is a difference in sending a message and deciding what to write down.

Writing margin questions is a skill that you must develop. Most likely, you won't be good at it for quite some time. If you have ever driven a car with a stick shift, remember when you first began to drive it? You had to really think yourself through it, and sometimes the ride was jerky. Now you shift without even thinking about it. The same is true with taking notes in shortened text-like form. At first you have to really think about what you are going to write. Sometimes it takes more time to think about what you are leaving out than it would to write it! Don't worry. You can think four times faster than most lecturers can talk, so you have time to determine what you will write. With practice, this shortened form of note taking will become natural. You'll do it without much effort. Don't get me wrong. Taking notes is hard work. You have to become involved in class both physically and mentally. At the end of class, you will probably be exhausted. You don't learn by passively sitting in the passenger seat. You process information only by becoming involved in what you are learning. Don't expect to be an expert immediately. It will take time to develop your skills .

Stop and reflect for a few minutes on how taking notes is like driving a stick-shift automobile. Write down as many comparisons as you can think of.

 VIRTUAL FIELD TRIP

Practice Using the Question in the Margin System

This field trip sends you to several online lectures by John Medina, who will provide you with some practice in taking notes.

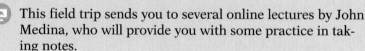

Exercise 6.6

Question in the Margin System

Study the step-by-step plan you devised in Exercise 6.1, "Modeling the Learning Process," at the beginning of the chapter. On the basis of your plan, what changes would you make to the Question in the Margin system?

What part of your plan corresponds to the Question in the Margin system? Fill in the chart below with similarities.

Question in the Margin System	Parts of My Learning Model That Correspond
Preparing for the system	
RECORD	
QUESTION	
RECITE	
REFLECT	
REVIEW	
SUMMARIZE	

Exercise 6.7

More Practice Using the Question in the Margin System

Have someone read this lecture to you as you practice taking notes using the Question in the Margin system.

Left Brain or Right Brain

There has been a lot of talk recently about left-brain, right-brain theory. The whole theory is somewhat confusing to students who want to know: "Am I left-brained or right-brained? How do I find out? Why should I care? Which is 'good'?" For a few minutes, let's talk about some of these questions.

To oversimplify things, the brain is primarily made up of two hemispheres. Although the right and left hemispheres work together, each side has a different function and processes information differently. Most people seem to have a dominant side. The catch is that we need to use both sides of the brain, so that left is not better than right; left is different from right. It appears that most classroom teaching is addressed to those who are predominantly left-brained, leaving those of us who are more right-brained feeling somewhat inadequate.

A closer look at the attributes of each side of the brain should clear up some of this confusion. The left brain processes material in a linear, sequential, logical way. The left brain is language oriented and also geared to mathematical reasoning. It responds to verbal instructions, sees things in parts that fit together neatly and logically into the whole. Learning rules, outlining, identifying and naming parts, sequencing events, arranging from part to whole, locating the main idea, and reading and following verbal instructions are all functions of the left brain. It is the left brain that pays attention to the mechanics of writing, such as spelling, punctuation, and agreement. Math, science, languages, writing, and logic are processed by the left brain.

The right brain, on the other hand, processes material in a more holistic, random, and intuitive way. The right brain is visual and creative. It responds by looking at a plan as a whole, not at the parts that make up the whole. Instead of memorizing vocabulary words, the right brain processes the words in context. Instead of sequencing events or numbering events in order, the right brain relates events to a whole theme. The right brain wants to see it, not be told about it. In writing, it is the right brain that pays attention to writing coherent sentences in meaningful sequence. Music appreciation, art appreciation, dance, perception, fantasy, and creativity are processed by the right brain.

If we are predominantly left-brained or predominantly right-brained, we should find ways to exercise the side of the brain that we use less. When learning new material, we should process the material in various ways, so as to use both sides of the brain. You may want to do some further research into your brain.

Summary Sheet for Question in the Margin: Lecture Notes

What You Do	When You Do It	Why You Do It
Input, or Gather, Information		
Record		
Listen carefully. Write down *important information* from the lecture in the wide margin of your page. Don't write whole sentences; be *telegraphic*.	Get out your paper and pen as soon as you come to class. Take notes from beginning to end of class.	Short-term memory will not hold what you hear in class, so you need a record. Use *selectivity* and *write telegraphically* because you can't write down everything. Taking notes also helps you *pay attention*.
Process Information Gathered		
Question		
Read over your notes. *Determine the main ideas* of each section and label them in the form of a possible test question. *Underline*, number, or clean up notes so that they are clear and legible.	Most students think that when they have taken notes in class, their job is over. But forgetting begins immediately; therefore, as soon as possible after class, begin a review of your notes.	Because you forget quickly, if you just take notes and do nothing, you'll end up relearning the material, rather than remembering it. Reading over notes begins to *process the information*. *Writing a question* ensures that you *understood* what you wrote and *organizes your notes* in a meaningful way.
Recite		
Cover up your notes. Use the labels as cues. *Say the main ideas out loud in your own words*.	This should be done as soon as you record and label your notes.	*Recitation* is the most powerful means you have of *transferring information from short-term memory to long-term memory*. You have begun to *learn* the material instead of merely recording it.
Reflect		
Think about the lecture. Make *connections* with things you already know. How does the lecture connect to the *textbook*? Make it *personal*. *Visualize*. Begin to *organize* your notes.	*As soon as you recite* or while you are reciting, begin to reflect. (You may want to reflect before you recite as well.)	*Reflection* makes the information *real* and *personal*. Therefore, you process information more deeply into your long-term memory.
Activate		
Review		
Go over your notes. *Recite* by making use of the narrow margin. Make *flash cards, mnemonic devices*, or *practice tests*, or *map* the ideas found in the notes.	Review *10 minutes after you finish going over your notes*, keeping recall fresh for one day. Review again in *one day*, in *one week*, and then once more *before the test*.	Periodic review keeps you from forgetting what you already know. Before a test, you will just need to review, not relearn, the material.
Summarize		
Condense main points in your own words at the end of each section or each day's notes, write a short summary, or make a summary sheet such as this one.	Summarize *during* one of your *reviews*.	Summarizing allows for *consolidation* and promotes a deeper *understanding* of the material.

Exercise 6.8

Learning Principles Used in the Question in the Margin System

One reason the Question in the Margin system works so well is that it uses all ten learning principles for learning. Use the following chart to explain how each principle is used in the Question in the Margin system. Be sure to consider all steps of the system. I have included a few to get you started. You will need to add to the list.

Learning Principle	How This Principle Is Used in the Question in the Margin System
INTEREST	When I take notes, my brain senses that the information is valuable. Other ways interest is used:
INTENT TO REMEMBER	Knowing that I will have to write a question and recite information later triggers intent to remember.
BASIC BACKGROUND	
SELECTIVITY	
MEANINGFUL ORGANIZATION	
VISUALIZATION	

Learning Principle for Learning	How This Principle Is Used in the Question in the Margin System
RECITATION	
ASSOCIATION	
CONSOLIDATION	
DISTRIBUTED PRACTICE	

The Question in the Margin system also fits nicely into the flowchart used on page XX in Chapter 5. Go back to the flowchart and label where each step of using the Question in the Margin system would fit on the chart.

 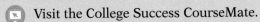

VIRTUAL FIELD TRIP

Expanding What You Know About Note Taking

Visit the College Success CourseMate.

Modeling the Learning Process

You learned the steps in the Question in the Margin system and created your plan at the beginning of the chapter in Exercise 6.1, "Modeling the Learning Process."

Gathering. You took notes in class.

Analyzing. You analyzed your notes, wrote questions in the margin, and looked for connections.

Creating New Ideas. You reflected and reviewed your notes and questions and predicted possible test questions, involving higher-order thinking skills.

Acting. You developed summary sheets, maps, PowerPoint presentations, and practice tests.

SUMMARY

To see if you grasped the major points of the chapter and to make a useful study guide, answer the following questions found in your reading. When you have written your answers, cover them and see if you can say the answer to each question in your own words. If you prefer to type your answers, you will find a Microsoft Word download for each summary on the College Success CourseMate for Practicing College Learning Strategies at www.cengagebrain.com.

Name and briefly explain what James Zull outlines as four essential functions for learning.

1. _____

2. _____

3. _____

4. _____

What are the five obstacles that keep you from listening well?

1. _____

2. _____

3. _____

4. _____

5. _____

Name five things you can do to improve your listening.

1. _____

2. _____

3. _____

4. _____

5. _____

What do you consider the three most important reasons for taking notes during a lecture?

1. _____

2. _____

3. _____

List and explain the six steps of the Question in the Margin system for processing information from lectures.

Step 1: _____

_____

Step 2: _____

_____

Step 3: _____

_____

Step 4: _____

_____

Step 5: _____

_____

Step 6: _____

_____

Case Study: What's Your Advice?

Sara is a first-year student taking 12 credit hours in college. She lives in the dorm, and it is her first time away from home. Sara was a very good student in high school and didn't have to study much to get As and Bs. Now she is doing exactly what she did in high school and is struggling even to pass. She listens in class and reads her assignments unless the instructor is going to lecture on them anyway. Then she thinks it isn't necessary to read the assignment. Sara does her homework at night in her room and usually finishes it before visiting her friends or watching TV. Her roommate suggested that Sara needed to take notes in class. Although she never had to take notes in high school, Sara decided it was worth a try. Her history professor talked so fast that when she tried to write down what he was saying, she couldn't write fast enough.

Fifteen minutes into the class, Sara was so frustrated that she quit writing. She started to take notes in her psychology class, but got so interested in the discussion that she forgot about taking notes. Sara took notes in biology class but was unable to read what notes she did manage to write when she got ready to study for a test. Although she reads all the assignments her English professor assigns, she has yet to pass the daily reading quiz.

You are sitting at Sara's table at the campus café. She is almost in tears and ready to give up and go home. Using what you have learned in this and previous chapters, can you help her make a list of things she might do? She has not had the benefit of taking this class and needs more instruction than a list. In addition to your list of what to do, you should suggest to her how to do it.

Parallel Parking

List each step of the Question in the Margin system and see if you can create a comparison to driving. For example, you might say that recording important information in class is like putting fuel in your car.

Evaluating Learning Outcomes

How successful were you in making it to your destination in this chapter?

Analyze what you learned in this chapter. Put a check beside each task you are now able to do. Now think of strategies that you learned that will help you save time and study more effectively. List them in the appropriate place on the back inside cover.

☐ **Use** the 10 learning principles to develop strategies for processing information from classroom lectures.
☐ **Appraise** your listening habits, and construct strategies for improving them.
☐ **Give** several reasons for taking notes in class.
☐ **Demonstrate** the six steps of the Question in the Margin system for taking notes: record, question, recite, reflect, review, and summarize.
☐ **Explain** how to use the Question in the Margin system to someone who has never used it.
☐ **Explain** the learning process modeled in this chapter.

Your Student Tip for This Chapter

Use the space below to write a tip you would give to other students about what you have learned in this chapter.

_____

_____

_____

Use this page to set specific goals for taking notes in each class.

7 Processing Information from Textbooks

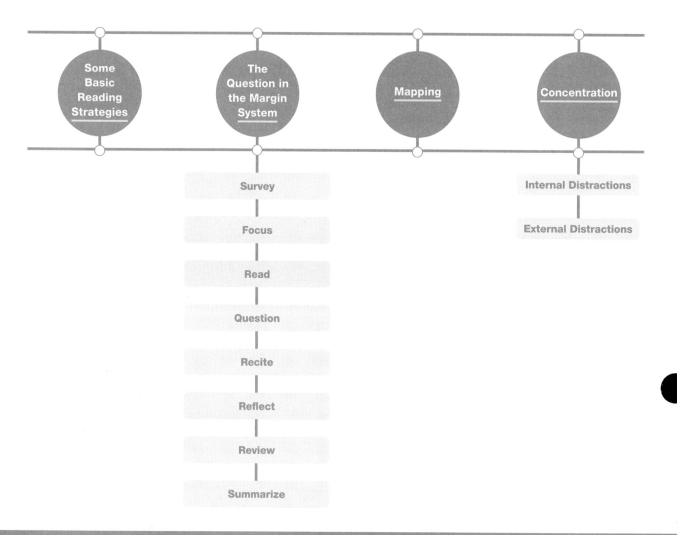

Some Basic Reading Strategies

The Question in the Margin System

- Survey
- Focus
- Read
- Question
- Recite
- Reflect
- Review
- Summarize

Mapping

Concentration

- Internal Distractions
- External Distractions

Using the Question in the Margin System for Textbooks

Now that you have the basics of the Question in the Margin system for taking notes in class and discovered how the process uses brain-compatible learning, let's look at how it works when reading a textbook. You have seen the importance of being the driver, not a passenger, in the classroom. Your role as driver takes on even more importance when

Learning Outcomes
for Chapter 7 Processing Information from Textbooks

Here's your destination for Chapter 7. When you complete Chapter 7, you are expected not only to understand the material presented, but also to be able to:

Demonstrate some strategies to use before, during, and after reading.

Explain how to use the Question in the Margin system to someone who has never used it.

Demonstrate how to use the Question in the Margin system for reading textbooks: survey, focus, read, question, recite, reflect, review, and summarize.

Explain how to survey a textbook assignment.

Explain the learning process modeled in this chapter.

Analyze the Question in the Margin system, and **explain** how the learning principles are used to complete the system.

reading your textbooks. The amount of material you are responsible for in your textbooks presents some real road hazards. There is a temptation to speed, to get to the end of the chapter. However, if you are to own the material in each chapter, you must plan your maneuvers carefully.

Remember that the first thing you want to do is to use as many learning principles as possible to gather the information. Using the chart on the following page, list several differences in gathering information from lectures and from textbooks.

Exercise 7.1

Differences in Gathering Information from Lectures and from Textbooks

Lectures	Textbooks

Some Basic Reading Strategies

Reading Strategy: before you read:

- Survey the chapter.

- Recall what you already know about the subject.

- Predict what you may be looking for by forming a question in your mind.

Reading Strategy: while you read

- Visualize what the author is saying.

- If it is complicated, read it aloud.

- Look for the answer to the question you predicted.

- Stop and look up any words you don't understand.

- Then rephrase it in your own words.

- Try to relate it to something you already know.

- Wait until you finish a paragraph before for you mark anything.

Reading Strategy: after you complete a paragraph

- Check to see if your predicted question was what the paragraph was actually about.

- Determine the main idea and supporting detail.

- Write a question in the margin that information in the paragraph is the answer to.

- After you write your question, mark the answer to your question by highlighting, circling, or numbering the text so you can quickly see the answer to your question. (Come up with a system that works for you.)

Reading Strategies: to use after you have marked your text:

- Cover the paragraph you have just read and marked. Using the question you wrote in the margin, test yourself.

- Recite the answer aloud.

- Reflect about what you read. Try to connect it to other things that you know. Try to make it personal. Predict what the next paragraph will be about and start the process all over again.

Before you put your book away:

- Review the key points of the selection.

- Make a summary or study guide for the selection.

Starting the Connections

Like listening to lectures, reading textbooks involves starting the connections. The three learning principles in this category are *interest*, *intent to remember*, and *basic background*. You want to make a conscious effort to use the learning principles before you begin to read. One of the best ways to get familiar with the road you are about to travel is to **survey** the material before you begin. Look at the title, major and minor topics discussed, and bold print; look at the pictures, study the graphs and charts, read the summary, and examine the review questions *before* you do any reading. As you are doing this, try to recall everything you already know about the subject. Surveying often builds interest; but most of all, it gives you a basic background about the material you are going to read. Knowing something about the subject makes it easier to pay attention and easier to remember. By knowing where the reading is going, you can make connections as you read the material for the first time.

Think for a moment about your concentration when you read. If someone gave you a page and said, "Read this," would you read it in the same way as if she said, "Read this page to find three ways to process information or five ways to save time"? If you know why you are reading something, you will probably get more out of it. An obvious study strategy to use when reading a textbook, then, is to note the headings or the topic sentence of each paragraph and try to determine what you are looking for as you continue through the paragraph. This **focusing** should be done after you survey and before you begin to read. Focus is the second step and requires no writing.

Controlling the Amount and Form of Information

As you begin to read, you can control the amount and form of the information you gather by reading not more than one paragraph at a time before you process that information. Remember that your short-term memory can hold only five to seven bits of information at a time. Each paragraph will likely hold about that amount. If you read the entire chapter without processing bits of information into long-term memory, you would probably have to go back and reread most of the chapter in order to process it. Instead, why not use distributed practice by processing information along the way?

Once you have read a paragraph, you want to process that information before you go on to the next one. The system works the same here as it did with taking notes. After you read a paragraph, to ensure you have gotten the main idea and selected the important points, write a question in the margin that labels those important points. Next, underline the answer to your question. Just as you were stingy with what you wrote while taking notes, you want to underline only the main words. You don't want to have to go back and reread the whole paragraph to find your answer. Underlining should be done *after* you read, *not while* you are reading, and the underlined words should answer the question you have written in the margin. This questioning and underlining is time-consuming, but you are going to have to process the information at some time before a test, so why not do it the first time?

The result of your efforts is that each paragraph is labeled with a possible test question or two, and you can quickly review the main points without having to reread the chapter. Know the speed limit. When you are responsible for knowing and using the information, speed-reading is not advisable. Stopping at the end of each paragraph slows you down enough to make sure you make connections and process what you have read. It also gives you an organized way to go back and review without rereading every word.

From here on, the system works the same as it did for lecture notes. You process the information by covering answers and asking yourself the question in the margin. You **recite** the answers until you are sure you have grasped the information. Before going on, **reflect.** Link the information to what you already know, relate it to the previous paragraph, and consider where the author may be going in the next paragraph. Make it personal. How will you use that information? How will you remember it for a test? If possible, make a mental video to help you *see* the information.

Once you are in control of the information in one paragraph, go on to the next and repeat the process. Because this system is demanding, you will probably want to do only several pages at a time. Make use of those minutes you used to waste. When you have labeled the entire chapter, review the chapter to get the whole picture.

The last step in the Question in the Margin system is to *summarize by bringing together the main ideas in your own words.* Many students find it more useful to study from their notes than from their marked textbook. Making a summary sheet to study for each chapter will be helpful. Your summary may be made by making flashcards from the questions you have written in the margin. Many students prefer to write their notes from each chapter on paper, as with lecture notes, instead of writing in the textbook or after marking their books. The summary at

Student Tip

❝*It was hard to break the habit of underlining as I read. Instead of just mindlessly underlining, now as I read, I am thinking what question I need to write. And I end up with something I can actually use for studying.*❞

the end of each chapter in this text illustrates this. In fact, you have probably already discovered that the questions in each chapter summary are the author's Question in the Margin questions moved to the end of the chapter. You can use this process as a model for summarizing chapters in your other textbooks. Writing a summary is a good check to make sure you understand the information enough to condense it in your own words. In addition, if you make a summary as soon as you finish a reading assignment, you will already have an aid to use to study for a test. This should really cut down on the amount of time needed to study for a test.

Student Tip

Don't try to mark a whole chapter at one time. It's easier to mark what you need to read throughout the day when you have a few minutes to read and mark a paragraph or two. When you get to your study time where you would have read the assignment, you've already read it and it's ready to study to make sure you understand it.

Exercise 7.2

Understanding the Steps

In order to gather the information from your assignment, you first **survey** what you need to read.	What does this involve?
The second step of this gathering is to **focus**.	How is this accomplished?
The third step needed in gathering the information is to **read paragraph by paragraph**.	Why read only one paragraph at a time?
Then you **label the margin with a question**. The answer to the question should be the main ideas in the paragraph.	Explain why this is a good method to use.
Next, you **underline the answer to the question in the textbook**.	Explain why you underline after, instead of before, you write the question.

Go back to the section in Chapter 6 on reviewing lecture notes (pp. 000–000) and apply this discussion to your textbook notes.

1. When should you review? _10 min after going over notes_

2. Why should you review? _periodic review keeps you from forgetting_

3. Name some ways to review. _make flash cards, go over notes, recite by making use of narrow margins practice test + map ideas found in notes_

4. List several methods of summarizing that are most effective for you. _Summarize during your reviews, condense main points in your own words write a short summary_

VIRTUAL FIELD TRIP

Learning More About Marking Your Textbook

Visit the College Success CourseMate.

Making Connections

Review what you know about using the Question in the Margin system for reading textbooks. Once you understand how the system works for textbooks, go back to Exercise 6.8. Check your list of learning principles and include your explanations of how the learning principles are used for the textbook model. You may want to use a different-color ink for the textbook items.

Exercise 7.3

Practice Using the Question in the Margin System for Textbooks

On the following pages, you will find textbook pages for you to practice on. You will want to use all of the steps; however, all that you will see is the question step with the question in the margin. The first paragraph has the questions noted for you. Be sure to write the margin questions throughout the entire excerpt.

In addition to writing your question in the margin and underlining the answer, you will probably develop other strategies, such as numbering major points, circling important dates, or starring items emphasized in class. You may want to use different-color highlighters to distinguish answers to different questions. If you are going to take the time to mark your textbooks with questions and answers, it is important that you be able to read it. Use a pen or highlighter, not a pencil.

Learning Styles: How a Person Learns Best

Everyone does not learn material in the same manner. And although we often have no control over how the instructor presents material in class, if as students we can analyze how we best learn, then we can make a conscious effort to reinforce what is taught in class by using our strengths.

What senses do auditory learners use?

Auditory learners use their voices and their ears as the primary mode of learning. If you are an auditory learner, you remember what you hear and what you yourself say. When something is hard to understand, you want to ¹talk it out. When you're excited and enthusiastic about learning, you want to ²verbally express your response. And when an assignment is given orally, you probably remember it without writing it down. You ³love class discussion, you seem to grow by working and ⁴talking with others, and you appreciate a teacher's taking time to ⁵explain something to you. You are also easily distracted by sound because you attend to all of the noises around you, but, ironically, you may often interrupt a quiet moment by talking because you find silence itself disturbing. When you want to remember something, you should ⁶say it aloud several times because the oral repetition will set it in your mind. You find it difficult when a teacher asks you to work quietly at your desk for an extended period of time or when you try to study in a quiet room. For some auditory learners,

What are six ways auditory learners learn?

their abilities serve them well in learning music, foreign languages, and in other areas that depend on good auditory discrimination.

Visual learners want to see the words written down, a picture of something being described, a time line to remember events in history, or the assignment written on the board. If you are a visual learner, you are very attuned to all the physical things in the classroom and appreciate a pleasant and orderly physical environment. You probably carefully organize your own materials and decorate your work space. You seek out illustrations, diagrams, and charts to help understand and remember information. You appreciate being able to follow what a teacher is presenting with material written on an overhead transparency or in a handout. You should review and study material by reading over your notes and by recopying and reorganizing them in outline form.

Kinesthetic learners prefer it and learn better when they touch and are physically involved in what they are studying. If you are a kinesthetic learner, you want to act out a situation, make a product, do a project, and in general be busy with your learning. You find that when you physically do something, you understand it and remember it. You may take lots of notes to keep your hands busy, but you probably never reread the notes! You learn to use the computer by trying it, experimenting, and practicing. You learn concepts in social studies by simulating experiences in the classroom. You may become interested in poetry by becoming physically involved in the thoughts expressed. You want to be as active as possible during the learning experience. You usually express your enthusiasm by jumping up and getting excited when something is going well. And when asked to sit still for long periods, you fidget and may have been labeled as having a behavior problem.

Mixed-modality learners are able to function in more than one modality. In terms of achievement, students with mixed-modality strengths often have a better chance of success than do those with a single-modality strength, because they can process information in whatever way it is presented.[1]

To be successful, learners need to understand how they learn best and how to use their modality strengths to transfer learning from the weaker areas.

Finding an Effective Way to Study Through Your Modality Strengths

Auditory

If you learn best by hearing, you should listen carefully in class. You should ask your instructor's permission to tape the lesson. Listen to the tape several times if the material is new or difficult. Keep the tape to review for tests. Another study technique is to discuss the material with another student. If no one is available, turn on the tape recorder and discuss the information as if you were explaining it to someone else. Then listen to the recording. Once you have listened

[1]Pat B. Guild and Stephen Garger, *Marching to Different Drummers* (Alexandria, VA: Association for Supervision and Curriculum Development, 1986).

Subjects good at?

Now it's your turn. Write questions in the margin; then, underline the answers in the text passage. Complete this through page 000.

to the lesson tape and your discussion tape, you should do some reading about the subject. Remember to write down notes concerning important items to remember. Listening, reading, and writing will help strengthen your understanding of the material. If the instructor announces the new subject ahead of time, ask if there are any tapes, sound films, or filmstrips available on the new material. If so, use the available material before the material is taught in class.

Visual

If you learn best by seeing the material, you should read the material to be discussed in class before you get to class. When you are reading, remember not only to read the words, but also to look at pictures, charts, maps, or graphs. You should take notes about the information while you are reading. You will probably benefit from mapping, clustering, outlining, or even using flash cards. Writing and placing information into maps, graphs, or the margin of your text will help you remember what you have read. Be sure to take notes while you are listening to class lectures and discussions.

Kinesthetic

If you learn best by doing something, you should write notes about what you are to learn. As you read, underline the important ideas *after* you have read a section or write notes in the margin. It may also help you to make flash cards or maps or to make charts, crossword puzzles, word bingo, picture puzzles, or mnemonic devices. Another effective way is to make a practice test about the material to be learned. Making a sample test will help point you to areas that are important and need to be studied more. You will learn best by using as many activities as possible.[2]

Summary Sheet for Question in the Margin: Textbooks

What You Do	When You Do It	Why You Do It
	Input, or Gather, Information	
Survey		
Skim the *title, major headings, bold print*, and *charts*, and read the *summary* and *review questions*.	Don't begin reading with the first page of the chapter. *Survey before you read*.	Surveying helps develop *interest* in what you are about to read. It gives you a *basic background*. Your subconscious begins to work.

[2]Adapted from J. L. Sanders, *How to Do Homework Through Your Own Perceptual Strengths* (Jamaica, NY: School of Education and Human Services, St. John's University, 1985).

What You Do	When You Do It	Why You Do It
Focus		
Turn each *major heading* into a *general question,* or use some other method of determining what you are looking for in the paragraph.	*Before you begin* reading each paragraph, determine what you will look for when you read.	Looking for the answer to a question rather than just reading promotes better *concentration* and *understanding*. In addition, you use the principle of selectivity.
Read		
Read each section *paragraph* by *paragraph* to find the answer to the question you have formulated. Look up any unfamiliar words. Read the section out loud if necessary.	*Do not go on to the next paragraph until you understand the one you are reading*. Do not underline or highlight at this time.	Reading paragraph by paragraph puts *small bits of information* into your memory so you need not try to remember the whole chapter at once. It ensures *understanding*.
Process Information Gathered		
Question		
Label the *main idea* by writing a *question* or brief statement *in the margin*. Then *underline* the answer to your question. Be stingy with your underlining.	*After you read* each paragraph, determine the main idea and put a question in the margin. Then *underline* the answers to your questions in the text. Do not underline while reading.	This step ensures that you *understand* the main ideas in each paragraph. *Selectivity* eliminates the need to reread the chapter and organizes it in a way that allows you to *process* it into *long-term memory*.
Recite		
Cover the underlined text and *recite* in your own words the answer to your margin question.	*Recite as soon as you complete the questioning and underlining*. Do not go on to the next paragraph until you can recite the main idea of this paragraph.	*Recitation* promotes consolidation, strengthens neural pathways, and gives you immediate feedback.
Reflect		
Think about what you have read. Make *connections* with things you already know. Make it *personal. Visualize.* Begin to *organize* your notes.	*As soon as you recite,* or while you are reciting, begin to reflect.	*Reflection* makes the information *real,* by processing it more deeply into your long-term memory. It is the difference between memorizing something and learning it.
Activate		
Review		
Go over what you have read. *Recite* margin questions. Make *summary sheets, flash cards, mnemonic devices,* and *practice tests,* or *map* the ideas found in the chapter.	*Review ten minutes after you finish* the whole chapter, keeping recall fresh for one day. Review again in *one day, one week,* and then once more *before the test.*	Periodic review keeps you from forgetting what you already know. Before a test, you will need to just *review, not relearn,* the material.
Summarize		
Condense main ideas in your own words by putting notes on paper, making a summary sheet, map, or time line.	Do this during one of your reviews.	*Summarizing* promotes the consolidation and understanding needed to use material that you have learned.

Summary for Both Lecture and Textbook Question in the Margin

Processing Stage	When Listening to Lectures	When Reading Textbooks
Get input or gather information.	1. **Listen** carefully. 2. Write down important information text message–like.	1. **Survey** the title, major headings, pictures, graphs, bold print, and summary. 2. **Focus** your attention on what you will read by turning each major heading into a question. 3. Read each section **paragraph by paragraph,** looking for the answer to the question.
Process information gathered.	1. **Read** over notes and **write a question in the margin.** 2. Cover notes and **recite** them. 3. Make the information personal by **reflecting.**	After completing each paragraph, label what the paragraph is about by writing a question in the margin. **Underline** the answer to the question. (Be stingy with your underlining!) 1. Cover your underlining in the text and **recite.** 2. Make the information **personal** by **reflecting.**
Activate	1. **Review** 10 minutes after going over the entire lecture. Review again in one day, in one week, and before a test. Use other methods such as flash cards, practice tests, and mnemonic devices. 2. **Summarize** at the end of each section of notes.	1. **Review** 10 minutes after finishing the chapter. Review again in one day, in one week, and before a test. Use other methods, such as flash cards, practice tests, and mnemonic devices. 2. Make a **summary sheet** for each chapter.

Exercise 7.4

Do You Understand How the Question in the Margin System Works?

Analyze the following situations and label with the correct *source* (classroom lecture or textbook reading), the correct *stage* (input or gather information, process information gathered, or activate), and the actual *step* within the system. The Summary Sheet should be helpful. Pay particular attention to what each student is doing. Identifying what is being done is not nearly as important as knowing what to do.

1. When he was finished reading, Julio went back through the entire chapter and tried to recite the answers to the questions he had written in the margin.

   Source _____ Stage _____ Step _____

2. After class, Lakeisha read over her lecture notes and wrote the key words and phrases on the left side of her paper.

   Source _____ Stage _____ Step _____

3. Sally wrote a question beside each paragraph in Chapter 3 of her History 201 textbook and then underlined the answer to each question.

   Source _____ Stage _____ Step _____

4. In order to study for his upcoming exam, Bobby covered up his lecture notes and recited the importance of the questions he had written.

Source _____ Stage _____ Step _____

5. When the instructor had concluded her lecture series on the different breeds of beef cattle, David wrote a summary at the end of that section in his notes, putting it into his own words.

Source _____ Stage _____ Step _____

6. To make sure he retained the information from the chapters he had read, Yuuki regularly went over the questions he had written in the margin of his textbook.

Source _____ Stage _____ Step _____

7. Jeff made summary sheets and flash cards and used mnemonic devices to refresh, rather than to relearn, the information from his German 210 class.

Source _____ Stage _____ Step _____

8. When class began, Curtis listened carefully to everything that the instructor said.

Source _____ Stage _____ Step _____

9. To begin her Psychology 141 reading assignment, Jane read the title, checked out the bold headings, and surveyed the graphs and the chapter summary.

Source _____ Stage _____ Step _____

10. While reading, Arya turned each major heading into a question, and then read each paragraph to answer the question.

Source _____ Stage _____ Step _____

11. When Beth's instructor said, "There are seven stages in Chickering's student development theory called vectors," Beth wrote "7 stages (vectors)—Chickering s.d. theory."

Source _____ Stage _____ Step _____

12. Mercedes took a few minutes to think about all of the information she had been reciting from Chapter 10 in her Sociology 310 textbook and tried to relate it to things she already knew.

Source _____ Stage _____ Step _____

Questions I need to ask about the Question in the Margin system for textbooks:

_____

_____

VIRTUAL FIELD TRIP

Let's Learn More About Critical Reading and Mapping

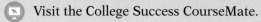

Visit the College Success CourseMate.

BRAIN BYTE

The human brain is not organized or designed for linear, one-path thought. Many brain researchers confirm that graphic organizers like mapping help learners understand and recall information better. Maps that are revised and color-coded boost learning and retention.

Mapping

If you find some information particularly difficult, you may want to use the learning principle of visualization to process it. **Mapping** is useful for students who learn well visually. Just as a road map gives you a clear picture of the main roads, connections, and possible routes, a concept map is a **visual representation** of important information selected from the text or lecture. It's like a picture outline. A map is usually hierarchical and shows the relationships among pieces of the whole. Once you have determined the topic or main idea of what you want to summarize as a map, make it the central focus of your map. Then you will select major and supporting points for each point.

Mapping can be used to organize information from sections of a chapter or even an entire chapter, depending on the complexity of the material. It serves best as a study aid by organizing information into manageable parts with observable relationships that can be easily understood and remembered. It is one of the best ways to create a summary for both lecture and textbook material. You have probably noticed that each chapter of this text begins with a map visually organizing the contents of the chapter.

Following is a paragraph given to students with the instruction to map the paragraph so that they can remember the material better. After the paragraph are several examples of mapping. It should be apparent that there is no one *correct* way to map. Each map looks different, but the relationship of the components in the passage (hierarchy) is the same in each map.

Four Kinds of Art

Each art form puts different demands on artists. Drama requires training of the voice and an ability to re-create life on stage. To excel in ballet, one must have great strength and endurance. A career in opera requires unique natural gifts and a willingness to spend years in training. Unlike these other arts, sculpture requires a talent for composing in three dimensions and a liking for manual labor. It is interesting how different countries bring a particular art form to mind. Because of Shakespeare, England comes to mind when one thinks of great drama. Russia recalls the performances of its spectacular ballet companies. Italy is synonymous with drama set to lush melodies of opera and with sculpture by the greatest artists who ever lived.

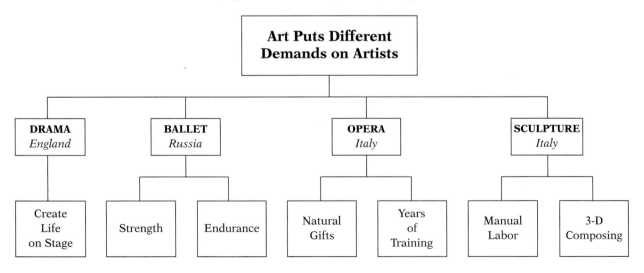

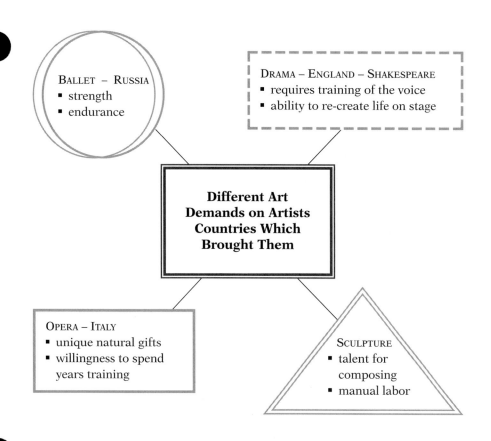

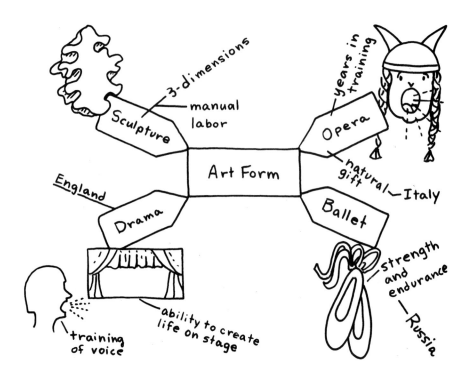

Exercise 7.5

Practice with Mapping

The two-paragraph article below describes things homeowners can do to save energy. Following the article, you will find a student's study notes on the first paragraph. The first example is how the information looked in her notes when her instructor was lecturing. The second is her version of the Question in the Margin system from this textbook. Then there are two examples of a map for the first paragraph. Your job is to examine the second paragraph. First, mark it as you would a textbook page using the Question in the Margin system. Next, using your marked text, map it on a separate sheet of paper. Because the goals of the Question in the Margin system and mapping are the same, the strategies used to process the information into long-term memory will also overlap. When mapping, I find it easier to put my questions in the margin before I map. Remember, you are mapping not to be artistic, but to help you remember the details you might need for a test.

Read the following article. First write your questions in the margin. Then use another sheet of paper to create a map.

All homeowners can take action if they are serious about saving on energy costs. Those with more than $100 to spend should consider any of the following steps. First, sidewalls and especially the ceiling of a home should be fully insulated. Proper insulation can save 30 percent or more of a heating or cooling bill. Next, storm windows should be installed throughout the house. They provide an insulating area of still air that may reduce energy loss by 10 percent or more. Finally, a homeowner might consider installing *a solar hot-water heating system. Four key factors in such a decision are geographical location, the amount of sunlight available, energy costs in the area, and the construction of the house.*

Homeowners with less than $100 to spend can take many energy-saving steps as well. To begin with, two kinds of inexpensive sealers can be used to reduce energy leaks around the house. Caulking will seal cracks around the outside windows, door frames, and at the corners of the house. Weather stripping can be applied to provide a weather-tight seal between the frame and moving parts of doors and windows. Another inexpensive step is to check that a home-heating or cooling system is clean. A dirty or clogged filter, for example, can make a furnace or air conditioner work much harder to heat or cool a house. In addition, a "low-flow" shower head can either be purchased separately or a small plastic insert available at the hardware store can be added to a regular head to limit water flow. Blinds and drapes can be used to advantage throughout the year. In winter, they can be closed at night to reduce heat loss. In summer, they can be closed during the day to keep the house cooler. Finally, a ceiling fan can be turned on in the summer to distribute cool air. When the thermostat is set at 78 degrees, the fan will make it seem like 72 degrees. If one reverses the blades to go clockwise in the winter, the fan will force heat down and circulate it throughout the room. A ceiling fan uses no more electricity than a 100-watt light bulb. These and other relatively inexpensive steps can be used to produce large savings.

Sample Notes If This Had Been a Lecture

What are three actions a homeowner with more than $100 can take to save energy?

Save energy cost > $100

1. Insulate sidewalls and ceilings, 30% sav
2. Install storm windows
3. Solar hot-water heater. Factors to consider:
   Geo location
   Amt sunlight avail Energy costs
   Construction of house

Sample of the Question in the Margin System for Textbooks

All homeowners can take action if they are serious about saving on energy costs. Those with more than $100 to spend should consider any of the following steps. First,[1] sidewalls and especially the ceiling of a home should be fully insulated. Proper insulation can save 30 percent or more of a heating or cooling bill. Next,[2] storm windows should be installed throughout the house. They provide an insulating area of still air that may reduce energy loss by 10 percent or more. Finally,[3] a homeowner might consider installing a solar hot-water heating system. Four key factors in such a decision are geographical location, the amount of sunlight available, energy costs in the area, and the construction of the house.

What are three actions a homeowner with more than $100 can take to save energy?

Sample Mapping

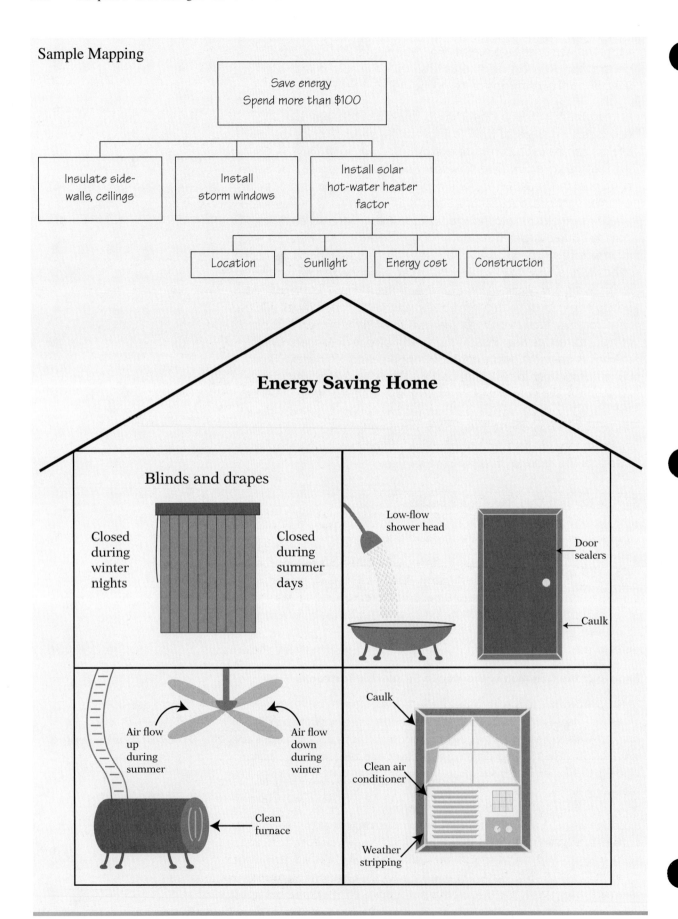

> ### Exercise 7.6
>
> ## Mapping the Question in the Margin System
>
> In order to study for a test on which you know you will be asked to name and explain the steps of the Question in the Margin system, on a separate sheet of paper construct a map of the Question in the Margin system as a summary sheet.

Promoting Concentration

Have you ever finished a chapter in a book and realized that you had no idea what you just read? Or have you ever sat in class and realized that 15 minutes had passed and, although your body was there, your mind had taken a vacation or dealt with something that was bothering you? These are examples of lapses in *concentration*. In addition to providing enough oxygen to the brain to promote concentration, checking the Big 3 of the BREATHE System reminds you to focus. You already know some strategies for promoting concentration. The learning principles used in the Question in the Margin system provide the basis for strategies that promote concentration. In order to develop the best plan for concentration, you need to determine which kinds of distractions prevent you from concentrating.

Internal Distractions

Many times the causes of your stress are the same things that cause a lack of concentration. These are usually referred to as **internal distractions**. There are so many things going on in your life that the balancing act you are performing may also bring about anxiety and other internal distractions that are detrimental to concentration. Internal distractions come from some source outside—your financial-aid check is lost, your mother is ill, your best friend has been in a car wreck—but you have internalized the problem.

List some things that are going on in your life that prevent you from concentrating.

_____

_____

_____

You can't always eliminate internal distractions, but you do want to be able to control them when you need to concentrate. Here are a few hints that will help you now:

1. **Keep an attention list.** When you are trying to concentrate and you keep thinking of something else, stop and make a note on your attention list. That way, you won't forget that something needs your attention, even though you have put it aside for the time being.

2. **Check your concentration.** Physically addressing breaks in concentration will help you get back on track. Try using the check mark technique in programming your mind to concentrate. In class or when reading an assignment, have a sheet of paper handy. When you note that you are not paying attention, put a check on the paper and immediately return to your task. The first time you check your concentration, you may fill up an entire sheet. But each subsequent time you use this technique, you will have fewer and fewer checks. (Popping a rubber band on your wrist when your attention strays would have a similar effect, but it's so much more painful!)

3. **Review the time-management and learning principles.** In particular, look for techniques that might be particularly effective for you—taking breaks, visualizing, reciting, and so on.

Exercise 7.7

Setting Goals to Promote Concentration

After reviewing the concentration, time-management, and learning principles discussed thus far, write three very specific goals that you think will help promote your concentration and that you will try to accomplish this week, each time you are in class and each time you study. (Review the elements of a useful goal before you write them. Give yourself clear directions for what you will do to promote concentration. "I'll try to pay better attention" won't do!)

1. _____

2. _____

3. _____

External Distractions

Often, there are **external**, or physical, **distractions** in your study environment. We know that studying every day at the same time and in the same place programs the mind and promotes concentration. Your time-management analysis should have helped you determine the best time for you to study each subject. Now, let's develop a plan for analyzing your place to study.

Your regular place should be one that you use exclusively for studying. If you studied in the chair where you normally watch TV, your mind would automatically want to know what's on TV. If you studied at the kitchen table, you would get hungry. If you studied in bed, even if you weren't sleepy before, you would become sleepy. Your regular study place should have a desk, a comfortable chair, the necessary supplies, good lighting, and so on. Obviously, your senses are involved. Examine each of them to determine the factors that might affect your concentration when you study.

Exercise 7.8

Identifying External Distractions

	Promote	Hinder
Sight		
Hearing		
Smell		
Taste		
Touch		

Now, write a short paragraph in which you describe your ideal study place.

Exercise 7.9

Discovering the Best Place for You to Study

This week choose two different times and places to do your regular studying that you think will promote concentration. Use the chart below to analyze the time and place for its effectiveness as a regular study time and place for you.

Time and Place 1

Place

Visual Distractions	Auditory Distractions

Time

Other Distractions	Features That Make This a Good Place to Study

Overall analysis of time and place for use as a regular study place (RSP): _____

_____

Time and Place 2

Place

	Visual Distractions	Auditory Distractions

Time

	Other Distractions	Features That Make This a Good Place to Study

Overall analysis of time and place for use as a regular study place (RSP): _____

_____

Exercise 7.10

Study Habits Analysis

Are you using all that you've learned so far about studying to learn things faster and better? We are creatures of habit, and often we don't realize that our habits are keeping us from being successful. Choose assignments from two different classes this week and use them to analyze your study habits. One check sheet is provided below. You will need to make copies of the check sheet for the other assignments and several extra copies to use at a later time. Remember to use the time-management and learning principles.

Assignment Check Sheet

Name: _____

Class chosen for assignment: _____

Analysis

1. Describe in detail the assignment you chose.
2. When did you begin working on the assignment in relation to when it was due?
3. Was this a good time to work on the assignment? Why?
4. Where did you work on the assignment?
5. Was this a good place? Why?

6. Did you

_____ take breaks?

_____ take notes even though it was not required?

_____ visualize as you were learning new concepts?

_____ give your full attention to studying?

_____ try to determine when you might be tested on this assignment?

_____ try your best?

VIRTUAL FIELD TRIP

Improve Your Concentration

 Visit the College Success CourseMate.

Modeling the Learning Process

The steps in the Question in the Margin system used for textbook reading also model the learning process.

Gathering. You surveyed the material you were responsible for and read it paragraph by paragraph.

Analyzing. You analyzed the paragraph, wrote questions in the margin, and looked for connections.

Creating New Ideas. You reflected and reviewed your marked text and questions and predicted possible test questions involving higher-order thinking skills, and you looked for connections with notes you had taken in class.

Acting. You developed summary sheets, maps, PowerPoint presentations, and practice tests.

SUMMARY

To see if you grasped the major points of the chapter and to make a useful study guide, answer the following questions found in your reading. When you have written your answers, cover them and see if you can say the answer to each question in your own words. If you prefer to type your answers, you will find a Microsoft Word download for each summary on the College Success CourseMate for Practicing College Learning Strategies at **www.cengagebrain.com.**

How does gathering information from lectures differ from gathering information from textbooks?

_____

_____

What are the three steps of gathering information from textbooks?

1. _____

2. _____

3. _____

How does the question step for reading a textbook differ from the question step for taking lecture notes?

_____

_____

Why should you survey before you read a chapter?

_____

_____

How do you focus on the paragraph you are reading?

_____

_____

Why should you process a paragraph before you go on to the next one?

_____

_____

Explain the rest of the Question in the Margin system for textbooks.

Recite

_____

Reflect

_____

Review

_____

Summarize

_____

What is the goal of mapping?

_____

_____

Explain how to check your concentration.

_____

_____

How can you eliminate or at least minimize physical or external distractions?

_____

_____

Describe what components would be included in an ideal study place for you.

_____

_____

Case Study: What's Your Advice?

This is KaToya's third semester at her university. She has done well, but this semester KaToya is having a difficult time. Four of her classes require a great deal of reading. So far she has managed to get all the reading done, but she rarely remembers what she has read. She has set aside every weeknight from 7:00 to 11:00 P.M. for reading assignments. As she reads, KaToya uses a highlighter and often finds that she has highlighted an entire page. One professor gives pop quizzes based on the reading, so KaToya saves that assignment for last, thinking she'll remember it more easily. She even reads it in bed where it is nice and quiet. She has yet to pass a quiz, and her exam scores are not much better. What advice can you give KaToya?

Parallel Parking

It is important to take responsibility for your reading assignments. Choose three of the driving analogies and compare each to things you know about processing information from reading assignments.

Reading the Map

_____

_____

_____

Going the Speed Limit

_____

_____

_____

Rush Hour Traffic

_____

_____

_____

_____

Side Trips

_____

_____

_____

_____

Finding a Mechanic

_____

_____

_____

_____

Evaluating Learning Outcomes

How successful were you in making it to your destination in this chapter?

Analyze what you learned in this chapter. Put a check beside each task you are now able to do. Now think of strategies that you learned that will help you save time and study more effectively. List them in the appropriate place on the back inside cover.

☐ **Explain** how to survey a textbook assignment.
☐ **Demonstrate** how to use the Question in the Margin system for reading textbooks: survey, focus, read, question, recite, reflect, review, and summarize.
☐ **Explain** how to use the Question in the Margin system to someone who has never used it.
☐ **Analyze** the Question in the Margin system, and explain how the learning principles are used to complete the system.
☐ **Explain** the learning process modeled in this chapter.

Your Student Tip For This Chapter

Use the space below to write a tip you would give to other students about what you have learned in this chapter.

_____

_____

_____

_____

8 Learning Styles

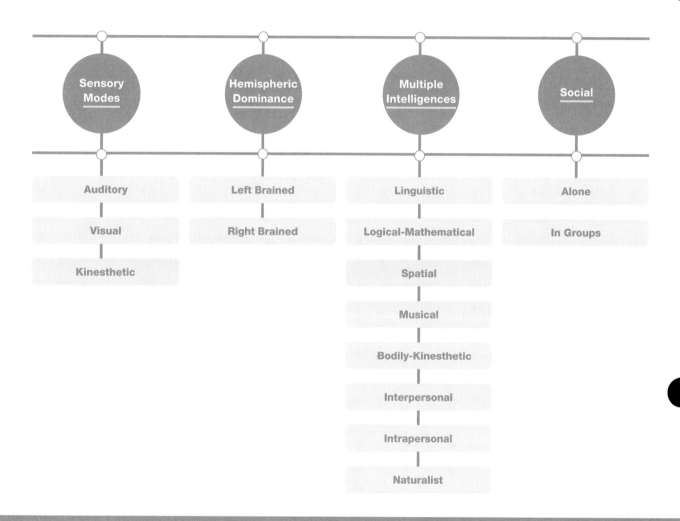

Sensory Modes	Hemispheric Dominance	Multiple Intelligences	Social
Auditory	Left Brained	Linguistic	Alone
Visual	Right Brained	Logical-Mathematical	In Groups
Kinesthetic		Spatial	
		Musical	
		Bodily-Kinesthetic	
		Interpersonal	
		Intrapersonal	
		Naturalist	

What Are Learning Styles?

The term **learning styles** refers to the preferred ways in which individuals interact with, take in, and process new stimuli or information. In other words, your preferred learning style is simply *how you learn best*. You have learned enough about the brain to know that your brain is unique. The structures, connections, and pathways in your brain are like those in no one else's brain. Educationally, *learning styles* is a loaded term. It means very different things to different people. There are literally hundreds of ways to measure learning styles. When I did a Google search recently, there were more than 9 million sites about learning styles. Learning styles are not so much about the style of car

Learning Outcomes
for Chapter 8 Learning Styles

Here's your destination for Chapter 8. When you complete Chapter 8, you are expected not only to understand the material presented, but also to be able to

Determine your preferred learning style, including sensory mode, hemispheric dominance, and type of multiple intelligence.

Explain the learning model used in this chapter.

Analyze a case study, and **construct** advice for a student having difficulty finding effective study methods.

Demonstrate ways to adapt new learning material to the preferred learning styles.

Practice the strategies presented in the chapter to determine the most efficient ones for you to process difficult material and to reinforce the initial learning.

you drive; rather, they are about the route you choose to take to get to your destination.

The learning specialist Eric Jensen says that there are six components you must consider if optimal learning is to occur. You have already developed strategies to address the first three—meaning, present circumstances, and personal history—in the strategies you use for interest, intent to remember, basic background, and other learning principles. This chapter will address the other three components and deal with finding your preferred learning styles for inputting information, processing information, and responding to that information. Of all the ways of looking at and addressing learning styles, these are the three that I think are most practical for students and most likely to produce optimal learning.

Why Determine Learning Style?

When you are driving to specific destinations, there are usually several routes you can take. I have noticed that when driving to my daughter's house, I usually take a different route than my husband takes. Neither route has a particular advantage. Our choices are either from habit or by preference. However, even when going to familiar places, I often discover a new or better route. Traffic conditions or road construction may make that route preferable. With that in mind, let's look at learning styles.

In previous chapters, you were briefly introduced to the idea of learning styles. You took practice notes about left-brain and right-brain theory in exercise 6.7 in Chapter 6 and you worked a Question in the Margin exercise from a textbook selection about modality strengths in Exercise 7.3. The way each individual processes information is unique, but because the Question in the Margin system is based on the learning principles and incorporates various learning strategies, it works for most learning styles. You may have found that you need to modify it slightly to better fit your learning style, or to rely heavily on one aspect of it because of your learning style. No one else processes information in exactly the same way you do.

There are several reasons for determining your learning style preference. (1) If you discover how you process information best, you can learn things both more efficiently and in less time. By applying strategies that address your learning style, you can study faster and better. (2) Now that you understand the cycle involved in the learning process, you can use your preferred learning style to go through the cycle in ways that are comfortable for you. (3) You can expand the strategies you use for learning and studying, just as you discover new or alternative routes when driving, and you can customize some of the strategies already discussed in this text. When learning something new or difficult, you naturally tend to use the learning style you prefer. It is good to know what your learning style is so that you can process information in the most efficient way. Even when material is not presented in the way you prefer, you can use your knowledge of learning styles to adjust and be flexible.

No matter who your instructor is or what the subject matter is, you need to know how to convert what you need to learn to the way you learn best. However, sometimes we need to leave our comfort zones and reinforce learning in as many different ways as possible. Going beyond your comfort zone forces you to drive more carefully and pay more attention. So, although knowing your style preference is good, you also need to expand your ways of learning. Knowing your learning style and being able to recognize and understand the learning styles of others who play a role in your learning—your professors, roommate or spouse, or those in your study group—is useful in getting the most out of any situation.

Sensory Modes of Learning: Input Preference

The most common way of looking at learning styles is for you to consider how you prefer to receive information through your senses, usually referred to as your preferred sensory mode. **Visual** learners find it easier to learn something new if they can see it or picture it. **Auditory** learners want to hear it, and **kinesthetic** learners acquire new information best by experiencing it. Most of us are **mixed-modality** learners. We learn using all of our senses. However, when something is new or difficult, you will probably have a preference as to how you can best learn it.

The inventory on the next few pages will help you determine the sensory mode in which you learn best. You will want to take this inventory before you read about each mode, even though you probably already know which one you prefer. When you are driving to an unfamiliar place, are you more likely to reach your destination with less hassle if you read the directions or follow a map (visual)? Would you prefer to have someone tell you how to get there (auditory)? Or would you be better off studying the directions and drawing a map for yourself or maybe just taking off and feeling your way (kinesthetic)? Consider what you already know about your learning preferences. What things do you automatically do if you want to remember something?

As noted, you probably prefer to learn new or difficult material within your strongest learning mode, but in order to get the fullest learning, you need to reinforce that learning mode with other modes. According to research done by Edgar Dale, people generally remember only 10 percent of what they read.[1] (Do you see why the Question in the Margin system is necessary?) They remember 20 percent of what they hear and 30 percent of what they see. Retention is increased to 50 percent if they hear *and* see something, as when watching a movie or a demonstration. People generally remember 70 percent of what they say or write and 90 percent of what they say as they do something. However, they remember 95 percent of what they teach to someone else.

BRAIN BYTE

A fire breaks out in the room. Your immediate reaction will be one of the following: (1) **visual** (quickly you size up the situation, looking for exits, others in need, etc.), (2) **auditory** (you start yelling "Fire" or giving directions or screaming), or (3) **kinesthetic** (you start running for an exit). Although you may do all three, one will be an instinctual first reaction. That's your preferred sensory mode or learning style.

Exercise 8.1

Create a PowerPoint Presentation

Pretend that your instructor has asked you to present the information about Edgar Dale's research (in the paragraph above) to your class as a PowerPoint presentation. Either actually make a PowerPoint presentation and print it for your instructor or make a pretend one using index cards as slides. Be sure to include illustrations.

You may find that developing PowerPoint presentations, even pretend ones, is an extremely effective way of learning new material. Why?

Exercise 8.2

Sensory Modality Inventory

There are 12 incomplete sentences and three choices for each. Score the three choices by rating them as follows:

3   The answer most typical of you
2   Your second choice
1   The one least like you

[1]Cited in Winman and Meierhenry, *Educational Media*, 1960.

1. When I have to learn something new, I usually:

    _____ a. want someone to explain it to me.

    _____ b. want to read about it in a book or magazine.

    _____ c. want to try it out, take notes, or make a model of it.

2. At a party, most of the time I like to:

    _____ a. listen and talk to two or three people at once.

    _____ b. see how everyone looks and watch the people.

    _____ c. dance, play games, or take part in some activities.

3. If I were helping with a musical show, I would most likely:

    _____ a. write the music, sing the songs, or play the accompaniment.

    _____ b. design the costumes, paint the scenery, or work the lighting effects.

    _____ c. make the costumes, build the sets, or take an acting role.

4. When I am angry, my first reaction is to:

    _____ a. tell people off, laugh, joke, or talk it over with someone.

    _____ b. blame myself or someone else, daydream about taking revenge, or keep it inside.

    _____ c. make a fist or tense my muscles, take it out on something else, or hit or throw things.

5. A happy experience I would like to have is to:

    _____ a. hear thunderous applause for my speech or music.

    _____ b. photograph the prize-winning picture for a newspaper story.

    _____ c. achieve the fame of being first in a physical activity such as dancing, acting, or a sport.

6. I prefer a teacher to:

    _____ a. use the lecture method with informative explanations and discussions.

    _____ b. write on the chalkboard, use visual aids, and assign readings.

    _____ c. require posters, models, in-service practice, and some activities in class.

7. I know that I talk with:

_____ a. different tones of voice.

_____ b. my eyes and facial expressions.

_____ c. my hands and gestures.

8. If I had to remember an event so that I could record it later, I would choose to:

_____ a. tell it to someone or hear an audiotape recording or song about it.

_____ b. see pictures of it or read a description.

_____ c. replay it in some practice rehearsal using movements such as dance, playacting, or drill.

9. When I cook something new, I like to:

_____ a. have someone tell me the directions (a friend or TV show).

_____ b. read the recipe and judge by how it looks.

_____ c. use many pots and dishes, stir often, and taste-test.

10. In my free time, I like to:

_____ a. listen to my iPod, talk on the telephone, or attend a musical event.

_____ b. go to the movies, watch TV, or read a magazine or book.

_____ c. get some exercise, go for a walk, play games, or post fun things on MySpace.

11. If I'm putting together a new bookshelf from IKEA:

_____ a. I want someone to tell me how to do it.

_____ b. I want to read the directions or watch someone else do it.

_____ c. I want to jump right in and do it. I'll figure it out sooner or later.

12. I like the classroom to be arranged:

_____ a. in a circle so I can interact with other students.

_____ b. in neat rows facing the instructor.

_____ c. in random order in case there are activities.

To interpret your sense modality, add your rating for each letter.

Total rating for:

a. _____ Auditory

b. _____ Visual

c. _____ Kinesthetic

If your highest category was:

a, you learn best through listening.

b, you learn best by seeing it in print or other visual modes.

c, you learn best by getting physically involved.

The Auditory Learner

If you learn best by hearing, you should, of course, listen carefully in class. However, just because you learn well by hearing doesn't mean you don't need to take notes; remember the nature of short-term memory? You need to keep a record. You may want to tape-record a difficult class. But be aware that taping a lecture is not a time-saver; you must still take time to process the information.

A better strategy would be to use your iPod, smart phone, or iPad to make audio flash cards. You might also be interested in the smartpens that are now on the market. Pens such as Livescribe allow you to take multimodal notes. An internal flash drive memory captures handwritten notes, audio, and drawings. The user can choose to record audio in addition to the hand-written text. Recorded audio is kept indexed with the handwritten text—tapping on a written word starts playback of the recorded audio from that part of the recording.

The recitation portion of the Question in the Margin system rein-forces your auditory learning. It gets you involved, provides feedback, and supplies motivation. This is especially true for the auditory learner. The auditory learner likes discussion and usually learns well in a study group or with a study partner. Auditory learners often need to hear what a difficult passage sounds like or to talk out a difficult concept. As an auditory learner, you should proofread your assignments out loud. Your ears seldom fail you. You may even want to try setting a long or difficult idea to music and singing it. (Remember how you learned the alphabet?) Your recall is best when you teach something to someone. And you will probably learn best by explaining something out loud to someone else.

The Visual Learner

Visual learners need to see something in order to remember it. If you are a visual learner, you want to see the words written down, a picture of something being described, a time line to remember events in history, or the assignment written on the board. You need to read the material being discussed in class. You also need to study the pictures, charts, maps, or graphs. You should take notes in class in order to see what you are hearing.

Of all the learning principles, visualization works best for you. You need to consistently make mental videos of things you want to understand and remember. You benefit from mapping, clustering, outlining, and using flash cards. You may want to illustrate your flash cards or notes. You should make use of color as much as possible. Most students, regardless of their preference, will benefit from this type of learning. The effect of a picture usually lasts longer than words for most of us. Because visual learning uses primarily the right side of the brain, this is a way for the left-brained student to involve both sides of the brain.

The Kinesthetic Learner

Kinesthetic learners prefer the sense of touch and learn better when they interact with what they are studying. Although the mapping strategies explained in the previous chapter are visual, they are also kinesthetic. As a kinesthetic learner, you find that when you are physically involved, you understand and remember. The simple act of doing it helps you understand. The Question in the Margin system will work for you as a kinesthetic learner because it requires physical involvement. You may find that during the recitation step you want to walk around. Making flash cards is a great strategy for kinesthetic learners. You will find that by making and using flash cards, you employ all 10 learning principles. No wonder they work so well. And as you learned in the time-management chapter, flash cards are also easy to carry as pocket work to make use of those bits of time that are normally wasted. In addition to maps, note taking, and flash cards, you may want to make charts, games, or mnemonic devices. As you will discover in the test-taking unit, making sample tests will help you physically select the main idea, and an added bonus is that taking these tests will cut test anxiety.

Yet learners with kinesthetic preference are not alone in benefiting from learning by doing. All learners seem to benefit. Remember that, as Edgar Dale noted, the highest level of remembering comes when you teach someone else. It appears that with all learners, the more actively involved in learning you are, the more you learn. If your instructors do not provide opportunities for active involvement with your learning, you will have to create those opportunities yourself.

Exercise 8.3

Sensory Mode Reflection

What specific learning strategies do you already use that involve **auditory** learning?

What are some others that you might try?

What specific learning strategies do you already use that involve **visual** learning?

What are some others that you might try?

List some ways you could create hands-on (**kinesthetic**) opportunities in a history class in which your professor always lectures.

Hemispheric Dominance: Processing Preference

A second way of looking at learning styles is to examine the way you prefer to process information in order to determine your hemispheric dominance. Are you more right brained or left brained?

Differences Between Left and Right Hemispheres

We know that the cerebral cortex is the part of the brain that houses rational functions. It is divided into two hemispheres connected by a thick band of nerve fibers (the corpus callosum), which sends messages back and forth between the hemispheres. And although brain research confirms that both sides of the brain are involved in nearly every human activity, we also know that the left side of the brain is the seat of language and processes information in a logical and sequential order. The right side is more visual and processes information intuitively, holistically, and randomly.

Most people seem to have a dominant side. Our dominance is a preference, not an absolute. When learning is new, difficult, or stressful, we *prefer* to learn in a certain way. It seems that our brain goes on autopilot to the preferred side. Just as it was more important for our purposes to determine that memory is stored in many parts of the brain, rather than learn the exact lobe for each part, likewise it is not so much that we are biologically right-brain or left-brain dominant, but that we are more comfortable with the learning strategies characteristic of one over the other.

What you are doing is lengthening your list of strategies for learning how to learn and trying to determine what works best for you. You can and must use and develop both sides of the brain. Sometimes driving alternative routes makes us more careful or deliberate. But because the seat of our preferences probably has more neuronal connections, learning may occur faster when we use our preferred mode.

This section will examine some differences between the left and right hemispheres and provide a few suggestions for both left- and right-dominant students. Be on the lookout for practical strategies that work for you. Following is an inventory to help you determine the balance of your hemispheres. It might be a good idea to take this inventory before you read the subsequent explanations.

Exercise 8.4

How Does Your Brain Process Information?

Check the answers that most closely describe your preferences.

1. Are you usually running late for class or other appointments?

   _____ a. Yes

   _____ b. No

2. When taking a test, you prefer the questions be:

   _____ a. objective (true/false, multiple-choice, matching).

   _____ b. subjective (discussion or essay questions).

3. When making decisions, you:

   _____ a. go with your gut feeling—what you feel is right.

   _____ b. carefully weigh each option.

4. When relating an event, you:

_____ a. go straight to the main point and then fill in details.

__✓__ b. tell many details before telling the conclusion.

5. Do you have a place for everything and everything in its place?

__✓__ a. Yes

_____ b. No

6. When faced with a major change in life, you are:

_____ a. excited.

__✓__ b. terrified.

7. Your work style is to:

__✓__ a. concentrate on one task at a time until it is complete.

_____ b. juggle several things at once.

8. Can you tell approximately how much time has passed without looking at your watch?

_____ a. Yes

__✓__ b. No

9. It is easier for you to understand:

__✓__ a. algebra.

_____ b. geometry.

10. Is it easier for you to remember people's:

_____ a. names.

__✓__ b. faces.

11. When learning how to use a new piece of equipment, you:

_____ a. jump in and wing it. (The instruction manual is a last resort.)

__✓__ b. carefully read the instruction manual before beginning.

12. When someone is speaking, you respond to:

    _____ a. what is being said (words).

    ___✓___ b. how it is being said (tone, tempo, volume, and emotion).

13. When speaking, you use:

    _____ a. few gestures (very seldom use your hands when you talk).

    ___✓___ b. many gestures (couldn't talk with your hands tied).

14. Your desk, work area, or laundry area is:

    ___✓___ a. neat and organized.

    _____ b. cluttered with stuff you might need.

15. When asked your opinion, you:

    ___✓___ a. immediately say what's on your mind (often foot in mouth).

    _____ b. think before you speak.

16. You do your best thinking while:

    ___✓___ a. sitting.

    _____ b. walking around or lying down.

17. When reading a magazine, you:

    ___✓___ a. jump in at whatever article looks most interesting.

    _____ b. start at page one and read in sequential order.

18. When you're shopping and see something you want to buy, you:

    ___✓___ a. save up until you have the money.

    _____ b. charge it.

19. In math, can you explain how you got the answer?

    ___✓___ a. Yes

    _____ b. No

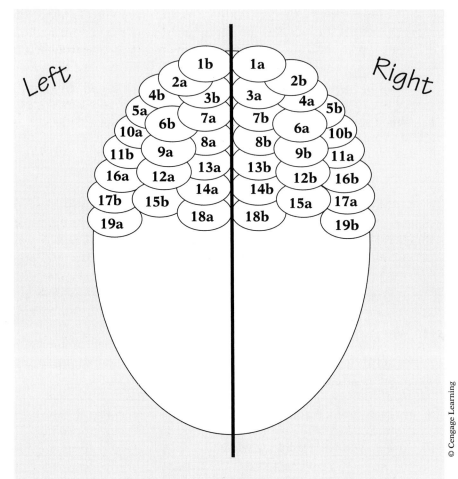

Now, using the diagram of the brain shown here, color in the sections that correspond to your answers on the questionnaire. For example, if your answer for question 1 is *a*, color in the area labeled *1a*, on the right side of the brain. Color all the sections that correspond to your answers. When you are finished, you will have a better sense of whether you are predominantly left or right brained or whether you use both sides equally.

Linear Versus Holistic Processing

The left side of the brain processes information in a linear manner. It processes from part to whole. It takes pieces, lines them up, and arranges them in a logical order; then it draws conclusions. The right brain, however, processes holistically, from whole to parts. It starts with the answer. It sees the big picture first, not the details. You can understand, then, why some of the strategies you have learned work well for right-brained students. If you are right brained, you may have difficulty following a lecture unless you get the big picture first. Do you now see why it is absolutely necessary for a right-brained person to read an assigned chapter or background information before a lecture or to survey a chapter before reading? If an instructor doesn't consistently give an overview before he or she begins a lecture, the right-brained person may need to ask at the end of class what the next lecture will be and how to prepare for it.

If you are predominantly right brained, you may also have trouble outlining. (You've probably written many papers first and outlined them later because an outline was required.) Mapping may be a better brainstorming and organizing method for you to use. You're the student who needs to know *why* you are doing something. Left-brained students would do well to exercise their right brain in such a manner!

Sequential Versus Random Processing

In addition to thinking in a linear manner, the left brain processes in sequence, that is, in order. The left-brained person is a list maker. If you are left brained, you were in your element when master schedules and daily planning were discussed. You complete tasks in order and take pleasure in checking them off when they are accomplished. Likewise, learning things in sequence is relatively easy for you. For example, the steps of the Question in the Margin system make sense to you, because they are a logical sequence for processing information from lectures and textbooks. Spelling involves sequence as well. If you are left brained, you are probably a good speller. The left brain is also at work in the linear and sequential processing of math and in following directions.

In contrast, the approach of the right-brained student is random. If you are right brained, you may flit from one task to another. You will get just as much done, but perhaps without having addressed priorities. An assignment may be late or incomplete, not because you weren't working, but because you were working on something else. You were ready to rebel when I suggested making a schedule and lists. But because of the random nature of your dominant side, you *must* make lists and you *must* make schedules. This may be your only hope for survival in college. You have probably abandoned the master schedule you created in Chapter 1. Remember, it is your guideline to make sure you have a certain time to complete things that you must do. Review your master schedule and try to get back on track. In addition, are you using an agenda or plan book to keep up with your assignments? Are you making a to-do list daily? You should also make a special effort to read directions. Oh, yes, the mention of spelling makes you cringe. Being right brained may be a reason you are not a great speller, but it is not an excuse. You just know that you need to be more careful and check your spelling more often. Use the dictionary, carry a Franklin speller, use the spell checker on your computer. Never turn in an assignment without proofing for spelling.

Because the right side of the brain is color sensitive, you might try using colors to learn sequence, making the first step green, the second blue, the last red. Or you may want to walk a sequence, either by physically going from place to place or by imagining it. For the first step of the sequence, you might walk to the front door; for the second, to the kitchen; for the third, to the den; and so on. Or make step 1 a certain place or thing in your dorm room or study place, and step 2 another. If you consistently use the same sequence, you will find that this strategy is transferable to many tasks involving sequence.

BRAIN BYTE

Researchers have discovered that musicians process music more on the left side, whereas nonmusicians process it on the right side. Musicians tend to analyze the music more, changing the function of the task.

Student Tip

❝ *I had real difficulty remembering things in order until I tried this trick. When I go to my dorm room, the first thing I do is unlock the door. So for the first thing on the list I need to remember, I picture my key. Next, I usually turn on my light. Number two, then, I picture the light switch. I put my books on my desk next, so the third item I picture my books. You get the idea. I actually have 10 steps I use. Try this with a routine you usually follow in a place that is personal. It works!* ❞

Symbolic Versus Concrete Processing

The left brain has no trouble processing symbols. Many academic pursuits deal with symbols, such as letters, words, and mathematical notations. The left-brained person tends to be comfortable with linguistic and mathematical endeavors. Left-brained students will probably just memorize vocabulary words or math formulas. The right brain, on the other hand, wants things to be concrete. The right-brained person wants to see, touch, or interact with the real object. Right-brained students may have had trouble learning to read using phonics. They prefer to see words in context, to see how the formula works. To use your right brain, create opportunities for hands-on activities. Use something real whenever possible to make connections. Consistently ask, What is this like that I already know? You may also want to draw a math problem or illustrate your notes. Mapping is another strategy you will definitely want to try.

Logical Versus Intuitive Processing

The left brain processes in a linear, sequential, and logical manner. When you process on the left side, you use information piece by piece to solve a math problem or work out a science experiment. When you read and listen, you look for the pieces so that you can draw logical conclusions. If you process primarily on the right side of the brain, you use intuition. You may know the right answer to a math problem but not be sure how you got it. You may have to start with the answer and work backward. On a quiz, you have a gut feeling as to which answers are correct, and you are usually right. In writing, it is the left brain that pays attention to mechanics such as spelling, agreement, and punctuation. But the right side pays attention to coherence and meaning; that is, your right brain tells you it feels right.

Verbal Versus Nonverbal Processing

Left-brained students have little trouble expressing themselves in words. Right-brained students may know what they mean but often have trouble finding the right words. A good illustration of this is to listen to people giving directions. The left-brained person will say something like, "From here, go west three blocks and turn north on Vine Street. Go three or four miles and then turn east onto Broad Street." The right-brained person will sound something like, "Turn right [*pointing right*] by the church over there [*pointing again*]. Then you will pass a McDonald's and a Wal-Mart. At the next light, turn right toward the BP station." So how is this relevant to planning study strategies? Right-brained students need to back up everything visually. If it's not written down, they probably won't remember it. And it would be even better for right-brained students to illustrate it. They need to get into the habit of making a mental video of things as they hear or read them. Right-brained students need to know that it may take them longer to write a paper, and the paper may need more revision before it says what they want it to say. This means allowing extra time when a writing assignment is due.

Reality-Based Versus Fantasy-Oriented Processing

The left side of the brain deals with things the way they are in reality. When left-brained students are affected by the environment, they usually adjust to it. Not so with right-brained students: they try to change the environment! Left-brained people want to know the rules and follow them. In fact, if there are no rules for situations, they will probably make up rules to follow! Left-brained students know the consequences of turning in papers late or of failing a test. But right-brained students are sometimes not aware that there is anything wrong with doing those things. So, if you are right brained, make sure you constantly ask for feedback and reality checks. It's too late to wait until the day before finals to ask if you can do something for extra credit. Keep a careful record of your assignments and tests. Visit with your professor routinely.

Although this fantasy orientation may seem a disadvantage, in some cases it is an advantage. The right-brained student is creative. In order to learn about the digestive system, you may decide to become a piece of food! And because emotion is processed on the right side of the brain, you will probably remember anything you become emotionally involved in as you are trying to learn.

Temporal Versus Nontemporal Processing

The left side of the brain seems to have a sense of time. Left-brained students are punctual and can usually tell you the time without even looking at a watch. The right brain is lost when judging time. The student who is perpetually late is probably right brained. You need to remember, of course, that although being right brained may be a reason for being late, it is never an excuse. A good strategy if you are a right-brained person may be to set your watch 10 or 15 minutes fast or use the alarm feature on your watch, iPod, or cell phone. Plan to leave home at least 30 minutes before you really need to. If you actually arrive at your destination early, remember to have pocket work with you. Timed tests are difficult for right-brained students. Be sure that you preview a test and budget your time before you begin the test.

These are just some of the differences that exist between the functioning of the left and right hemispheres, but you can see a pattern. Because left-brained strategies are the ones used most often in the classroom, right-brained students sometimes feel inadequate. However, you now know that you can be flexible and adapt material to the right side of your brain. Likewise, those of you who are predominantly left-brained know that it would be wise to use both sides of the brain and employ some right-brained strategies.

Student Tip

" *After I was unable to complete a psychology test on time even though I knew the answers, I went to my professor's office and explained how difficult it is for me to sense how much time has passed. I asked him on the next test to announce at intervals how much time was left. This really made a difference, and the professor didn't mind. Now the day before any test, I ask my professor in that class to announce time left.* "

Exercise 8.5

Left Brain–Right Brain Reflection

Linear Versus Holistic Processing

List some *specific strategies* described in the linear versus holistic paragraph that would use the right side of the brain.

Carry this beyond study strategies. When you are dealing with right-brained professors, classmates, spouses, children, or bosses, it is important to give the big picture before you begin details. Describe a situation where giving the big picture first might have been helpful to you.

Sequential Versus Random Processing

Time management and stress management can be improved by noting the random nature of the right side of the brain, making a plan, and taking action. What are two specific things you can do to combat the random nature of the right brain?

1. _____

2. _____

List some specific strategies students can use when trying to process something that involves sequence.

_____

_____

_____

Symbolic Versus Concrete Processing

Think of a class you are taking. List some specific strategies you can use in that class to make things more concrete.

_____

_____

_____

Logical Versus Intuitive Processing

How can you use the left side of your brain to proofread your papers?

_____

_____

How can you use the right side of your brain to proofread your papers?

_____

_____

Verbal Versus Nonverbal Processing

What are some ways to visually back up things you need to learn?

_____

_____

_____

Reality-Based Versus Fantasy-Oriented Processing

List some ways to create reality checks for yourself throughout the semester.

_____

_____

_____

Temporal Versus Nontemporal Processing

It is often said that the first five minutes of class are the most important. Can you think of a time that you were late for class and this proved true? Give specific examples of what you missed and the consequences.

_____

_____

Let's have some fun with this. To check your understanding of the characteristics of left and right dominance, read the descriptions of drivers below and try to determine if the driver is left brained or right brained. Circle left or right and in the blank below write an explanation of your choice.	
Left Right	Which driver would more likely draw a colorful map of the route?
Left Right	Which driver would prefer to be given landmarks in directions?
Left Right	Which driver would have a trunk that is neat and organized?
Left Right	Which driver would be more likely to make unplanned stops?
Left Right	Which driver would make a list before leaving home?
Left Right	Which driver is likely to reach the destination on time?
Left Right	Which driver may take a vacation that is really unaffordable?

Multiple Intelligences: Response Preference

Howard Gardner and other Harvard researchers speak of intelligence in terms of multiplicity.[2] They say that instead of thinking about intelligence in terms of what IQ tests measure, people should be aware that there are many kinds of intelligences. Gardner lists eight kinds of intelligences and says that everyone possesses all eight kinds. Individuals will have some of the intelligences more developed than others, but they can develop all the intelligences to a certain degree of proficiency.

[2]Howard Gardner, _Frames of Mind: The Theory of Multiple Intelligences,_ 10th anniversary ed. (New York: HarperCollins, 1993).

Although these intelligences are not usually referred to as learning styles, they are certainly related to the ways we learn and process information and usually indicate ways of responding to or using new information learned. An examination of these intelligences may be useful for several reasons. First, as a student, you are seeking ways to process information so that you own it. Second, you are seeking ways to learn things faster and more efficiently. Third, the theory of multiple intelligences gives you opportunities to look at your abilities in a different way. What you thought was simply a talent may, in fact, be an intelligence and a way to learn something. Fourth, recognizing your strongest intelligences may be of help in choosing a major and, ultimately, a career that is satisfying. Just as you examined your preferred sensory mode and hemispheric preference, you also need to check your multiple intelligences. The idea is to find your strengths. It is easier to learn something new within your strengths and then to reinforce that learning in as many ways as possible. The more ways you learn something, the more likely you are to remember it.

Thomas Armstrong defines intelligence as "the ability to respond successfully to new situations and the capacity to learn from one's past experiences."[3] In short, intelligence is about solving problems. Basic background becomes especially important here, and drawing on the particular intelligences needed in a real-life situation is essential. Let's very briefly examine the eight kinds of intelligence you possess.

Eight Kinds of Intelligence

- **Linguistic intelligence** involves your verbal skills. Will you learn something best by using words or playing with the verbal structure? Do you need to create a mnemonic to remember something?
- **Logical-mathematical intelligence** deals with your ability to reason. Can you determine the cause? Can you follow the logic in order to learn something?
- **Spatial intelligence** uses pictures and images to learn. Do you benefit from drawing or mapping something?
- **Musical intelligence** deals with rhythms and melodies. Can you set what you are trying to learn to music—give it a beat?
- **Bodily-kinesthetic intelligence** is where hands-on activity is required. Do you need to do something in order to learn it? Intuition, or "gut feeling," is associated with this intelligence.
- **Interpersonal intelligence** involves working with and understanding others.
- **Intrapersonal intelligence** determines how well you are attuned to your inner self.
  (The last two types of intelligence mentioned determine your social learning style.)
- **Naturalist intelligence** involves your ability to discriminate among living things (plants and animals), as well as your sensitivity to other features of the natural world (like clouds and rock configurations).

[3]Thomas Armstrong, *Seven Kinds of Smart: Identifying and Developing Your Many Intelligences* (New York: Penguin Books, 1993).

You possess all eight intelligences in varying degrees.

Using multiple intelligences may be compared to taking different routes to get to the same destination. Some drivers are uncomfortable driving in traffic on the interstate. Others are annoyed by the stopping and starting caused by driving through cities. Some drivers prefer the scenic route and would go well out of their way to travel a more interesting route.

Exercise 8.6

Multiple Intelligences

To say that there is a test to determine what your strongest intelligences are would be to limit the scope of the theory. However, the more you understand about what each intelligence involves, the more you can determine your strengths. Use the following exercise to determine which intelligences you use. More than one intelligence may be involved. In the space before the situation described, list the intelligences you used.

1 Linguistic	5 Bodily-kinesthetic
2 Logical-mathematical	6 Interpersonal
3 Spatial	7 Intrapersonal
4 Musical	8 Naturalist

_____ **1.** Singing in the choir at church

_____ **2.** Working a jigsaw puzzle

_____ **3.** Working a crossword puzzle

_____ **4.** Solving "who done it" in a mystery

_____ **5.** Giving advice to people at work

_____ **6.** Writing poetry

_____ **7.** Knowing the words to many popular songs

_____ **8.** Enjoying having time for yourself

_____ **9.** Humming a jingle you've heard on TV

_____ **10.** Doodling while talking on the phone or taking notes

_____ **11.** Computing numbers in your head

_____ **12.** Reading for pleasure as often as possible

_____ **13.** Playing a sport

_____ **14.** Sewing

_____   **15.** Framing a house

_____   **16.** Writing an essay

_____   **17.** Keeping a personal journal or diary

_____   **18.** Taking photographs

_____   **19.** Meditating

_____   **20.** Arguing

_____   **21.** Appreciating the color and balance of a picture

_____   **22.** Creating mnemonics

_____   **23.** Rearranging a room

_____   **24.** Categorizing objects

_____   **25.** Perceiving the moods of others

_____   **26.** Working alone on a problem

_____   **27.** Keeping rhythm to a song

_____   **28.** Studying in a group

_____   **29.** Using concept maps, graphs, or pictures to learn

_____   **30.** Organizing collections

_____   **31.** Finding a rational explanation for an occurrence

_____   **32.** Having trouble sitting still

_____   **33.** Noticing changes in the environment

_____   **34.** Showing someone how to do something

_____   **35.** Visiting with friends

_____   **36.** Spending a weekend alone

Exercise 8.7

Determining Your MI Strengths

Using the list from Exercise 8.6, circle the 12 items that you do most often. How many did you circle for each of the following intelligences? The higher the number, the stronger that intelligence is. Use the chart below to record the number of times each intelligence is part of your choices.

_____ Linguistic   _____ Bodily-kinesthetic

_____ Logical-mathematical   _____ Interpersonal

_____ Spatial   _____ Intrapersonal

_____ Musical   _____ Naturalist

VIRTUAL FIELD TRIP

Learning More About Multiple Intelligences

Visit the College Success CourseMate.

Making It Concrete

If for a biology test you need to learn the seven major taxonomic categories, or taxa, used in classification—(1) kingdom, (2) phylum, (3) class, (4) order, (5) family, (6) genus, and (7) species—you might use each of the intelligences to learn them. (Remember to learn new material in your strength, but reinforce it in as many ways as possible.) Below is a list of the multiple intelligences. For each one, give a concrete example of how you might use it to learn the classification system for your biology test. Then put into practice what you suggested. For example, if you suggested singing, for the classification musical intelligence, think of a specific tune and try it.

Linguistic: _____

_____

Logical-mathematical: _____

_____

Spatial: _____

_____

Musical: _____

_____

Bodily-kinesthetic: _____

_____

Interpersonal: _____

_____

Naturalist: _____

_____

BRAIN BYTE

Although we possess all eight intelligences, high performance in one is not necessarily a predictor of high performance in another domain. Outstanding performance by people in two or more domains is rare. Pierce Howard asserts that employers should not expect high performance in all domains. Asking a human resources expert (interpersonal) to be a financial expert (logical-mathematical) is like asking a starting quarterback (bodily-kinesthetic) to be a best-selling writer (linguistic).

Using Multiple Intelligences to Make Decisions

Not only can you use the assessment of your learning style and multiple intelligences to develop study strategies, but you will also find there is a parallel in multiple-intelligence strengths and job skills and preference. Following is a brief list of job skills and sample professions for each of the eight intelligences. Can you add to the list? Do your goals parallel your strongest intelligence? Can you add college majors you would suggest for each intelligence? Knowing your strongest multiple intelligence may be useful in choosing a major in college and ultimately a career. We usually find that performing tasks that employ our strengths provide the most satisfaction. Study the job skills and sample professions that are suggested for your strongest intelligences.

Linguistic

- **Job skills:** talking, telling, informing, giving instructions, writing, verbalizing, speaking a foreign language, interpreting, translating, teaching, lecturing, discussing, debating, researching, listening (to words), copying, proofreading, editing, word processing, filing, reporting
- **Sample professions:** librarian, archivist, curator, editor, translator, speaker, writer, radio/TV announcer, journalist, legal assistant, lawyer, secretary, typist, proofreader, English teacher

Logical-Mathematical

- **Job skills:** financing, budgeting, doing economic research, accounting, hypothesizing, estimating, counting, calculating, using statistics, auditing, reasoning, analyzing, systemizing, classifying, sequencing
- **Sample professions:** auditor, accountant, purchasing agent, mathematician, scientist, statistician, actuary, computer analyst, economist, technician, bookkeeper, science teacher

Spatial

- **Job skills:** drawing, painting, visualizing, creating visual presentation, designing, imagining, inventing, illustrating, coloring, drafting, graphing, mapping, photographing, decorating, filming
- **Sample professions:** engineer, surveyor, architect, urban planner, graphic artist, interior decorator, photographer, art teacher, inventor, cartographer, pilot, fine artist, sculptor

Musical

- **Job skills:** singing, playing an instrument, recording, conducting, improvising, composing, transcribing, arranging, listening, distinguishing (tones), tuning, orchestrating, analyzing, criticizing (musical styles)

- **Sample professions:** disc jockey, musician, instrument maker, piano tuner, music therapist, instrument salesperson, songwriter, studio engineer, choral director, conductor, singer, music teacher, musical copyist

Bodily-Kinesthetic

- **Job skills:** sorting, balancing, lifting, carrying, walking, crafting, restoring, cleaning, shipping, delivering, manufacturing, repairing, assembling, installing, operating, adjusting, salvaging, performing, signing, miming, dramatizing, modeling (clothes), dancing, playing sports, organizing outdoor activities, traveling
- **Sample professions:** physical therapist, recreational worker, dancer, actor, model, farmer, mechanic, carpenter, craftsperson, physical education teacher, factory worker, choreographer, professional athlete, forest ranger, jeweler

Interpersonal

- **Job skills:** serving, hosting, communicating, empathizing, trading, tutoring, coaching, counseling, mentoring, assessing others, persuading, motivating, selling, recruiting, inspiring, publicizing, encouraging, supervising, coordinating, delegating, negotiating, mediating, collaborating, confronting, interviewing
- **Sample professions:** administrator, manager, school principal, personnel worker, arbitrator, sociologist, anthropologist, counselor, psychologist, nurse, public relations person, salesperson, travel agent, social director

Intrapersonal

- **Job skills:** carrying out decisions, working alone, self-promotion, setting goals, attaining objectives, initiating, evaluating, appraising, planning, organizing, discerning opportunities, looking inward, understanding self
- **Sample professions:** psychologist, cleric, psychology teacher, therapist, counselor, theologian, program planner, entrepreneur

Naturalist

- **Job skills:** observing, understanding, organizing various types of environments, classifying, collecting, diagnosing
- **Sample professions:** molecular biologist, herbalist, chef, criminologist, mechanic, historian

VIRTUAL FIELD TRIP

Career Guide

 Visit the College Success CourseMate.

Making Connections

Do you think the information you either learned or confirmed about your learning style and multiple intelligences is significant when it comes to your choice of major or career? Discuss your reasons.

_____

_____

_____

A college advisor recently told me that she finds many college students choose a major and set career goals without ever talking to anyone who has majored in that subject at their college. She added that many students set career goals without talking to someone in that career. For example, because June was good at drawing, she decided to become an architect without ever knowing an architect. Discuss some of the dangers inherent in this. What plan of action do you need to make to ensure that you have done all you can to be prepared?

_____

_____

_____

Social Learning Preference: Alone or in Groups

We have now examined three ways to view your learning style in terms of which sense you prefer, whether you process information predominantly with the left or right side of your brain, and the strongest of your multiple intelligences. This knowledge may help you determine how best to initially study new material. The social inventory that follows will give you an indication of whether you should first study in a group or by yourself. Successful students study both alone and with a group; however, your learning style will determine if you need a group to help you learn new information or reinforce what you already have learned.

Again, you will want to learn new information in your strengths and reinforce your learning with as many other methods as possible. If the following inventory indicates you learn best alone, you will need to make sure you understand the concept you are striving to learn before you study with others. You need to customize your study environment for minimum distractions. Reciting by writing questions and answers or in the traditional manner of saying it out loud is a good strategy for you to use alone. If the social inventory in Exercise 8.8 indicates that you learn best with a group, you want to be careful that your study group or study partner shares your study goals. A few guidelines may be helpful. Notice in class who the dedicated students are. Who takes good notes? Who asks logical questions? Who turns in completed assignments on time? Who makes good grades on tests? Although studying with friends is nice, it can lead to visiting instead of studying. For each class you are taking, find three or four people you think would make up a good study group. Set a time and place to meet.

At the study session, you may want to do the following:

1. Make sure your goals are the same.

2. Determine what the test will cover. Comparing notes is a good way to do this.

3. Divide up your assignments so that each person is responsible for certain material. (Teaching material to others is a very effective way of making sure you know it.)

4. Predict test questions. Come up with a test that is similar to the one you will take.

5. Ask others in the group to help with material that is confusing or difficult for you.

6. Drill out loud on possible test questions.

7. Decide if another session would be profitable, and set a time. Make assignments for the next session. For example, ask each member to create a practice test for the next time.

Student Tip

"*I used to think that it was better to study by myself. I know that I need to self-test and make sure I know the material, but I also discovered it worth the effort to form a group to study. You get different approaches to the same problem and opportunities to teach someone. Someone in my groups always thinks of something I would have forgotten if I had just studied alone.*"

Exercise 8.8

Social Inventory: Study First Alone or in a Group?

Check *a* or *b* in the following questions:

1. When shopping, running errands, or working, I:

    _____ a. usually try to go with friends.

    _____ b. seldom go with friends.

2. When something is very important to me, I:

    _____ a. seek the advice of others.

    _____ b. do it myself.

3. For a grade in chemistry class, I would prefer to:

    _____ a. work with a lab partner.

    _____ b. work alone.

4. When working with groups in class, I would rather:

    _____ a. work with the group on the whole task.

    _____ b. divide the task up so that each individual does one part.

5. I prefer instructors who:

_____ a. include discussion and group activities as part of the class.

_____ b. allow students to work on their own.

6. When listening to a speaker, I respond more to:

_____ a. the person speaking.

_____ b. the ideas themselves.

7. When faced with difficult personal problems, I:

_____ a. discuss them with others.

_____ b. try to solve them myself.

8. For a summer job, I would prefer:

_____ a. working in a busy office.

_____ b. working alone.

Add the number of *a*'s and of *b*'s. If you checked more *a*'s than *b*'s, you would rather work with someone than alone. If you checked more *b*'s than *a*'s, you would rather work independently.

You now want to use what you have discovered about your learning style to develop more effective ways to study. Don't, however, lock yourself into one way. *Be flexible.*

Exercise 8.9

Your Learning Profile

Beginning with your strongest intelligence, list what you think your multiple intelligences are in order of their strength.

1. _____

2. _____

3. _____

4. _____

5. _____

6. _____

7. _____

8. _____

Do you process information primarily in the left or right hemisphere, or equally? _____

List the sensory modes you use in order of preference (auditory, visual, and kinesthetic).

1. _____

2. _____

3. _____

Do you prefer to work alone or with others? _____

Given the preceding information, list **specific learning strategies** in the order that you should be using them to process new material.

1. _____

2. _____

3. _____

4. _____

5. _____

Modeling the Learning Process

The information you learned in this chapter will help in modeling the learning process because you confirmed your learning style preference for each step.

Gathering. When you gather information, you will want to begin with your preferred sensory mode, but you will also want to reinforce it with the other two. The sensory modes include visual, auditory, and kinesthetic. You gathered information about three ways of looking at learning styles.

In analyzing and creating you will begin with your preferred hemisphere and use strategies that are most natural for you. However, you should also try strategies that are not your preference to help you concentrate and to expand ways of learning.

Analyzing. You made the styles more personal by determining what your preferences are.

Creating New Ideas. You predicted strategies that you should start with and those you should add as reinforcement.

Acting. The acting step, your response to your predictions, uses one or more of the multiple intelligences.

You created a song, drew a map, constructed a PowerPoint exercise, and so on, using the strategies you developed.

If you haven't already begun, make a conscious effort to re-create the learning process with what you are learning in other classes.

SUMMARY

To see if you grasped the major points of the chapter and to make a useful study guide, answer the following questions found in your reading. When you have written your answers, cover them and see if you can say the answer to each question in your own words. If you prefer to type your answers, you will find a Microsoft Word download for each summary on the College Success CourseMate for Practicing College Learning Strategies at www.cengagebrain.com.

What does the term "learning styles" refer to?

_____

Why is it important to determine your learning style?

_____

What did Edgar Dale discover about how much people generally remember?

_____

Explain some study strategies that a visual learner should use.

_____

Explain some study strategies that an auditory learner should use.

_____

Explain some study strategies that a kinesthetic learner should use.

_____

What are some characteristics of left-brain processing?

_____

What are some characteristics of right-brain processing?

_____

List and briefly explain the eight kinds of intelligences.

1. _____

   _____

2. _____

   _____

3. _____

   _____

4. _____

   _____

5. _____
_____

6. _____
_____

7. _____
_____

8. _____
_____

What are good strategies for those students who learn best alone?
_____

Name several ways to determine who might potentially be a good member for your study group.
_____
_____
_____

Name several guidelines for group study.
_____
_____
_____

Case Study: What's Your Advice?

Jon and Mandy are having a difficult time studying for their psychology test, so they formed a study group with two other classmates. From inventories they had taken in a previous class, Jon discovered that his left hemisphere is dominant. He prefers auditory input and his multiple-intelligence strengths are logical, linguistic, and intrapersonal. Mandy, on the other hand, is right brained and prefers visual and kinesthetic input, and her strengths are interpersonal, musical, and kinesthetic. They had memorized what their learning styles were for the final exam, but really didn't understand what those meant. The preferences and strengths of the two other students (Marc and Amanda) were not known. The upcoming test is about how the brain learns.

1. List some strategies that the group could use to study.

2. Assign specific tasks to each group member to complete before the study session.

3. Make specific suggestions for strategies to use during the session.

4. Make specific suggestions for strategies each should use after the session.

Parallel Parking

We covered different ways of looking at learning styles in this chapter. As a review, let's go back to the driving analogy. Can you compare the parallel parking terms to things you learned about learning styles? Choose at least three. Remember there is no *right* answer. I have left a blank space for you to fill in with one of your own if you choose.

Buying a New Car: _____

_____

Taking the Scenic Route: _____

_____

_____

Asking for Directions: _____

_____

_____

Taking the Interstate or Freeway: _____

_____

_____

Buying Insurance: _____

_____

_____

Evaluating Learning Outcomes

How successful were you in making it to your destination in this chapter?

Analyze what you learned in this chapter. Put a check beside each task you are now able to do. Now think of strategies that you learned that will help you save time and study more effectively. List them in the appropriate place on the back inside cover.

☐ **Determine** your preferred learning style, including sensory mode, hemispheric dominance, and type of multiple intelligence.
☐ **Practice** the strategies presented in the chapter to determine the most efficient ones for you to process difficult material and to reinforce the initial learning.
☐ **Demonstrate** ways to adapt new learning material to the preferred learning styles.
☐ **Analyze** a case study, and construct advice for a student having difficulty finding effective study methods.
☐ **Explain** the learning model used in this chapter.

Your Student Tip for This Chapter

Use the space below to write a tip you would give to other students about what you have learned in this chapter.

_____

_____

9 Test-Taking Strategies

Test-Taking Strategies	Strategies for Objective Tests	Strategies for Essay Tests
Budgeting Your Test-Taking Time	True/False	Planning Your Answer
Predicting Test Questions	Multiple-Choice	Direction Words
Preparing for Finals	Fill-in-the-Blank	Writing Winning Essay Answers
	Matching	

In previous chapters, you discovered the importance of critical thinking, you learned how to use what you know about your brain to develop wise study strategies, and you acquired a system for processing information from both lectures and texts. In other words, you know the fundamentals for preparing for a test. You filled your tank, checked your tires, plotted your course, and are ready for another leg of your college road trip: taking a test about material you have learned.

Learning Outcomes
for Chapter 9 Test-Taking Strategies

Here is your destination for Chapter 9. When you complete Chapter 9, you are expected not only to understand the material presented, but also to be able to:

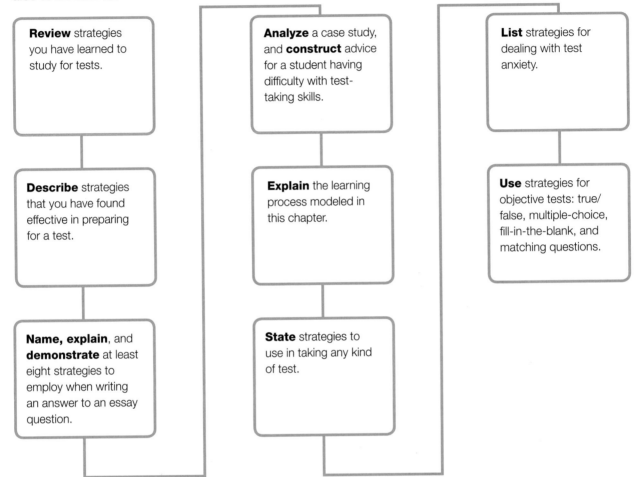

Review strategies you have learned to study for tests.

Analyze a case study, and **construct** advice for a student having difficulty with test-taking skills.

List strategies for dealing with test anxiety.

Describe strategies that you have found effective in preparing for a test.

Explain the learning process modeled in this chapter.

Use strategies for objective tests: true/false, multiple-choice, fill-in-the-blank, and matching questions.

Name, explain, and **demonstrate** at least eight strategies to employ when writing an answer to an essay question.

State strategies to use in taking any kind of test.

 Making Connections

Before we begin looking at strategies for taking tests, let's review some of the strategies we have learned for preparing for tests.

Below is a list of study aids that we have discussed. Review the classes you are taking and determine which aid might be the best strategy for each course. Use the questions below the strategy to make the strategies personal. Make the strategies part of your routine study. Remember that the more strategies you use, the more successful you will likely be.

Strategy	Notes about Strategy
Routinely Set Goals for each class	At the end of each week, review what assignments and tests you have due the next week. Determine what you will need to do to accomplish each task successfully. Map out a specific time to have each task completed. Think through what study aids you may need to make for each test. Develop a form for this or use your planner.
This strategy works for all classes. How do you think this would affect your success in each class?	
Class Notes	As you Use the Question in the Margin System, anticipate possible test questions. Once you have had a test in a course, compare your questions to those on the test. Let your professor check your notes to make sure you are getting what you need.
You can adapt QMS to any class. What classes do you have notes for? What classes do you wish you had notes for?	
Marked Textbooks	As you use the Question in the Margin System, anticipate possible test questions. Check your textbooks. Have you developed an effective way to mark them? Are you marking too much? Are you marking enough? Are you comparing what you marked to the notes you took? Remember, it will be easier to take notes in class if you have carefully read the assignment.
What courses are you taking that reading and marking your textbook would make you more successful?	
Study Guides	Don't just look over study guides. Use them to make some of the specific study aids below. Don't forget that many textbook sites have study guides.
In which classes do your instructors give you study guides?	
Study Groups	Even if you prefer to study alone, some study in a group assures you haven't missed something and provides you with different perspectives
In which classes do you have study groups?	
Flash Cards	Flash cards use all 10 learning principles and are effective for all learning styles. You can make them with index cards or electronically from Internet sites or apps. They provide pocket work to use anywhere. Anticipate test questions as you learn the material and create flash cards as your summary. Although flash cards are most useful for vocabulary and terms, they work for almost any type of course.

What classes have you made flashcards for?	
Mapping	Mapping uses all 10 learning principles and is effective for all learning styles—a must for visual learner.
	Maps can be made from textbooks or class notes. There is also mapping software available.
Mapping lets you see how everything fits together as a whole. What classes are you taking that you can map as a summary?	
Time Lines, Charts, and Diagrams	Time lines, charts, and diagrams serve to summarize and condense information to a manageable size.
Time lines are important when you need to manage information chronologically. What classes would this be useful for? What classes are you taking that a chart or diagram would help you better understand the material?	
Making Practice Tests	Making a practice test uses most of the 10 learning principles and promotes practice of actual tasks you will be asked to perform on the test. Use previous tests to model your test. This means that if you have an essay question, you practice actually writing your answer.
	Have each member of your study group make a version.
What classes have you made practice tests for? Did you notice that you had less test anxiety?	
Making Review Games	Make your own Jeopardy, matching, or Who Wants to Be a Millionaire-type games or check websites and apps that make them for you.
Would playing games with the information get you more interested?	
PowerPoints	Review PowerPoint slides used in classes or make your own. Have each person in your study group make a PowerPoint and teach something to your group.
Which classes could you make PowerPoints for?	

It is especially important that you be in the driver's seat when taking tests. This chapter addresses some strategies for taking tests.

There are two basic categories of tests. The first is objective. For each item in an objective test, there is one correct answer. This kind of test usually depends on *recognition* to get the answer out of your long-term memory. In other words, there are clues within the question to jog your memory. Objective tests include true/false, multiple-choice, fill-in-the-blank, and matching questions.

The other category of tests is subjective. There is a correct answer for each question on a subjective test but also a range of possible ways to give this answer. Discussion questions, essay questions, and many short-answer questions fall into this category. They depend on *recall*, not just recognition. Recall requires that you bring the information out of your long-term memory and organize it in a way that effectively answers what has been asked. There is no substitute for having studied thoroughly and knowing the answers. However, certain strategies can be used with each kind of test so that you get the most out of your effort. Just as different road conditions require different driving strategies, different test types require different strategies in both studying for and taking tests.

Exercise 9.1

Preparing for Tests

Before you begin practicing specific test-taking strategies, make sure you are effectively preparing for tests. Below is a list of ways that successful students use to prepare for tests. They are strategies you have learned in previous chapters. Be deliberate in your evaluation. You know the strategies, but are you using them? Rate yourself on how well you practice each of them. A *5* means that you almost always do it; *4*, that you usually do it; *3*, that you sometimes do it; *2*, that you rarely do it; and *1*, that you never do it. Be totally honest in your evaluation.

_____ **1.** Keep up to date with assignments.

_____ **2.** Take notes in every class every day. This includes asking questions when you don't understand.

_____ **3.** Process information as you come to it. Learning information is very different from becoming acquainted with it.

_____ **4.** Process information systematically. The Question in the Margin system works well for most people. Adapt it to suit your learning style. Capitalize on the discipline that this system requires, and make it a habit to process information from texts and lectures, not just go over it.

_____ **5.** Have a study place that is free of distractions.

_____ **6.** Have a specific time for the initial study of each subject. You may need more than this time, but having a set time will save you time in the long run.

_____ **7.** Make summary sheets, flash cards, and practice tests.

_____ **8.** Always carry some kind of pocket work so that you can make use of what would otherwise be wasted spare minutes by reciting and thinking about what you are learning.

_____ **9.** Learn something new or difficult in your strongest intelligence or sense or in your dominant hemisphere. Reinforce it in as many different ways as possible.

_____ **10.** Find a study partner or two in each class, and routinely take turns teaching each other the material.

_____ **11.** Prepare for each class as if there will be a pop quiz.

_____ Total your score.

When you have totaled your score, choose the appropriate writing assignment from the list that follows.

Writing Assignment for Exercise 9.1

- If your score is from 44 to 55, write a paragraph or two in which you describe the results of using the study strategies listed. Be specific. A comparison of the benefits of your old study habits and your new ones might be one approach.

- If your score is from 33 to 43, write a paragraph or two in which you describe both your good and bad study habits. Discuss reasons for both and goals for incorporating more of the strategies listed above.

- If your score is below 33, write a paragraph or two in which you try to determine why you have not used the strategies listed above to your advantage and which strategies you think you might be able to use effectively. Set some realistic goals and discuss how you might achieve them.

Critical Thinking About Tests

In Chapter 2 on critical thinking, you learned that there are levels, or depths, of thinking and learning. You used Bloom's taxonomy as a model: **knowledge, comprehension, application, analysis, synthesis,** and **evaluation.** You may want to review these concepts. When taking a test, it is important to know what *level* of learning will be tested. You can study all night memorizing definitions for a test; however, if the test asks for analysis, synthesis, or evaluation of those definitions, you are sunk!

Identify the level of learning being asked for in the following test questions:

_____ What evidence can you present to support the idea that the Confederate Army was unprepared in the Battle of Shiloh?

_____ Where were the first Olympic Games held?

_____ Name and explain each step of the Question in the Margin system.

_____ What would happen if you combined sulfur with iodine?

_____ Demonstrate that you know how to take notes using the Question in the Margin system.

_____ What were the merits of Hannibal's plan to take Rome?

Exercise 9.2

Self-Analysis: Preparing for Tests

Now that you know some strategies that will help you study for tests, let's discuss taking a test. Many students feel that one reason they are not top students is that they are poor test takers. The following diagnostic inventory is designed to help you rate your present test-taking skills and habits. It will also serve as an overview of the topics discussed in this test-taking unit. It is divided into three sections: strategies used to prepare for a test, general test-taking strategies, and strategies for specific types of tests. *Be totally honest. This is not a test!*

Write the number in the column that best describes you.

Strategies Used to Prepare for a Test

	1 Never	2 Infrequently	3 Generally	4 Frequently	5 Always
1. Do you find out as much about the test as possible?				✓	
2. As you review material, do you anticipate possible test questions?			✓		
3. Do you have notes to review?				✓	
4. Do you review your notes systematically?		✓			
5. Do you make summary sheets?					✓
6. Do you recite or write down material in your own words?					
7. Do you use mnemonic devices and other memory principles for lists, dates, and so on?			✓		
8. Do you avoid cramming the night before?			✓		
9. Do you get plenty of rest the night before a test?					✓
10. Do you try to do your best on every test you take?					✓
11. Do you take tests without too much anxiety?		✓			
12. Do you find other people in your class to study with?		✓			
13. Do you arrive early to your classroom the day of the test?			✓		

General Test-Taking Strategies

	1 Never	2 Infrequently	3 Generally	4 Frequently	5 Always
14. Do you preview the test before writing anything?				✓	
15. Do you plan test-taking time? (How much time do you allow for each task?)			✓		
16. Do you make sure you are following directions by underlining or circling key words?				✓	
17. Do you answer the easiest questions first?				✓	

Strategies Used to Prepare for a Test (cont.)

	1 Never	2 Infrequently	3 Generally	4 Frequently	5 Always
18. Do you answer all questions (unless the directions say otherwise or you are penalized for wrong answers)?	____	____	____	____	____
19. Do you check all answers carefully? (This means reworking each question if time permits.)	____	____	____	____	____
20. Do you use all the time allotted for the test?	____	____	____	____	____
21. Do you use specific strategies in taking objective tests such as multiple choice, true/false, fill-in, and matching?	____	____	____	____	____
22. Do you use specific strategies to answer essay questions?	____	____	____	____	____
23. Do you review returned tests to see how you might do better on future tests?	____	____	____	____	____
Subtotals	____	____	____	____	____

Add the numbers you've written in each column to find your subtotals. Add your subtotals to find your final score: _____

How testwise are you?   **Rating Scale**

27–49	Poor
50–71	Fair
72–93	Good
94–115	Excellent

Personal analysis: On another sheet of paper write a paragraph in which you analyze your strengths and weaknesses in the test-taking strategies specifically covered in the preceding inventory.

Budgeting Your Time When Taking Tests

One of the most important strategies for taking any kind of test is budgeting your time. Too often we hear students say that they knew the answers but ran out of time or that they made careless mistakes because they rushed. Taking a test without budgeting your time is like driving to an important meeting without determining how much time it will take to drive there. Because you want to get the most points on a test for the time you spend, you should analyze each test and budget your time accordingly. Stopping to analyze a test before you begin to work on it puts you in control and may have a calming effect.

Preview the Test

1. Determine the types of questions.
2. Calculate the point value of questions.

BRAIN BYTE

The Big 3 of Dr. Hillman's BREATHE System should also improve your test taking by supplying your brain with sufficient oxygen and giving you a feeling of self-confidence. You've prepared your mind for the test by studying. Now prepare your body: Maintain proper posture, relax neck and shoulder muscles, and take cleansing breaths.

3. Look for questions you need to make notes about; if necessary, use a mnemonic or another review strategy you have learned.

4. Locate easy questions to answer first.

Budget Your Time

1. When calculating the point value of questions, determine the percentage of the total score toward which it counts. (If it counts 30 points, it's worth 30 percent of a 100-point test.)

2. From the total amount of time allowed for the test, subtract some time for preview and review. (If you have 60 minutes to take a test, you might subtract 5 minutes for previewing the test and 5 minutes for reviewing it. This would leave 50 minutes base time to take the test.)

3. Calculate the percentage of the base time (time remaining after you've subtracted preview and review times) that you should allow for each question or set of questions. If a question counts for 30 percent of the test, multiply 0.30 (percent) × 50 (base time). Allow 15 minutes to answer that question. Use the entire time allotted for the test.

Exercise 9.3

Budgeting Your Time

How much time would you allow for the following?

Total Time for Test: 2 Hours

Time allowed for preview _____

Time allowed for review _____

2 essays (20 points each) _____

25 multiple-choice (1 point each) _____

15 matching (1 point each) _____

20 true/false (1 point each) _____

Total Time for Test: 50 Minutes

Time allowed for preview _____

Time allowed for review _____

20 true/false (1 point each) _____

2 essays (10 points each) _____

Matching (30 points) _____

Fill-in-the-blank (10 points) _____

Short answer (20 points) _____

Following Directions

One of the most common reasons for getting lost is not following directions. One of the most common mistakes students make on tests is that they don't follow directions. It is important to follow directions carefully even if the test is timed. Never assume that you know what the directions say. For example, true/false questions may ask you to correct the false ones to make them true. As practice, take the following test.

Exercise 9.4

Following Directions

Directions: Read all questions before answering anything. This is a timed test. Your instructor will tell you at the beginning how much time you are allowed. You *must* complete it in the given time.

1. Write your name and section number in the top right corner of this paper.

2. In the top left corner, write today's date in *numbers*.

3. Under today's date, write "Following Directions, Timed Test."

4. If $3 \times 4 \times 2 = 25$, write *green;* if not, write *purple.* _____

5. Count the number of empty desks in this room. _____

6. Draw a house with two chimneys, two windows, and one door.

7. Stand and say in a very loud voice, "I have reached question 9. I am the leader in following directions."

8. Spell the name of your hometown backward. _____

9. Circle one: True or false: Following directions is easy.

10. Underline one: True or false: Following directions is essential.

11. Now that you have read all the questions, do only questions 1, 2, and 3. Then turn your page over and wait for the rest of the class to finish.

Exercise 9.5

Strategies for Taking Any Test

Carefully review the survival tips for taking tests above. Then create a summary sheet using the Question in the Margin system. Write the questions below in the margin and put your answers on the notes side. The self-testing employed in the Question in the Margin system simulates a testing situation.

1. Why should you preview your test before answering any questions?

2. What specifically does doing a "mind dump" involve?

3. Why is it important to read directions? Does this step just waste important time?

4. List several reasons why you would want to answer the easy questions first.

5. Why should you skip the harder questions and go back to them later?

6. Name several things you might do if a question is unclear.

7. Why is it important to use the entire test-taking time allotted?

The strategies in your summary sheet can be used for taking any test. Now, however, we consider some strategies you can use for specific kinds of tests.

Survival Tips for Taking Tests

Below is a list of helpful strategies for you to use when taking tests. The suggestions are common sense, but the strategies will help you establish a routine for taking tests.

Before You Begin

1. Preview the test before you answer anything. This gets you thinking about the material. Make sure to note the point value of each question. This will give you some ideas on budgeting your time.

2. Do a "mind dump." Using what you saw in the preview, make notes of anything you think you might forget. Write down things such as formulas, mnemonics, or lists you used in learning the material that might help you remember it. Outline your answers to discussion questions.

3. Quickly calculate how much time you should allow for each section according to the point value. (You don't want to spend thirty minutes on an essay question that counts only five points.)

Taking the Test

4. Read the directions. (Can more than one answer be correct? Are you penalized for guessing? And so on.) Never assume that you know what the directions say without reading them.

5. Answer the easy questions first. This will give you the confidence and momentum to get through the rest of the test. You are sure these answers are correct.

6. Go back to the difficult questions. While looking over the test and doing the easy questions, your subconscious mind will have been

working on the answers to the harder ones. Also, later items on the test may give you useful or needed information for earlier items.

7. Answer all questions (unless you are penalized for wrong answers or unless the directions say otherwise).

8. Ask the instructor to explain any items that are not clear. Do not ask for the answer, but phrase your question in a way that shows the instructor that you have the information but are not sure how you are expected to present it.

9. Try to answer the questions from the instructor's point of view. Try to remember what the instructor emphasized and felt was important.

10. Use the margin to explain why you chose a particular answer if the question does not seem clear or if the answer seems ambiguous. Express a difficult question in your own words. Rephrasing can make a question clear to you, but be sure you don't change the meaning of the question.

11. Circle key words in difficult questions. This will force you to focus on the central point.

12. Use all of the time allotted for the test. If you have extra time, cover your answers and rework the questions.

Strategies for Objective Tests

Because you are looking for clues to the best or correct answers when taking objective tests, the strategies you use will differ from those for subjective or essay tests. With that in mind, let's look at strategies for specific kinds of objective tests.

Strategies for True/False Tests

You have a 50:50 chance of guessing the answer to a true/false question even if you don't read the question. So you can be sure that when a test maker writes true/false test questions, there will be some tricky questions. This section will help you build strategies for looking at the way true/false questions are written and help you anticipate possible tricks. **No amount of guessing can replace knowing the answer.** Nevertheless, you should be aware of strategies to use if you are not sure. Although these strategies won't apply every time, they will make you aware of possible tricks that test makers use.

Negatives and Double Negatives

Testing makes most of us somewhat anxious and more prone to making careless errors and errors in reading. If the statement has a negative word in it and you leave it out, your answer will be wrong. Double negatives are a test maker's trick to catch students unaware.

A negative is a word or part of a word, such as *no*, *not*, or *non-*, that indicates negation. Negation, in its most basic sense, changes the truth value of a statement to its opposite. Because a **negative word** or **prefix** (*not, cannot, un-, dis-, il-, non-, in-*) used in a statement makes the statement's

BRAIN BYTE

Apparently, testing gives the learner an opportunity to practice effective learning procedures simultaneously. Tests do not have to be graded to be effective. It is the act of taking the test that is helpful.

opposite, a good strategy to use is to circle all negatives so that you are sure of what the statement says. Consider the following:

A koala bear is a kind of bear.
A koala bear is not a kind of bear.

The first statement is false, but the addition of *not* in the second makes it true. The effect of negatives is to make the sentence the opposite of what it would be without the negative.

Not is the most commonly used negative. Other negative words include *no, none, nothing, nowhere, neither, nobody, no one, hardly, scarcely,* and *barely;* however, you should also be on the lookout for prefixes that make a word negative. In the following list, fill in the blanks with the negative of the word given:

1. Truthful   Untruthful
2. Alcoholic   _____
3. Direct   _____
4. Saturated   _____
5. Perfect   _____
6. Responsible   _____
7. Agreeable   _____
8. Legal   _____

A **double negative** is the nonstandard use of two negatives in the same sentence so that they cancel each other and create a positive. Sometimes double negatives are used for emphasis such as "he can't just do nothing." For our consideration, double negatives are often one of those nasty tricks test writers use on tests to confuse or to make sure a student is paying attention.

Because we rarely hear double negatives, our brain processes them much like a foreign language. Therefore, we need to simplify the question by getting rid of *double* negatives. **You can cross out both negatives *without changing the meaning* of the word, phrase, or statement they appear in.** If a question says, "You won't be unprepared," change it to say, "You will be prepared." If a question says, "This is not an imperfect method," change it to say, "This is a perfect method." If a sentence has three negatives, you can cross out two without changing the meaning of the statement.

Exercise 9.6

Practice with Double Negatives

Read the following statements. Circle all negatives. If two negatives occur, eliminate both. You won't change the meaning; you will simply clarify the statement. Then read and decide if the statement is true or false.

_____ 1. Most students are not unwilling to leave class early.

_____ 2. It is not unusual for students to have math anxiety.

_____ 3. It is not illegal not to drive on the left side of the road in the United States.

_____ **4.** Most students would not be dissatisfied with an *F* on an exam.

_____ **5.** The cost of an SUV is usually not inexpensive in comparison to the cost of a sedan.

Qualifiers

Words that limit or change the meaning of a word or sentence are called **qualifiers** and are often used in tricky true/false questions. Understanding the difference between absolute and general qualifiers or modifiers should help you be more confident in your answers.

If you are talking about a child doing chores at home, you can start with the sentence, "He does his chores." You can qualify that sentence in several ways.

If you begin with the negative, you can say:

He *never* does his chores.	
He did *none* of his chores.	These are *absolute* qualifiers. They mean 100 percent.
He did *no* chores.	The child didn't do *any* chores—not even one.

Then you can move toward the positive.

He *seldom* does his chores.	
He did *few* of his chores.	
He did *some* of his chores.	
He *sometimes* does his chores.	These are *general* qualifiers. They do not include 100 percent.
He *generally* does his chores.	
He did *many* of his chores.	
He *usually* does his chores.	
He did *most* of his chores.	

When you get to the other end of the continuum, you get back to absolutes on the positive side.

He *always* does his chores.	
He did *all* of his chores.	These are *absolute* qualifiers. They mean 100 percent.
He did *every* chore.	The child did *all* the chores—every one.

We need to understand about qualifiers because they make a great deal of difference in answering a true/false question.

No, never, none, nobody, only	Few, seldom, some, generally, many, usually, most	Always, all, every, best
100%	General	100%
Absolute		Absolute

If **general qualifiers** are present (*generally, probably, usually, many,* or *sometimes*), there is a **good chance that the statement is true.** If **absolute qualifiers** (*all, always, no, never, none, every, everyone, only, best, entirely,* or *invariably*) are used, **the statement is probably false.** Consider these examples.

Honda makes cars. Honda makes *only* cars.

All pit bulls are aggressive.

Absolutes are words for which there are no exceptions—100 percent words. Learn the absolutes well. Otherwise, you are likely to be confused. When you see absolutes in a true/false statement, you can be sure that 99 percent of the time the statement is false.

Other Educated Guesses

If any part of a statement is false, then the whole statement is false. This is always the case. You should, then, carefully read each statement, looking for any part that may be false. For example, for a true/false test question:

_____ George Washington, Abraham Lincoln, and Benjamin Franklin were U.S. presidents.

While Washington and Lincoln were presidents, Franklin was not a president.

True/false statements that give reasons tend to be false (*because the reason is incorrect or there may be additional reasons*).

_____ Children today get lower grades because they watch too much television.

This may be one reason but not the only reason. Be wary of statements that include words such as *reason, because, due to,* or *since.* They may be indicators of reasons that could very well be false.

Assume statements are true unless you know they are false. (If you absolutely must guess, guess *true.* It is easier to write a true statement than a false one. Unless they make a real effort, test writers will usually have more true than false questions.)

Summary of Strategies for True/False Statements

Negatives	Circle all negatives so that you are sure of what the statement says. Simplify the question by getting rid of *double* negatives.
Qualifiers	If **general qualifiers** are present (*generally, probably, usually, many,* or *sometimes*), there is a **good chance that the statement is true.** If **absolute qualifiers** (*all, always, no, never, none, every, everyone, only, best, entirely,* or *invariably*) are used, **the statement is probably false.**
Guess false	If any part of a statement is false, then the whole statement is false. Carefully check items in a series.
Guess false	True/false statements that give reasons tend to be false. Be on the lookout for phrases introduced by *reason, because, due to,* or *since.*
Guess true	Assume statements are true unless you know they are false (or unless they include the two exceptions above).

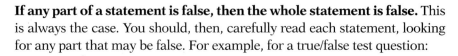

Exercise 9.7

Mapping True/False Strategies

On a separate piece of paper, use what you learned about mapping in Chapter 7 to make a map that summarizes the strategies to use for true/false questions.

Exercise 9.8

Practice with True/False Tests

Use the methods just discussed to determine whether the following statements are true or false. Write *T* on the lines in front of the true statements and *F* on the lines in front of the false statements. In the blank following each statement, explain the strategy you used to determine if the statement was true or false.

_____ **1.** We should eat protein for breakfast because it gets oxygen to the brain.

_____

_____ **2.** Most collisions happen within a short distance from home.

_____

_____ **3.** As a general rule, one should study two hours for each hour of class time.

_____

_____ **4.** July is never a winter month.

_____

_____ **5.** A master schedule should never be changed during a semester.

_____

_____ **6.** Average drivers commit 2.5 traffic violations every mile they drive!

_____

_____ **7.** Short-term memory appears to function in the hippocampus as a clearinghouse that selects chunks of data to remember.

_____

_____ **8.** Most students drop out of college because they are not smart enough.

_____

_____ **9.** You should always answer the easy questions on a test first because you might forget the answers.

_____

_____ **10.** The Question in the Margin system should be used for all reading.

_____

_____ **11.** An absolute qualifier will always make a true/false question false.

_____

_____ **12.** In taking class notes, students are not unlikely to miss the point if they try to write down everything.

_____

_____ **13.** A good study environment should include good lighting, a comfortable seat, quiet music, and plenty of food.

_____

_____ **14.** A chunk of information is defined as an unfamiliar array of only seven pieces or bits.

_____

_____ **15.** Left-brained students are always smarter than right-brained students.

_____

_____ **16.** For most students, getting a good night's sleep is more important than cramming all night.

_____

_____ **17.** *Most, few, some, all,* and *rarely* are general qualifiers and usually make a statement true.

_____

Strategies for Multiple-Choice Tests

1. **Realize that there is not always a perfect answer.** You must choose the best answer.
2. This means you need to **read all possible responses.**
3. **Cross out the incorrect answers.** Incorrect answers are called *distracters*. Crossing them out will focus your attention on reasonable options.
4. **Treat each option as a true/false question.** Read the stem and then the first answer. Read the stem again and then the second answer. Read the stem again and then the third answer. And so on. Apply the true/false strategies each time. By doing this, you will keep track of the question in the tangle of answers.
5. **Use educated guesses only as a last resort.** Although there is no substitute for knowing the material, becoming familiar with certain tendencies can be of value when you do not know the answer. Such tendencies are often referred to as test cues or test flaws and require you to use an educated guess. As a general rule, the following types of options tend to be *incorrect* answers:

    • **Options with absolutes** (*Can you name ten absolutes?*)

       _____ _____ _____ _____

       _____ _____ _____ _____

- **Options with unfamiliar terms** (*Of course, if you haven't read the assignment or listened in class, all terms may sound unfamiliar!*)

- **Options with jokes and insults or are just plain silly**

- **Options with highest and lowest numbers** (*except on math quizzes*)

And the following types of options tend to be *correct* answers:

- **Options that read "all of the above"** (*especially when you know that two options are correct*)

- **Options with more complete or inclusive answers**

_____ Physical attractiveness is likely to vary among

    a. Italians.   **b.** female bank tellers.

    c. high school cheerleaders.   **d.** women over thirty.

(*Which group includes the most people?*)

- **One of two similar-looking options**

_____ In the brain, logical and linguistic functions are processed by

    a. the right hemisphere.   **b.** the left hemisphere.

    c. habeas corpus.   **d.** the cerebellum.

Exercise 9.9

Practice with Multiple-Choice Questions

Use the strategies just discussed to select the correct answer to the following questions. Write *a*, *b*, *c*, or *d* on the line in front of the question. Use the line following the question to explain the strategy you used.

_____ **1.** Research has found that the ideal length of a nap:
    a. is only 15 minutes.
    b. is as long as your history professor is talking.
    c. is 30 minutes.
    d. One should never take naps.

_____

_____ **2.** A sonnet is a:
    a. lyric poem of 14 lines.
    b. love poem with 25 lines.
    c. seven-line rhyme.
    d. flowery hat.

_____

_____ **3.** Common driving distractions are:
    a. applying makeup and talking on a cell phone.
    b. adjusting the radio or changing CDs.
    c. dealing with rambunctious or misbehaving kids.
    d. all of the above.

_____

_____ **4.** An excise tax is a tax:
   a. imposed on health clubs.
   b. imposed on goods, especially luxuries and cars.
   c. imposed only on diamonds.
   d. added to all incomes over $100,000.

_____ **5.** Calvin Coolidge:
   a. was vice president under Warren Harding.
   b. became president in 1923 when Harding died.
   c. was elected president on his own in 1924.
   d. all of the above.

_____ **6.** Potassium:
   a. is never found in red meat.
   b. is the only chemical necessary for pH balance.
   c. should never be combined with vitamin C.
   d. is abundant in many fruits and vegetables.

_____ **7.** Once a long-term memory has formed, which factor interferes with retrieving it?
   a. clogging at the synapse
   b. deterioration of the neuronal pathways involved
   c. stress
   d. all of the above

_____ **8.** During the fifth and sixth centuries, Germanics migrated to England. They were called:
   a. Angles.
   b. Saxons.
   c. Jutes.
   d. Angles, Saxons, and Jutes.

_____ **9.** Henry Clay is classified as:
   a. a great boxer and poet.
   b. a war hawk.
   c. a war hawk and the Great Compromiser.
   d. entirely responsible for the War of 1812 and the Treaty of Ghent.

_____ **10.** The most effective time to study for a lecture class is:
   a. before class.
   b. after class.
   c. right before you go to bed.
   d. irrelevant; it is not necessary to study for a lecture class.

_____ **11.** Prolonged stress produces high levels of cortisol, which can:
  a. cause the hippocampus to shrink.
  b. significantly reduce the production of neurons.
  c. affect memory, mood, and mental functions.
  d. all of the above.

_____ **12.** If you cover 1.47 feet per second for each mile per hour you are driving and if you are driving at 60 miles per hour, every second that elapses, you cover:
  a. 60 feet.
  b. 147 feet.
  c. almost 30 yards.
  d. 1.47 yards.

Strategies for Fill-in Questions

1. Read the question to yourself so that you can hear what is being asked.

2. If more than one answer comes to mind, write both in the margin. Come back later and choose the one you want.

3. Make sure that your choice fits in logically and grammatically.

4. Remember that your answer may require more than one word.

Exercise 9.10

Practice with Fill-in Questions

1. One should answer _____easy_____ questions, unless you are penalized for wrong answers.

2. _____, _____, and _____ are three kinds of objective tests.

3. Answer the _____ questions first.

4. True/false statements that give a reason tend to be _____.

5. True/false statements with absolutes will almost always be _____.

6. The incorrect choices in a multiple-choice question are called _____.

Strategies for Matching Questions

With true/false questions you have a 50 percent chance of guessing the correct answer. With multiple-choice questions, you have a 25 percent chance before you begin to eliminate distracters. Although most students think that matching is one of the easier ways to take a test, your chances of guessing the correct answers are very small.

Following are some strategies for matching tests:

1. Preview all of the possibilities before answering anything.
2. Determine whether an answer can be used more than once.
3. Answer the questions you are sure of first.
4. Cross out options as you use them.
5. Use logic to determine what is being asked for. A person? A place? A date?

Exercise 9.11

Practice with Matching Questions

Use the strategies for matching to match the U.S. president with his vice president.

_____ 1. Jimmy Carter   **a.** George H. W. Bush

_____ 2. Ronald Reagan   **b.** Dan Quayle

_____ 3. George H. W. Bush   **c.** Dick Cheney

_____ 4. Bill Clinton   **d.** Walter Mondale

_____ 5. George W. Bush   **e.** Al Gore

VIRTUAL FIELD TRIP

Objective Tests

Visit the College Success CourseMate.

Reviewing Returned Test

A Dozen Reasons to Review a Returned Test

1. Check the point total to make sure it is right. Look for mistakes in grading.
2. Know what questions you missed, what the correct answers are, and why you missed them. The reasons you missed these questions are often as or more important for your performance on the next test as knowing the correct answers.
3. Study the instructor's comments, especially for essay questions, so that you will know what is expected next time.
4. Figure out what kinds of questions (including tricky questions) the instructor likes to use.
5. See if the questions you missed came from the text or the lecture. Concentrate more on that source when you study for the next exam.

6. Correct and understand what you missed. This is information you need to know. It may appear on a later test or the final exam.

7. Determine which type of questions you missed so you can review strategies for that type.

8. Review to get an idea about what kind of test the instructor may give next time.

9. Review to put information back into your long-term memory.

10. Ask questions of your instructor while the test is fresh in your mind.

11. Review how you studied for the exam. Look for better ways to study next time.

12. Reviewing gives you a good reason to talk to your instructor and let her or him know you want to improve.

 Making Connections

It is important to remember that not all objective test questions fall into the lower thinking levels of Bloom's taxonomy. Memorizing definitions, dates, and places will probably not be enough to answer all the questions. Here are some examples of test questions that use the higher-order thinking skills of analysis, synthesis, and evaluation.

_____ 1. You can gain time by:
  a. doing a job in less time than usual.
  b. using blocks of time you usually waste.
  c. obeying your alarm clock.
  d. all of the above.

_____ 2. The most effective time to study for a lecture class is just:
  a. before the class.
  b. after the class.
  c. before the test.
  d. after a party.

_____ 3. Rereading:
  a. is a quick, efficient way to review a chapter.
  b. is better than reciting because you cover more material.
  c. should always be done before major tests.
  d. none of the above.

_____ 4. John was assigned to read a chapter in his psychology textbook. He should begin his assignment by:
  a. turning to the first page of the chapter and reading through from beginning to end.
  b. reading the chapter's introduction, headings, and summary and examining the graphic material in it.
  c. underlining the information that he eventually wants in his notes.
  d. waiting until after the lecture so he will know what's important to the professor.

_____ **5.** Which is the best plan for completing a long reading assignment for your history class?

    a. Find a quiet place and read the assignment at one sitting. Mark it as you read.

    b. Read parts of the assignment throughout the day when you have a few minutes. When you finish a paragraph, write a question in the text's margin and underline the answer. Then review when reading is complete.

    c. Read the summary and mark the text in class as the instructor lectures.

    d. Survey the assignment, then read it in one sitting. Write a question for each paragraph and underline the answers.

Copyright © 2013 Wadsworth, Cengage Learning. All rights reserved.

BRAIN BYTE

Brain researchers talk about knowledge as being *state bound*, meaning that how and where we learn may be as important to the brain as what we learn. This is why taking a practice test (which simulates the real situation) is a great way to study. What does it say about cramming for an exam?

Exercise 9.12

Summary for Objective Test Strategies

Either add to the map you created for true/false questions or create a new map so that it includes all the strategies you learned about objective tests.

Predicting Test Questions

One of the most important study skills you can develop is predicting what will be on a test. Knowing this with confidence can make your study time more effective, as well as cut down on test anxiety. By using the Question in the Margin system for taking notes from lectures and textbooks, you have already begun to use the essential strategies needed to predict what will be on a test.

Here are some important guidelines to remember in predicting questions that will be on a test.

1. Notice clues to test questions from lecture material.
    a. What an instructor says and how he or she says it (verbal cues)
    b. Ideas that are repeated
    c. Ideas written on the board, in an overhead, or in a handout
    d. "This is important"; "You'll see this again."
    e. Questions the instructor asks

2. Notice clues to test questions from textbook material.
    a. Material in **bold** print
    b. Information in summary section
    c. Problems or questions at the end of chapters

3. Save all tests, quizzes, homework, and so on. Look for patterns.

4. Find out if previous tests are available and analyze the material covered.

Exercise 9.13

Possible Test Questions Dealing with Test-Taking Strategies

Examine the test-taking strategies on the previous pages. Look closely at the strategies described in the diagnostic inventory and strategies for any test: true/false, multiple-choice, fill-in, and matching questions. Now predict 10 true/false questions and 5 multiple-choice questions dealing with these strategies. Use the numbered blanks for your questions.

True/False

_____ 1. _____

_____ 2. _____

_____ 3. _____

_____ 4. _____

_____ 5. _____

_____ 6. _____

_____ 7. _____

_____ 8. _____

_____ 9. _____

_____ 10. _____

Multiple Choice

_____ 1. _____
         a.
         b.
         c.
         d.

_____ 2. _____
         a.
         b.
         c.
         d.

_____ 3. _____
         a.
         b.
         c.
         d.

_____ 4. _____
         a.
         b.
         c.
         d.

_____ 5. _____
         a.
         b.
         c.
         d.

Strategies for Essay Tests

Many students dread essay exams and discussion questions. Whereas objective tests require you to choose the correct answer or fill in a specific blank, subjective tests require you to recall and to organize. The main idea is to make sure that the grader knows that you know the answer to the question. Leave nothing to chance.

Basic Strategies for Writing Answers to Essay Tests

 The check list presented below is an important guide for you to use when writing answers that require or paragraph. You need to understand each point so that when you write an essay for history class or psychology class, you have a guideline to make sure you get the most points for what you know. Use the following as your GPS to guide you in writing the answers and as a checklist after you have written the answers.

Check List for Essay Tests

_____ 1. Do I really understand what the question asks me to do?

_____ 2. Have I done any preliminary planning of my major points?

_____ 3. From reading the first sentence of my answer, does the reader know both what the question is and how I will develop my answer?

_____ 4. Do the major points stand out?

_____ 5. Are the major points supported with examples and facts?

_____ 6. Are there clear transitions between the major points?

_____ 7. Would someone who has not taken this class be able to understand the concept discussed in the way I explained it?

_____ 8. Have I completely covered all major points needed to answer the question?

_____ 9. Did I stick to the question?

_____ 10. Have I concluded with a summary statement?

_____ 11. Did I proofread for misspelled words, sentence fragments, run-on sentences, comma splices, subject-verb or pronoun-antecedent agreement errors, and other errors that might prevent the reader from understanding what I have written?

_____ 12. Is my handwriting readable, and have I left enough space for comments or additions?

Direction Words

Often students lose points on essay tests, not because they don't know the answer, but because they do not answer the question being asked. The key to what your professor is asking you to do is to understand exactly what

BRAIN BYTE

Leslie Hart argues that subjective tests are superior to objective tests because learners have to identify patterns and select strategies for using them.

the directions ask for. On page XX is a list of 15 commonly used direction words. Make flash cards to help you remember them. Write a direction word on the front of the card and put the definition and examples on the back or use your flash card app.

Direction Word	Definition	Example
1. Compare	Emphasize similarities but also present differences.	*Compare* the strategies used in taking true/false tests with those used in taking multiple-choice tests.
2. Contrast	Give differences only.	*Contrast* the functions of the left brain and the right brain.
3. Criticize	Give your judgment of good points; then give the limitations with evidence.	*Criticize* the Question in the Margin system for taking lecture notes.
4. Define	Give meaning but no detail.	*Define* objective tests.
5. Describe	State particulars in detail.	*Describe* your weaknesses as tested by LASSI.
6. Discuss	Give reasons pro and con with details.	*Discuss* what you have done to overcome your weaknesses that were pinpointed by LASSI.
7. Evaluate	Discuss advantages and disadvantages along with your opinion.	*Evaluate* the implementation of the on-line catalog in the library.
8. Give cause and effect	Describe the steps that lead to an event or situation and the impact of the event or situation.	*Give the cause* of our forgetting what we read in textbooks and the *effect* that the Question in the Margin system has on this forgetting.
9. Give an example	Give a concrete illustration from your book, notes, or experience.	*Give an example* of a reference book that you think will be helpful in other courses.
10. Illustrate	Give an example.	*Illustrate* how the principle of meaningful organization will help transfer information from short-term to long-term memory.
11. Justify	Prove or give reasons.	Most students will not use the Question in the Margin system for reading a textbook because it takes too long. *Justify* its use.
12. Relate	Show how things interconnect.	*Relate* the Question in the Margin system for reading textbooks to the Question in the Margin system for taking lecture notes.
13. Summarize	Organize and bring together main points only.	*Summarize* what you have learned in this course.
14. Support	Back up a statement with facts and proof.	Researchers say that recitation is the most powerful means for transferring information from short-term to long-term memory. *Support* this statement.
15. Trace	Give main points from beginning to end of an event.	*Trace* ideas from when they first enter the brain to active memory.

Exercise 9.14

Applying the Direction Words

Below are descriptions of what different instructors want you to write on a test. Identify which direction words they are likely to use in their directions. There is a self-grading version of this exercise on-line at http://www.quia.com/tq/215781.html to use if you prefer.

compare

1. In your composition class, the instructor asks you to show how the modes of narration and description are alike and how they are different.

critize
evaluate

2. In a political science class, you are asked to give your judgment on the good points of the electoral college system while acknowledging its limitations.

contrast
compare

3. Your study skills instructor asks for you to point out differences between your study habits now and your study habits at the beginning of the semester.

define

4. In an algebra class, the professor asks you to give the meaning of the term _slope_.

describe

5. In a literature class, the professor asks you to depict in detail the setting of the novel _Sula_ by giving particular details.

discuss
criticize

6. An aerospace instructor asks students to give a detailed analysis (both pros and cons) of the reasons NASA was faced by problems during the 1980s.

evaluate
compare

7. Your study skills instructor asks you to discuss the advantages and disadvantages of using the Question in the Margin system for reading textbooks.

cause + effect
discuss

8. Your political science professor asks you to discuss the steps that led to the resignation of Richard Nixon and what the consequences were for the Republican Party.

example

9. Your nursing professor asks you to give concrete illustrations of the effects of smoking on human health.

girtlustrate

10. Your physical fitness teacher asks you to give an example showing the link between aerobic conditioning and good health.

cause + effect
justify

11. An education professor asks you to prove or give reasons why teachers should use the "whole language" method of teaching reading.

~~Compare~~
relate

Summarize

~~trace~~

12. Your psychology professor asks you to demonstrate how Freud's theories of childhood development interconnect with Jung's theories.

13. Your biology professor asks you to organize and bring together the main points regarding the process of photosynthesis.

Support

14. Your history professor asks you to use facts to prove that the South was technologically unprepared to win the Civil War.

~~discuss~~
Trace

15. Your music history professor asks you to briefly discuss the main composers of the Jazz Age from its beginning to its end.

One reason to know this list of commonly used direction words is to understand exactly what test questions or instructions ask you to do. In addition, being familiar with direction words is also helpful in predicting and preparing for possible questions or instructions about the topics that your tests will cover. Practicing writing questions or instructions using direction words for a topic you think will be on a test helps you be better prepared.

For example, suppose your topic is memory principles. Here are a few possibilities.

Define	Define each of the memory principles.
Discuss	Discuss how the memory principles are used in the Question in the Margin system.
Give an example	Give an example of using visualization.
Evaluate	Evaluate your use of the memory principles.
Compare	Compare association with basic background.

Exercise 9.15

Practice with Direction Words

Your topic is defensive driving. Following the preceding example, choose six of the direction words and write a test question for each about defensive driving.

Direction Word	Possible Discussion Question or Instruction

Making Connections

Review your notes about Bloom's taxonomy. Remember that each level of learning requires a different level of thinking. First, as a review, list the levels to match the descriptions. Then examine the list of commonly used direction words. In the third column decide which level of thinking each direction word may require. (Some direction words may fit into more than one level, so you may use them more than once.) Try to place each direction word in an appropriate box.

Level of Bloom's Taxonomy	Description	Possible Direction Words
	Lower-Order Thinking Skills	
	Recall data or information, not necessarily understand it	
	Understand it enough to explain in own words	
	Actually use the information	
	Higher-Order Thinking Skills	
	Subdividing to see how it is put together	
	Put information back together in a unique way	
	Making value judgments	

Exercise 9.16

Practice with Topic Sentences and Direction Words

The first sentence of your answer to an essay question is crucial. It should show the grader both that you understand the question and how you will develop your answer. In addition, it becomes your guide as well. It keeps you on track. Pay particular attention to the direction word. You will pay a severe penalty if you know the material but answer the wrong question because you did not pay attention to what the question asked you to do. For each question below, plan what your answer would say, and write a clear topic sentence showing both that you understand the question and how you will develop your answer.

1. *Compare* the role of a defensive driver to the role of a successful college student.

_____

_____

2. *Contrast* the role of student as passenger to that of student as driver.

_____

_____

3. *Evaluate* your computer skills.

_____

_____

4. The cost, time, and effort involved in getting a college education is enormous. *Justify* your decision to come to college.

_____

_____

_____

5. *Relate* what you have learned in this course to your other courses.

_____

_____

_____

6. *Summarize* your responsibilities when you miss a class.

_____

_____

_____

7. *Trace* the steps necessary to register for next term.

_____

_____

_____

After planning what should be included in each of these seven answers, choose one and write a complete answer to the question. Use a separate sheet of paper to write your answer.

 VIRTUAL FIELD TRIP

Essay Tests

 Visit the College Success CourseMate.

Practice with Evaluating Answers to Essay Questions

One way for you to better understand what the grader is looking for is to examine essay questions from a grader's point of view. Following are four answers to the same question asked on a learning strategies test. The instruction is to discuss how to write an effective answer to an essay question. You are the grader. The question is worth 20 points. Use the checklist (see page XXX) as your guide for what to look for in the student's answer and which elements the answer should contain (the content). Use the Grade Sheet as a rubric, or guide, in grading the essay answers. For each student answer, give your score, with the highest possible score being 20. Write your comments as to why the student received those points. You will need to make a copy of the rubric for each essay.

Rubric or Grade Sheet for Essay Test

Content	**8 points**	A point for each item that is actually on the "Checklist for Essay Tests" that you use as a major point in your answer (up to 8 points)
Organization	**2 points**	If from reading the first sentence of your answer, the reader knows both what the question was and how you will develop your answer
	2 points	If major points stand out and transitions are used
	2 points	If major points are supported with examples, reasons, and facts
	1 point	If there is a concluding statement
Clarity	**2 points**	If someone who has not taken this class could use this as a guide for writing an effective essay
Grammar, spelling	**3 points**	
Total score		

Use the back of the rubric to make comments to the student about how she or he could improve her or his answer.

Student 1 Score _____

To write an effective answer to an essay question includes several steps. The first step is to answer by rewriting the question in a complete sentence. The second step is to write your answer in complete sentences. The third step is to support you answer with examples and facts. The fourth step as to conclude with complete sentences. Those are the four steps to answering an essay question. With these steps it lets the reader know how the answers were developed.

Comments:

_____

_____

_____

Student 2 Score _____

In order to write an effective answer to an essay question, you must know the topic. Always answer the question being asked in the first sentence of the answer. Have a strong thesis statement. The thesis statement should be what the paper is about. When you begin the actual essay, you must have proper facts. Detail sentences should support any topics brought up in your paper. Last, you should sum up your paper, not bring up new ideas. This is my idea of how one should write an effective essay.

Comments:

_____

_____

_____

Student 3 Score _____

My instructor says it is important to use the checklist for answering essay questions in order to make sure I get the most points possible for what I know. It's a bunch of stuff to memorize, but after analyzing the list more carefully, I think she may be right. I do need to understand what the question is asking; otherwise I probably won't get any credit even if I know something about the topic. The best way to do this is to plan my answer and then show the grader both that I understand what the question is asking me to do and how I will answer it. The grader knows I know the answer, and it provides a guide for me to follow so I make sure I cover all the points and don't get off the subject. Major points should stand out so that I know I've covered them and the grader can check off points he or she is looking for. If I don't support the major points, I come up with just a list. That's not good. I need to make sure my writing is readable and that I have checked for mistakes. I know, when it's a test situation, I may make more mistakes than usual and not even know I've made them. A concluding statement lets me double-check that I answered the question and reminds the grader again that I know what the answer is. The checklist may be overkill, but if I want to get the most points for what I know, I probably will do better if I do everything on it.

Comments:

_____

_____

_____

Student 4 Score _____

In order for someone to write an effective answer to a discussion question, she must include at least these nine strategies which fall into the categories of developing, supporting and concluding the essay. The first category is to develop and plan your answer. You need to read the question over to see that you fully understand what is being asked of you. Next, you do any preliminary planning that needs to be done in order to organize your answer before you start, and then you make the first sentence of your essay repeat the question and show how you will answer it. The second stage is to support your answer. You need to make sure that you list all your major points and they are supported by examples. You must also make sure that anyone who is not in this class would be able to read your essay and know what the discussion is about. The last and sometimes most important thing to do is conclude your essay. Now this category consists of several items on the checklist. First, did you cover all the major points? Did your completely answer the question? Have you reread your essay and proofed for any spelling or grammar errors? Most importantly you should make sure your handwriting is neat and legible for someone to read and understand, without guessing, what you are saying. If you can include most, if not all, of these strategies in your essay, then you should be able to write an exceptional answer to a discussion question.

Comments:

_____

_____

_____

VIRTUAL FIELD TRIP

Dealing with Test Anxiety

Visit the College Success CourseMate.

  Making It Concrete

Suppose your team is going to participate in a championship game a week from Saturday. Your coach calls you together and says, "We have a week to prepare, and I want you to do your best, so we will take it easy and not practice until Friday night. On Friday night, report for practice at midnight. We will practice all night long."

What do you think the results would be for the game on Saturday morning?

Compare how you should prepare for the championship to how you should prepare for your exams. List at least four similarities.

1. _____

_____

2. _____

_____

3. _____

_____

4. _____

_____

Final Exams

You should, of course, begin preparation for finals the first day of class. Most of us, however, need a bit of organizing to get ready for finals. The following study organizer may be just what you need for each of your classes to be used a week or so before finals. List each class you are taking, and fill in the information asked for about each class. *Be very specific*. Make copies so that you will have one sheet for each class.

20

Class _____   Date and time of exam _____

Instructor _____   Office and telephone number _____

What percentage of the final grade will the final exam count? _____

What will be covered on the final exam? (Be specific.)

  1. _____

  2. _____

  3. _____

  4. _____

  5. _____

What kind of exam will this be (multiple-choice, true/false, essay, and so on)?

_____

What is the best way to study for this exam? (Be specific.)

_____

_____

I need to have flash cards covering

  1. _____

  2. _____

  3. _____

I will use these mnemonics (and why)

  1. _____

  2. _____

  3. _____

Summary sheets will be useful to study (specific concepts)

  1. _____

  2. _____

  3. _____

Name and telephone number of a person in the class with whom I will study for at least an hour.

_____

Modeling the Learning Process

Gathering. You gathered strategies for taking specific tests.

Analyzing. You analyzed examples and took practice tests.

Creating New Ideas. You predicted what questions might be included and planned possible answers.

Acting. You wrote essay answers and a practice test.

SUMMARY

To see if you grasped the major points of the chapter and to make a useful study guide, answer the following questions found in your reading. When you have written your answers, cover them and see if you can say the answer to each question in your own words. If you prefer to type your answers, you will find a Microsoft Word download for each summary on the College Success CourseMate for Practicing College Learning Strategies at www.cengagebrain.com.

What is the difference between *recognition* and *recall* when answering test questions?

_____

_____

Name four specific strategies that you already use to *prepare* for tests.

1. _____

2. _____

3. _____

4. _____

Why is it important to budget your time when taking a test?

_____

Explain how to budget your time when you take a test.

_____

Explain the effect negatives have on true/false statements.

_____

What is a double negative?

_____

What is the difference between a general qualifier and an absolute qualifier?

_____

In true/false statements, why should one carefully check items in a series?

_____

What educated guess can you make when a true/false statement gives reasons?

_____

Why are there usually more true statements than false ones?

_____

What are four basic strategies to use with multiple-choice questions?

1. _____

2. _____

3. _____

4. _____

What options in multiple-choice questions tend to be the incorrect choice?

_____

What options in multiple-choice questions tend to be the correct choice?

_____

What are basic strategies for fill-in questions?

_____

What are basic strategies for matching tests?

_____

Name some clues used to predict test questions from lecture material.

_____

What clues can you use to predict test questions from textbooks?

_____

Why is it important to know the meaning of direction words?

_____

Describe what the first sentence of the answer to an essay question should do.

_____

List some strategies to use when preparing for final exams.

_____

_____

Case Study: What's Your Advice?

LaNita, Bill, and Charlene have a midterm exam next week in Dr. Watts's philosophy class, one of only two tests in the course for the entire semester. The difficulty of Dr. Watts's exams is legendary on campus, but he is the only instructor who teaches this course, a requirement in their major. Because it is important for them to do well, the three students decide on their first day of class to meet weekly for a study session. The students promise to take notes in class, question them after class, and keep up with reading assignments by writing possible test questions in the margins and underlining the answers in each paragraph.

At their weekly study session, they compare their marked notes and textbooks and take turns answering questions out loud. At the end of each weekly session, LaNita is responsible for making a practice test for next time using that week's material. Bill's responsibility is to come up with as many visual study aids as he can for the material—comparison charts, maps, time lines, and so forth. Charlene's job is to create mnemonics and use her computer program to make flash cards or games involving the information for the week. Because they keep up with weekly sessions, their tasks are relatively simple.

At the class period before the exam, Dr. Watts tells the students that the test will have several discussion questions asking students to compare or just to contrast various philosophies, trace the development of certain philosophies, or discuss how certain philosophers might react to a statement. In addition, there will be a multiple-choice section, a true/false section, and a matching section. They will have 1 hour and 15 minutes for the test.

When the three students meet for a final study session, they agree that they have prepared well but they are worried about taking the test. LaNita says that she usually does great on the objective parts of a test but somehow fails to get full credit on the discussion parts even though she knows the material. For Bill and Charlene, it is just the opposite. They ask for your advice on test-taking strategies they can use. Please make them a guide for taking the test.

Parallel Parking

Choose two of the following and compare the driving term to test-taking strategies:

Going Over a Speed Bump

_____

_____

Planning a Trip Before You Leave Home

_____

_____

Finding a Parking Place

_____

_____

Fueling Up, Checking Tires, Oil, etc.

_____

_____

Missing the Turn You Needed to Make

_____

_____

Taking a Detour

_____

_____

Evaluating Learning Outcomes

How successful were you in making it to your destination in this chapter?

Analyze what you learned in this chapter. Put a check beside each task you are now able to do. Now think of strategies that you learned that will help you save time and study more effectively. List them in the appropriate place on the back inside cover.

☐ **Describe** strategies that you have found effective in preparing for a test.
☐ **State** strategies to use in taking any kind of test.
☐ **Use** strategies for objective tests: true/false, multiple-choice, fill-in-the-blank, and matching questions.
☐ **Name,** explain, and demonstrate at least eight strategies to employ when writing an answer to an essay question.
☐ **List** strategies for dealing with test anxiety.
☐ **Analyze** a case study, and construct advice for a student having difficulty with test-taking skills.
☐ **Explain** the learning process modeled in this chapter.

Your Student Tip for This Chapter

Use the space below to write a tip you would give to other students about what you have learned in this chapter.

_____

_____

_____

_____

10 Managing Stress

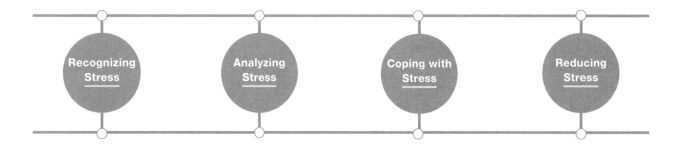

Recognizing Stress   Analyzing Stress   Coping with Stress   Reducing Stress

As a driver you know how to plan your route, schedule your car maintenance, and drive defensively. But one factor that may make your trip almost frightening is the stress caused by being stuck in traffic, lost, late for an appointment, or even having rowdy passengers. As a developing college student, you are learning how to manage your time, process information, and take tests; likewise, there is an additional factor that may determine your success as a college student. How well do you deal with stress? Almost 50 percent of American students who enter college never graduate. Although finances and life circumstances play a role, stress must be considered as a factor.

Stress: What Is It?

If you are not feeling stress at this point in the term, there is something wrong. Stress is completely normal and is our response to our changing environments. Therefore, not *all* stress is bad. There are as many

BRAIN BYTE

Researchers O'Keefe and Nadel have found that positive forms of stress occur when we are challenged to rise to the occasion. Your body releases adrenaline and noradrenaline, which actually heighten perception, increase motivation, and even enhance physical strength.

Learning Outcomes
for Chapter 10 Managing Stress

Here's your destination for Chapter 10. When you complete Chapter 10, you are expected not only to understand the material presented, but also to be able to:

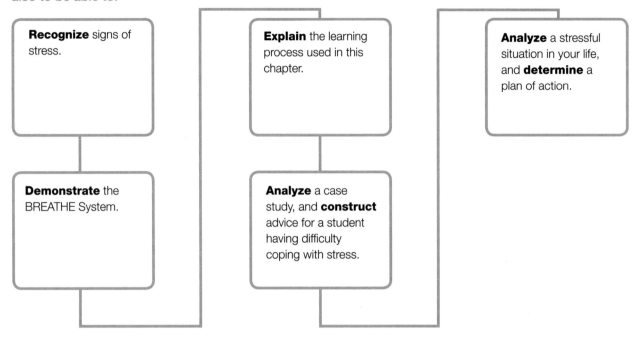

Recognize signs of stress.

Explain the learning process used in this chapter.

Analyze a stressful situation in your life, and **determine** a plan of action.

Demonstrate the BREATHE System.

Analyze a case study, and **construct** advice for a student having difficulty coping with stress.

different ideas about stress as there are people who experience it in their lives. **Stress** refers to the way you react physically, emotionally, and mentally to stressors. **Stressors** are physical, psychological, or social forces that put real or perceived demands on the body, emotions, mind, or spirit of an individual . In other words, stressors are anything that causes stress!

You may be going about your daily life and not realize the effect that stress is having on you. But the fact is, stress can make itself known in every aspect of a person's life. When you snap at your roommate, spouse, or children, when you have trouble concentrating, when you feel that you just want to be left alone—all may be symptoms of stress. These symptoms can be reflected in your health, your mental and emotional well-being, and your behavior. Let's look at a list of common symptoms of stress. *Check those in the following table that apply to you.*

Recognizing Possible Signs of Stress

	Health or Medical		Mental and Emotional		Behavioral
	Migraine or tension headache		Irritability		Sleeping badly
	Upset stomach, diarrhea		Losing sense of humor		Snapping or shouting at those around you
	High blood pressure		Often on the verge of tears		Fiddling with your hair
	Shortness of breath		Crying spells		High-pitched or nervous laughter
	Loss of appetite		Feeling that you can't cope		Trembling, shaking, excessive blinking
	Frequent or lingering colds		Being suspicious of others		Finding it difficult to talk to people
	Acne or pimples		Difficulty concentrating		Having trouble completing tasks
	Cold sores on mouth		Difficulty making decisions		Overeating
	Dizziness		Making poor decisions		Drinking or smoking more than usual
	Lack of energy		Not being able to think		Reduced sex drive
	Dryness of the throat and mouth		Not being able to stay on task		Grinding the teeth or clenching the jaw

If you checked more than four or five of these items, you are overly stressed and need to read further for help in managing your stress.

Analyzing Your Stress

As you have learned from critical thinking, if you are going to solve a problem or make a decision, you first need to determine exactly what the problem is. Accordingly, in order to manage stress, it's helpful to know what causes it. At the risk of getting you even more stressed out, let's look at a few of the stressors many college students face.

Financial Stress	Students worry about paying for tuition, as well as other living expenses.
Multitasking Stress	Students must juggle classes, job, family responsibilities, and extracurricular activities.
Peer Pressure	For those who choose not to experiment with drugs, alcohol, sexual activity, or other potentially harmful behaviors, resisting pressure can be stressful. For those who do participate in such behavior, there is both physical and emotional stress.
Independence and Responsibility	Dealing with change and added responsibility, living away from home, or making decisions about one's life and future is stressful.

(Continued)

Academic Pressure	The course work can be demanding, and the amount of time required to be successful is stressful, as is the pressure of keeping a scholarship or getting into grad school.
Social Stress	Going to college means creating new social networks. Often it means finding and living with roommates and balancing friends with school work. These types of things are stressful.

   Making It Concrete

Remember step 2 of the decision-making process, gathering information? Let's gather information about your stress. Choose two of the categories above, expand on them as necessary, and write a well-developed paragraph in which you describe stress you have experienced this semester.

The study strategies you have developed so far are ways of dealing with situations that are common for college students. Let's review some things you already know about relieving stress:

- You have developed study strategies that use what you know about how the brain processes information in order to process information more efficiently.
- You have developed a system for taking notes and reading textbooks.
- You have developed strategies for studying for and taking tests.
- You have developed a master schedule for help with time management.
- You know how to write goals in order to solve stress-related problems.
- You know how to use the BREATHE System to relax and focus.

Are you using these strategies? Remember that if you have a plan or strategy for dealing with stressors, their impact on you will be reduced.

 Critical Thinking About Stress

When you think about stress in your daily life, what images, people, places, and so on, come to mind? List at least five causes of stress in your life.

1. _____
2. _____
3. _____
4. _____
5. _____

Step 3 in critically solving problems is to determine your options. Examine the major causes of stress in your life, and try to determine what your options are for dealing with each. Choose one of the causes you listed, and write down what you think some of your options are. Ask others to help if you are stuck.

Cause of stress: _____

Possible options I have for dealing with this stress:

1. _____
2. _____
3. _____
4. _____

BRAIN BYTE

The body responds to negative stress by releasing the hormone cortisol. Too much cortisol negatively affects the hippocampus, which is very sensitive to this hormone. The result is to weaken the brain's local memory and indexing systems. The hippocampus is the part of the brain that enables the body to fight disease, so the release of cortisol weakens the body's immune system.

Exercise 10.1

Developing a Plan of Action

Now return to the options you listed for dealing with one of the causes of your stress. Weigh each option carefully and choose one. Using what you know about goal setting, write a plan of action in the form of a useful goal.

Goal for dealing with _____

_____

 VIRTUAL FIELD TRIP

Let's Find Out More About Managing Stress

Visit the College Success CourseMate.

Coping Strategies for Alleviating Stress Symptoms

When stress is constant and unrelieved, it can become negative and even destructive. But you can break the cycle of negative stress by learning ways to help yourself relax. By taking the time to practice simple relaxation techniques on a regular basis, you can give yourself a chance to unwind and get ready for life's next challenge.

1. **Musical background.** CDs can be purchased at most department or music stores or downloaded to your iPod. The content of these CDs ranges from soothing music to sounds of nature (oceans, thunderstorms, forest wildlife, and so on). You can also buy CDs that incorporate music and nature sounds, as well as those with a relaxation narrative.

2. **BREATHE System.** The Big 3 of Hillman's BREATHE System were presented in Chapter 1. Hopefully, they have become a habit for you. An overview of the system is presented here.

Breathe	Use the Big 3: (1) straighten your posture and elevate your rib cage, (2) relax your neck and shoulder muscles, and (3) breathe by moving your ribs sideways and not raising your shoulders while inhaling to make calming breaths possible. Inhale completely (through your nose) and blow out (through your mouth) as much air as possible with each exhale.
Repeat	Take another calming breath, using the Big 3. Focus on the breathing.
Emotion	Become aware of and identify your emotional condition and the emotions of others. Evaluate their effectiveness. Are those emotions working for or against you? Allow your emotional state to reduce in intensity or transform to a more effective emotional state.
Assess	Assess your actions and behaviors and those of others in the situation. Are those behaviors beneficial? Make the choice to change, regain personal control, and redirect your behavior to be more consistent with your goals. Focus on the breathing.
Talk	Clarify what the wants/needs/concerns are by asking questions. Be careful how you ask the questions. Use good voice quality and falling inflection, and don't let your voice reflect a negative emotional condition. Is what you are saying, feeling, and doing right now helping you achieve your goals? How might it help you? Focus on the breathing.
Hear	Focus on the concepts expressed or implied by the speaker (even if it is you). Look beneath the words to determine what is really being said. Continue to talk and listen as you seek additional options that might resolve this situation. Focus on the breathing.
Exit	Seek agreement about how to resolve this situation and return to the learning community, back to a place of security, calmness, and hope. Continue to breathe.[1]

3. **Progressive relaxation routine.** This is a three-step technique. It can be done while sitting or lying down and takes only 15 minutes or so. It helps if you can practice the technique in a quiet, relaxing place. First, *tighten your hand muscles* and make a fist; then, notice how it feels. Your muscles are taut and strained, and your hand may even be trembling slightly. You may feel tension in your hand, wrist, and lower arm. Hold the tension for a few seconds before relaxing. Now, *release your hand*, relax your fist, and let the tension slip away. You may notice that your hand feels lighter than it did

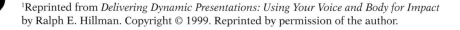

[1]Reprinted from *Delivering Dynamic Presentations: Using Your Voice and Body for Impact* by Ralph E. Hillman. Copyright © 1999. Reprinted by permission of the author.

while your muscles were tensed and that your wrist and forearm also feel relieved of pressure. *Notice the difference* between how your hand felt when tensed and how it felt when you released the tension. Does your hand tingle or feel warm when relaxed? Did the throbbing you felt while tensed disappear when you relaxed? It is best to do this exercise on each of the major muscle groups of your body. The basic technique remains the same throughout.

Tighten the muscle, release the tension, then notice the difference. You can start with your hands, then progress to other muscles; or you can move from head to toe, tightening and relaxing the muscles in your face, shoulders, arms, hands, chest, back, stomach, legs, and feet.

4. **Visualization.** Visualization can be thought of as a mental vacation, a license to daydream. You can produce feelings of relaxation simply by using your imagination. Visualization allows your imagination to run free. Try to visualize yourself feeling warm, calm, and relaxed. Picture a tranquil setting that has particular appeal for you, and try to imagine all of the details. Are you lying on a warm beach? How does the sun feel on your back? Do you hear waves lapping on the shore? Is there a fragrance in the air? Do you see sailboats on the water? Just by using your imagination, you can give yourself a mental vacation whenever you feel the need to take a moment to relax and enjoy life.

5. **Clearing your mind.** Giving yourself a mental break can help relax your body as well. When you clear your mind, you let your worries slip away. *Reduce distractions*, noise, and interruptions as much as possible as you begin this exercise. Try to set aside 5 to 10 minutes daily to practice clearing your mind. *Sit comfortably*, loosen any tight clothing, kick off your shoes, and relax yourself. Then, close your eyes and begin to breathe slowly and deeply. *Mentally focus* on one peaceful word, thought, or image. If other thoughts should enter your mind, don't be discouraged; relax, breathe deeply, and try again. *Stretch and exhale* as you complete the exercise. With practice, clearing your mind can help you feel refreshed, energetic, and ready to tackle the next challenge.

6. **Energy-release activities.** Just about anything requiring physical activity will release energy. Get involved in a hobby or sport. Good old-fashioned exercise (jogging, weight lifting, calisthenics, and so on) also works wonders. Aerobic exercise or any exercise that keeps the heart pumping at elevated levels for 12 to 30 minutes is best. But don't fail to exercise just because you can't get in 30 minutes; lesser quantities do have a positive effect on stress. Check out what recreational activities your campus offers.

7. **Talking it out.** Talking with a friend or counselor about a problem will prevent it from becoming bottled up inside, thus giving you a better chance of dealing with it rationally. You will have counseling services on your campus.

8. **Laugh.** Many brain researchers have found that humor and laughter help relieve stress.

Student Tip

" *I found that having a regular exercise routine prevents stress as well as relieving it. I made time for water aerobics three times a week in my master schedule. The times I skipped it, I really felt the stress. When I did go, I felt energized. It is definitely worth the effort.* "

Exercise 10.2

Using the Strategies for Alleviating Stress

Name three specific situations that occur in your life in which you might find it necessary to use one of the techniques for alleviating stress discussed on pages 252-254.

1. _____
2. _____
3. _____

Analyze the eight strategies for alleviating stress. List, in order of probability of use, four that you might try.

1. _____
2. _____
3. _____
4. _____

Do you think you may need additional or individual help on stress management?

_____

Lifestyle Habits That Help Reduce Stress: Try a Few!

Stress can cause certain brain functions to literally shut down. Higher-level thinking skills and memory are most affected. Because stress involves both emotional and physical reactions to change, the better you feel in body and mind, the better you'll be able to deal with the stress in your life. When you learn to think positively, exercise, eat well, and rest regularly, you'll be taking care of the most important person you know—you. Just as you can make defensive driving a habit, there are lifestyle habits you can develop to help reduce stress.

Exercise 10.3

Analyzing Lifestyle Habits

Read this list carefully. Choose *three* or *four* of the following habits that relate to your lifestyle. On the line below each of those habits, write about a time in your life that you *should have* used that habit.

1. Don't take on more than you can handle. Try to complete one task at a time.

_____

2. Schedule quiet time and time for relaxation and planned exercise.

_____

3. Be assertive and stand up for yourself—or no one else will. Learn to say no.

_____

4. Distinguish between situations you can control and those you cannot.

_____

5. Accept the fact that you can't be perfect and will not always be right.

_____

6. Educate yourself about proper nutrition and how it can affect your mind and body.

_____

7. Use time management to set priorities and allow enough time to complete a task. Eliminate something if too much is happening at once.

_____

8. Don't make too many life changes at once.

_____

9. Analyze your values, and accept yourself for who you are.

_____

10. Make efforts to develop close friendships and support systems.

_____

11. Develop a stress-management program and stick to it!

_____

12. Get enough sleep.

_____

13. Seek help with conflict resolution.

_____

VIRTUAL FIELD TRIP

What You Need to Know About Sleep

 Visit the College Success CourseMate.

 Making Connections

You have already developed some strategies that will help you deal with stress. Recall the following topics we have studied and briefly describe how each could relate to your handling of stress.

Time management

Goal setting

Memory principles

Question in the Margin system

Your learning style

Test-taking strategies

Student Tip

My roommate seems to never sleep. She is either partying to all hours of the night one night or studying all night for a test the next. The first two or three weeks of the semester, I tried to do the same. What a disaster! When I could stay awake in class, I couldn't focus. Even though I studied all night long, I couldn't remember the answers. Then someone in speech class gave a speech on sleep deprivation. I discovered why I was so stressed. I went back to my master schedule, made sure I have time to do everything, and set a goal to get at least seven hours of sleep. Wow, what a difference!

Modeling the Learning Process

Again we modeled the learning process in learning about managing stress.

Gathering. You gathered information both about what causes stress and ways to deal with stress.

Analyzing. You analyzed your situation and strategies you learned in previous chapters and tried to determine how to best manage your personal stress.

Creating New Ideas. You predicted some things that might work for you in preventing and relieving stress.

Acting. You made a plan to deal with your stress and put it into practice to see if it worked.

SUMMARY

To see if you grasped the major points of the chapter and to make a useful study guide, answer the following questions found in your reading. When you have written your answers, cover them and see if you can say the answer to each question in your own words. If you prefer to type your answers, you will find a Microsoft Word download for each summary on the College Success CourseMate for Practicing College Learning Strategies at **www.cengagebrain.com**.

What is stress?

_____

What are stressors?

_____

Name some common symptoms of stress

_____

Name three things that cause stress in your life.

1. _____

2. _____

3. _____

What is your plan of action for dealing with one of your stressors?

_____

This chapter presents eight coping strategies to alleviate stress symptoms. Discuss the four that you think will be most useful to you.

1. _____

2. _____

3. _____

4. _____

Case Study: What's Your Advice?

Several students are gathered in the hall before class. It is midterm, and everyone is talking about being stressed out. Most of the class, however, is managing to deal with stress.

John is not sure that's possible for him. He never has time to do his class work. Besides, he thinks most of it is just busy work. His boss is constantly on his back to work more hours, and his parents are always nagging him about money. John's girlfriend complains that he doesn't spend enough time with her. His roommate is a bore, and there is always something broken in their rented house. If he doesn't pass all his classes, John will lose his financial aid. He has frequent headaches and can't seem to concentrate for more than five minutes at a time. He's smoking up to two packs of cigarettes a day and hasn't really slept well in what seems like months.

Obviously, John needs more help than you can give him, but he would really like some suggestions from you of ways that you deal with *your* stress that might work for him.

Parallel Parking

After reviewing this chapter on managing stress, choose two of the following driving situations and explain specifically how managing stress is similar.

Making Sure Your Car Gets Routine Maintenance

_____

_____

_____

_____

_____

Adjusting to the Road Conditions

_____

_____

_____

_____

Making a Rest Stop

_____

_____

_____

_____

_____

Carefully Planning Your Route So You Are Not Late for Something Important

_____

_____

_____

_____

_____

Evaluating Learning Outcomes

How successful were you in making it to your destination in this chapter?

Analyze what you learned in this chapter. Put a check beside each task you are now able to do. Now think of strategies that you learned that will help you save time and study more effectively. List them in the appropriate place on the back inside cover.

☐ **Recognize** signs of stress.
☐ **Analyze** a stressful situation in your life, and determine a plan of action.
☐ **Demonstrate** the BREATHE System.
☐ **Analyze** a case study, and construct advice for a student having difficulty coping with the stress.
☐ **Explain** the learning process used in this chapter.

Your Student Tip For This Chapter

Use the space below to write a tip you would give to other students about what you have learned in this chapter.

_____

_____

_____

Use this page to develop a plan for combating stress this week.

11 Information Literacy

- What Is Information Literacy?
- A Systematic Approach to Information Literacy and the Research Process
  - Identifying and Finding Background Information
  - Using the Library Catalog
  - Using Indexes and Databases
  - Finding Internet Resources
  - Evaluating Your Sources
  - Citing Your Sources
- Finding Books
- Finding Periodicals
- Using Subject-(Discipline-) Specific Databases
- Finding Newspapers
- Using the Internet for Research
  - Quick References
  - Biographical Resources

Learning Outcomes
for Chapter 11 Information Literacy

Here's your destination for Chapter 11. When you complete Chapter 11, you are expected not only to understand the material presented, but also to be able to:

Explain the elements involved in information literacy.

Access library resources from an off-campus site.

Locate reliable biographical sources by using various library biographical databases.

Identify library databases used to find books, general periodicals, subject-specific periodicals, newspapers, and Internet sources.

Explain how to evaluate an Internet site for accuracy, authority, objectivity, currency, and coverage.

Explain the learning process modeled in this chapter.

Follow a systematic approach to a research topic, including identifying and narrowing the topic; finding book, periodical, and Internet sources; and evaluating each source and listing information that should be cited.

Indicate the appropriate use for Kane's *Famous First Facts, World Almanac, The Statesman's Yearbook, Congressional Directory, Statistical Abstract of the United States, Bartlett's Familiar Quotations,* and *Benét's Reader's Encyclopedia.*

What Is Information Literacy?

One of the most important parts of your college journey is getting familiar with things that make your journey easier. A map does you no good if you can't orient yourself with it, and a GPS is useless if you can't program your destination. As a college student in what is often called the "information age," you will find that you sometimes have too much information to deal with. The very volume of information available makes it necessary to find ways to sort through it in order to find what is relevant. Being able to manage and organize all this information is called **information literacy**. The University of Idaho Library site defines *information literacy* as (1) the ability to identify what information is needed, (2) understand how the information is organized, (3) identify the best sources of information for a given need, (4) locate those sources, (5) evaluate the sources critically, and (6) share that information (University of Idaho – Library http://www.lib.uidaho.edu). This chapter will address some things you need in order to be an effective student in an information age. Databases in your college library provide valuable resources that will help you with this task. Practice in using some of these databases should build the confidence and skill you will need for assignments that require research.

Each college library is unique. But there are basic resources in all libraries that you will need to use with proficiency, no matter how large or small or technologically up-to-date your library is. If you have not already done so, take time to learn both what resources are available in your library and how to access them. On some campuses, a library orientation is offered. In addition, handouts and printed instructions are often available, or you can ask the librarians to help you. Do not hesitate to ask. You are certainly not the first or only student who needed help.

Making It Concrete: What is a database?

When using the library, you will use many different databases. It is important that you have a concept of what a database is. A **database** is a collection of information about a specific subject or related subjects. Databases exist for the purpose of organizing like information into one place. For example, the telephone book for your city is a database of the telephone users in that area with telephone numbers and addresses. The database that tells you what books and periodicals your library has is the library catalog, which is electronic in most libraries today. In the library, you will also use databases for finding articles in journals, magazines, and newspapers or databases for finding information about certain subjects such as education, medicine, or psychology.

A Systematic Approach to the Information Literacy and the Research Process

The critical-thinking skills you have developed are crucial when searching for specific information that you need amidst all the information that is available. It is important that you have a systematic, well-thought-out way of finding relevant sources. When you have an assignment that requires research, you want to cover all your bases and get results as quickly but as efficiently as possible. There are several steps you can follow to ensure a minimum amount of frustration and results of which you can be proud.

Step 1: Identifying and finding background information on your topic

The first step in research is to *identify and develop your topic*. The instructor who gave the assignment is the best source of information for determining your topic. Take time to discuss the assignment before you begin. Make sure you understand exactly what the assignment asks you to do and the scope of the research necessary. You have learned that the more you know about a subject, the easier it will be to gather new information about it. An important step, then, is to make sure you have enough information about the topic before you leap in.

This usually involves finding background information in one or more sources. The most common background sources are *encyclopedias and dictionaries* from the print and online reference collection. *Class textbooks* also provide background information. Students often go straight to Wikipedia for background. Actually, Wikipedia is acceptable to use as long as you remember that Wikipedia is a general encyclopedia whose authors are unpaid and usually anonymous. There is no way of knowing the author's level of expertise. You should never cite Wikipedia as a source; however, it often provides an overview, a place to start and perhaps some references.

To make sure that you understand your topic and that you know specifically what you are looking for, it is a good idea to put it in the form of a question. For example, if your topic is global warming, you need to determine what it is you need to know about global warming. What causes global warming? What are the impacts of global warming? What solutions are there for global warming? What are some issues involving global warming? You may use what you learned about mapping to brainstorm or draw a clear picture of possible ways to narrow your topic.

Step 2: Using the library catalog to find books

There are several types of sources of information in any library. The one we usually think of first is *books*. Depending on its size, your library has from several hundred thousand to several million books. The system used to organize and classify books may also vary. Your library will use either the Library of Congress Classification System or the Dewey Decimal System.

Books are usually shelved in stacks in the main collection, the reference section, or special collections.

To find the location and call number for a book, you will use your library catalog. You may find that there are too many books about your topic for you to use them all. Frequently review the question you developed about your topic to help you analyze the relevance of each source.

When you use a book for research, you want to check the date it was written and the credentials of the author. For example: Is it important that the information in the book be up to date? What is the author's background? What makes him or her an expert on the subject? Also remember that when you use a book in your research, you will need to document it. Be sure to write down the entire title, the author's name, and the date and place of publication, as well as the publisher's name. Note what pages you use as well. Doing so will save you valuable time when you document your research.

Step 3: Using indexes and databases to find periodical articles

Periodicals are continuous publications, such as journals, newspapers, or magazines, so called because they come out periodically (weekly, monthly, annually). The advantage of using periodicals over books is that they maybe be more up to date, and more manageable in size. There are three broad types of periodicals. First, *scholarly journals* generally have a somewhat academic appearance. Cornell reference librarian Michael Engle says that someone who has done research in the field or is an authority on the subject writes the articles for these journals. The writers in scholarly journals use discipline-specific language and assume that the reader has the background to understand it. "The main purpose of a scholarly journal," Engle says, "is to report on original research or experimentation in order to make such information available to the rest of the scholarly world." Writers in scholarly journals authenticate their work by *always* citing their sources in the form of footnotes or bibliographies.[1]

The second type, *substantive news* or *general interest periodicals* may have a magazine or newspaper format. Engle describes the content of these as having articles that are "often heavily illustrated, generally with photographs." News and general-interest periodicals sometimes cite sources, though more often they do not. A member of the editorial staff, a scholar, or a freelance writer may write these articles. The language of such publications is geared to any educated audience. There is no specialty assumed, only interest and a certain level of intelligence. Commercial enterprises or individuals generally publish them, although some may be published by specific professional organizations. The main purpose of periodicals in this category is to provide information, in a general manner, to a broad audience of concerned citizens.[2]

[1]See http://www.library.cornell.edu/olinuris/ref/research/skill20.html.
[2]See http://www.library.cornell.edu/olinuris/ref/research/skill20.html.

The third type, *popular periodicals* come in many formats, although most often they are somewhat slick and attractive in appearance and contain lots of graphics (photographs, drawings, etc.). Engle says:

These publications rarely, if ever, cite sources. Information published in such journals is often second or third hand and the original source is sometimes obscure. Articles are usually very short, written in simple language and are designed to meet a minimal education level. There is generally little depth to the content of these articles. The main purpose of popular periodicals is to entertain the reader, to sell products (their own or their advertisers), and/or to promote a viewpoint.[3]

The index or database you choose may vary, depending on the type of periodical article you are looking for. Your library probably subscribes to thousands of periodicals. One reason for using periodicals in your research is that they are often more up-to-date than books; another is that the article takes less time to read than a book.

Most libraries have copies going back to the early publication of the periodicals, either physically bound or on microfilm. If you want a historical view of an event, don't forget to research periodicals from the era in question.

Step 4: Finding Internet resources

The Internet is, of course, a virtual reference desk. By using a Web browser, such as Mozilla Foxfire, Microsoft's Internet Explorer, Apple Safari, Google Chrome, or America Online, you should be able to find up-to-date information on almost any subject. Once you log on to your Internet provider, unless you know the URL of a specific site, you will use a search engine to locate sites that are related to your subjects. You are already familiar with some search engines, such as Google, Bing, Ask, Yahoo, or AOLFind. New search engines appear almost daily. In a recent random check, I located more than 15,000 search engines.

A **search engine** is a type of software that creates indexes of databases or Internet sites on the basis of the titles of files, keywords, or the full text of files. The search engine has an interface that allows you to type what you're looking for into a blank field. It then gives you a list of the results of the search. When you use a search engine on the Web, the results are presented to you in hypertext; this means you can click on any item in the list to get the file. Some sites allow you to use more than one search engine at a time. After using various search engines, you will find one or two that you prefer. Although the results will be similar, each search engine will probably identify some hits that are different. If your library subscribes to Google Scholar, you may want to try it. Google Scholar provides a search of scholarly literature across many disciplines and sources, including theses, books, abstracts, and articles.

A very important fact to remember is that a search engine cannot read your mind or identify specific information you need. The search engine simply tries to locate sites that contain your search word, and

[3]See http://www.library.cornell.edu/olinuris/ref/research/skill20.html.

these sites may or may not be relevant. The search engine Google came up with 68,400,000 hits to my search for *time management*. The engine located anything with the word *time* or *management*. Critical thinking is extremely important in both performing and limiting a search and when evaluating the usefulness of a site on the Internet. It's tempting to just get on the Web and surf. But you can waste a great deal of time if you don't know what you are doing. Before you use any search engine, click on the *search tips* or *help* link for the engine you have chosen. Even if you have frequently used the Internet for research, you will find time-savers and ways to minimize the number of hits you get that are not relevant to your search.

As you search for resources to use, you should keep in mind the value and appropriateness a source adds to your search. The databases you use in the library for books, journals, and other resources have been reviewed, evaluated, and selected by scholars, but what about the sites on the Internet? The fact is that anyone can put virtually anything on the Internet. It doesn't have to be truthful, reliable, or accurate.

It is important, then, that you determine, among other things, where the information came from and the accuracy or bias of the information. Just as the type of information you get from a popular magazine and a scholarly journal will differ, the type of information you get from internet sites will also differ. The domain name often gives such clues to the validity of the information on a site. The **domain** is the three-letter code following the "dot." It will tell you the type of organization that sponsors the site. Below is a list of the most commonly used domain names. You want to look for domains that are appropriate for your topic.

Domain Name	Type of Organization
.edu	**U.S. college or university**
	Information here will come from faculty or students at an educational institution. Check the authority of the source.
.com	**Commercial enterprise**
	Companies advertise, sell products, and publish annual reports and other company information on the Web. Many online newspapers or journals also have .com names.
.gov	**Government**
	Federal and state government agencies use the Web to publish legislation, census information, weather data, tax forms, and many other documents.
.org	**Nonprofit organizations**
	Nonprofit organizations use the Web to promote their causes. These pages may be useful when comparing different sides of an issue.
.net	**Internet service providers**
	General-purpose domain often used as an alternative to .com
.mil	**U.S. military**
	United States Department of Defense and its subsidiary or affiliated organizations.

For most of your research projects, you will use primary resources in the form of books, periodicals, and newspapers. You may also use the Internet. It is always a good idea to consult with the professor who assigned the topic or project for suggestions about types of sources he or she wants included and for what bibliographical format to use. Again, be sure to write down all information you will need to document your sources.

Step 5: Evaluating your sources

Evaluating the reliability and appropriateness of information and sources is crucial. The questions you ask about books, periodicals, and webpages will be similar. Because so much information is readily available, an important part of information literacy and of research is to make sure the information you find is reliable and appropriate for your topic or argument. Evaluating a source involves a great deal of detective work. Preliminary investigation will save you time by eliminating sources you don't want to use before you waste too much time with them. Your primary tool for investigating is AAOCC—accuracy, authority, objectivity, currency, and coverage.

Is the information **accurate**? What clues can you use to tell? Check the author. What are his or her credentials? Is the author an **authority**? Is the information **objective**? Why is the author writing the book or article? What is the domain of a website? Is it fact, opinion, or propaganda? Is it trying to sell you something? Does it appear to be well researched? The next thing to investigate is the **currency**. When was the information published? Do you need the most up-to-date information for the topic you are researching? Is this the most recent edition? An additional thing to investigate is **coverage.** Does it cover the information you need in enough depth to substantiate your research? Later in the chapter, you will be asked to take a virtual field trip to discover more about evaluating sources.

Step 6: Citing your sources

It is important that you give proper credit to the source of information. Instructors will usually indicate whether to format the citations using examples from the Modern Language Association (MLA) or the American Psychological Association (APA). Follow the format chosen exactly as shown. It is extremely important to record the information you need as you are researching. If you don't write down your source then, you may never find it again when you need it.

Finding Books

In order to find books for an assignment that requires research, you will need to use your library's catalog, which is the database where books and other materials in the library are listed. Libraries buy cataloging software from venders. They are alike in general, but not in detail. Your library may use Infosearch, Voyager, World Cat, or some other system. Because so many

Student Tip

Don't just jump to the exercises. Read the information in the text and the directions first. Some of the answers are in the reading. This made the difference between actually learning something from the assignments and busy work.

people use them, library catalog databases are generally user-friendly. You will need to determine how to use your library's system and then practice a bit to make sure you understand how to make it work for you.

Exercise 11.1

Using Your Library Catalog

What is the name of your library's online catalog?

_____

Use the library catalog in your library to find the following:

1. Use a keyword search to find a book about *careers*.

   _____ Title

   _____

   _____ Author

   _____ Call number

   _____ Number of pages

   _____ When published

   _____ Where published

   _____ Publisher

   _____ Is it illustrated?

   _____ Does it have a bibliography?

   _____ Is it currently available for checkout?

   _____ How do you check it out?

2. Do an author search to find out how many books your library has by Toni Morrison: _____. Choose one and provide the following information about it.

   _____ Title

   _____

   _____ Call number

   _____ Number of pages

   _____ When published

   _____ Where published

   _____ Publisher

   _____ Is it currently available for checkout?

3. Use a title search to find out if your library has *The Floating Opera*: _____. If yes, provide the following information about it.

_____ Author(s)

_____

_____ Call number

_____ Number of pages

_____ When published

_____ Where published

_____ Publisher

_____ Is it currently available for checkout?

_____ How do you check it out?

We have said that encyclopedias and reference materials are good sources for background information. Don't stop with the general encyclopedias; check the library catalog or ask your librarian for other reference materials that might be useful.

Exercise 11.2

Providing Background

Enter *encyclopedia* as a keyword search into your library's electronic catalog.

How many books are on the list? _____

List several that are interesting to you. _____

_____

_____

Following are five general topics for research. *Choose one.* You will use this topic in several exercises, so choose one you are interested in, *or ask your instructor if you want to use a topic that is not listed here.*

Autism	GPS (Global Positioning System)	Obesity	Road Rage	Car Insurance

Now look up the topic in an encyclopedia to get some background information. How might you narrow your topic?

Topic: _____

Name of Encyclopedia: _____

Possible way to narrow topic: _____

Exercise 11.3

Finding Books About Your Topic

Find two books that contain information about the topic you chose in Exercise 11.2.

Topic chosen: _____

	Author (or Editor):	Title:	Place of Publication:	Publisher:	Date of Publication:
Book 1					
Book 2					

Finding Periodicals

Deciding which index or database to use may depend on the type or date of the periodical you need. Before databases were computerized, researchers used indexes such as the *Readers' Guide to Periodical Literature* to find periodical articles on their subject. The *Readers' Guide* indexes 300 popular magazines in yearly volumes. Other print-version indexes, such as the *Education Index, Humanities Index,* and *Social Sciences Index,* are more subject-specific.

With print versions of periodical databases, you must physically find the periodical in the bound periodical section of the library or on microtext. However, most libraries have an electronic database such as InfoTrac, EbscoHost, and ProQuest Direct (all of which are expanded academic indexes such as General OneFile or EBSCO's Academic Search Premier), and many of these databases will have the full text of the article online. Because most electronic databases begin around 1980, you may need to use *Readers' Guide* or other print-version indexes if you are searching for articles before 1980. Or your library may have *Readers' Guide Retrospective,* an electronic version that covers the years 1890 to 1982.

Locate the *Readers' Guide* in your library. Describe where it is and what it looks like.

_____

_____

You will find that the periodical resources available to you in computerized databases are expansive. For example, the *Readers' Guide* indexes 300 popular periodicals; General OneFile, Thomson Gale's electronic resource for access to periodical and news content, includes over 5,000 full-text titles (more than 9,200 titles in all). It contains full indexing of some of the world's greatest newspapers and 89 wire services covering worldwide current events. When you use the *Readers' Guide,* you must look separately at each yearly volume and then locate a hard copy of the periodical. When you use an electronic database, you direct the search to cover the years you want to research. General OneFile's integrated back-file coverage is from 1980 to the present. It is important to remember, then, if you need periodical resources before 1980, you will need to use *Readers' Guide* or *Readers' Guide Retrospective*. Remember that when you read the full text of an article online, you still need to cite the source of the original article. I cannot emphasize enough that writing down that information when you first access it will save you time and grief later.

Exercise 11.4

Practice Using Periodicals

_____   What is a periodical?

1. _____   Name three types of periodicals.

2. _____

3. _____

Locate the electronic database for periodical articles in your library and answer the following questions:

_____   Name of the database (If your library has General One File, write it in the blank.)

_____   What specifically is indexed in the database—how many periodicals?

_____   What does it mean by full-text titles?

_____   To what year does the database go back?

_____   How do you access the database?

Use the electronic database General OneFile or the electronic database for periodical articles in your library to find two articles on the **same topic** you chose in Exercise 11.3, "Finding Books About Your Topic."

Autism   Obesity   GPS   Road Rage   Car Insurance

_____   Subject chosen

Article 1

_____   Subheading (if any)

_____   Title of article

_____   Author(s) of article (if any)

_____   Title of periodical

_____   Volume of periodical

_____   Page number

_____ Date of periodical

_____ Is an abstract or the text available online?

Article 2

_____ Subheading (if any)

_____ Author(s) of article (if any)

_____ Title of periodical

_____ Volume of periodical

_____ Page number

_____ Date of periodical

_____ Is an abstract or the text available online?

Using Subject-(Discipline-) Specific Databases

When you choose a major, you will find that there are discipline- or subject-specific databases that narrow the scope of your search and are likely to be authoritative and reliable. Some of the databases may be electronic, some on CD-ROM, and some in a print version. On your library's website, you will find a list similar to the one shown here (sometimes called a *research gateway* or *gateway to databases*).

Exercise 11.5

Practice Using Subject-Specific Databases

Choose one of the following majors and list as many subject-specific databases and resources as you can find on your campus.

Accounting	Engineering tech.	Nursing
Aerospace	Fashion/design	Nutrition/food science
Agriculture	Foreign languages	Philosophy
Anthropology	Geography	Physics
Art	Geology	Political science
Biology	History	Psychology
Business	HPERS	Radio/TV/photography
Chemistry	Journalism	Recording industry
Computer science	Law	Social work
Criminal justice	Literature	Sociology
Current issues	Mathematics	Theater
Education	Music	Women's studies

Major or subject:

_____

Databases specific to that subject:

_____

_____

_____

_____

_____

What topic did you choose for the previous exercises? _____

What subject category from the preceding list could you search to find other databases for your topic? _____

_____

Finding Newspapers

An additional source of information you may need to use in your research is newspapers or news periodicals. Most libraries subscribe to several major newspapers and have back copies on microfilm. Your library will probably have several electronic newspaper databases online. National Newspaper Index, ProQuest Newspapers, and LexisNexis are a few.

LexisNexis covers general news and information and legal, business, and medical resources. It gives mostly full-text access to newspapers and magazine articles, state and federal law, company financial information, industry news, and more and is a good place to start your search for news articles. I like it because full text is given for most articles. If you don't find full text online, you will have to read the article on microtext. Note that you library may have historical newspaper databases that may be useful as well. For example, you might read the actual newspaper account of the assassination of Lincoln.

Exercise 11.6

Practice Using Newspaper Sources

As practice using newspaper sources, use the same subject you used for periodicals and find two news articles about that subject from different newspaper databases. Use LexisNexis or another newspaper database of your choice. Because LexisNexis covers more than newspaper articles, make sure you click on the News tab and narrow the search to meet your needs. _Choose the same topic used in the previous exercises._

Autism   Obesity   GPS   Road Rage   Car Insurance

_____   Subject chosen

Article 1

_____   Newspaper database

_____   Newspaper

_____   Headline of article

_____   Date of article

_____   Page numbers of article

Short summary of article

Article 2

_____   Newspaper database

_____   Newspaper

_____   Headline of article

_____   Date of article

_____   Page numbers of article

Short summary of article

Using the Internet for Research

VIRTUAL FIELD TRIP

Internet Searches

 Visit the College Success CourseMate.

Exercise 11.7

Practice Using the Internet for Research

As practice using the Internet as a resource, *use the same subject you used to practice finding books, periodicals, and news articles*. Find three websites that will give you the following information about the subject. For this exercise, limit your sources to URLs that end in .edu, .org, or .gov.

Autism   Obesity   GPS   Road Rage   Car Insurance

_____   Subject chosen

_____   Search engine used

_____   URL of **website 1**

Describe what information you found and how it was presented.

_____   List who is responsible for the material on the site.

_____   List date information was posted, if you can determine it.

_____   URL of **website 2**

Describe what information you found and how it was presented.

_____   List who is responsible for the material on the site.

_____   List date information was posted, if you can determine it.

_____   If available, use Google Scholar for this search.

_____   URL of **website 3**

Describe what information you found and how it was presented.

_____   List who is responsible for the material on the site.

_____   List date information was posted, if you can determine it.

VIRTUAL FIELD TRIP

Evaluating Sites

Visit the College Success CourseMate.

Making Connections

Use your critical-thinking skills to make a list of things you should consider in deciding if a source is appropriate to use.

_____

_____

_____

Then take the Virtual Field Trip for other ideas.

Exercise 11.8

Choosing a Database

Before you begin this exercise, make a list of the databases that are appropriate for your library.

_____   Database you use to locate books

_____   Database you use to locate periodical articles

_____   Database you use to locate newspaper articles

_____   Database you use to locate subject-specific indexes

_____   Internet search engine

Knowing which database to use is the most efficient way for you to use resources; it will save you many hours in the library or online. Analyze the following and tell what the best database to use in your library is.

_____   **1.** You need to know if your library has a book or books about astronomy.

_____   **2.** You are looking for some general periodical articles about global warming.

_____   **3.** You want to find a book by George Eliot.

_____ **4.** Your education professor has asked you to research technology in the classroom.

_____ **5.** For your nursing classes you need technical information about juvenile diabetes.

_____ **6.** You want to know if your library has *Sports Illustrated*.

_____ **7.** You need the call number for *Benét's Reader's Encyclopedia*.

_____ **8.** You want information about a recent accident in London.

_____ **9.** You want weather information about your favorite ski resort.

_____ **10.** You need general periodical articles about the candidates for the senate in your state.

Quick References

Several terms ago, I conducted a survey of colleagues who teach general studies courses on my campus. I asked them which library reference books their students use most often. In the list that follows are the eight reference books that my colleagues cited most often. These reference books should be in any library. Some of these are available online. For each of them, I have provided a brief explanation of the purpose of the book and one or more examples of information that can be found in the book.

Exercise 11.9

Quick, Reliable References

Your assignment is to locate each book in your library and, after investigating the index and contents, pretend that you are an instructor. Write a question that you want your students to answer by using the book and include the answer. Use the most recent copy you can find.

1. Joseph Nathan Kane's *Famous First Facts* records first happenings, discoveries, and inventions in the United States. You could use this book to find out who was the first African American woman to be awarded a medical degree.

   Call number: _____

   Your question and answer:

   _____

   _____

2. The *World Almanac and Book of Facts* is probably the most comprehensive and most frequently used U.S. almanac of miscellaneous information. It is published yearly. You might use it to discover the world's tallest building, the zip code of a certain city, or the parent company for Jim Beam whiskey.

   Call number: _____

   Your question and answer:

   _____

   _____

3. *The Statesman's Yearbook* contains information on the countries of the world (large and small) including history, area and population, type of government, defense, international relations, economy, energy and natural resources, industry and trade, communications, justice, religion, education, and welfare. It is published yearly, so it often contains the most up-to-date information on a country. You might use *The Statesman's Yearbook* to determine the currency of Greece, the official language of Malta, or the area in square miles of Rwanda.

   Call number: _____

   Your question and answer:

   _____

   _____

4. The *Congressional Directory* contains biographical sketches of members of the U.S. Congress and the president's cabinet, a section on the diplomatic and consular service, and small maps showing congressional districts. You might use the most current edition to find who your U.S. representative is.

   Call number: _____

   Your question and answer:

   _____

   _____

5. The *Statistical Abstract of the United States* as prepared by the chief of the Bureau of Statistics is a standard summary of statistics on the social, political, and economic organization of the United States. It is published annually. You might use this reference to determine the median family income in the United States or the life expectancy for a white female born in 1960.

   Call number: _____

   Your question and answer:

   _____

   _____

6. The *United States Government Manual* is the official handbook of the federal government. It contains comprehensive information on the agencies of the legislative, judicial, and executive branches of government. In it you can find out who the secretary of the interior is or the chairperson of the Tennessee Valley Authority.

Call number: _____

Your question and answer:

_____

_____

7. *Benét's Reader's Encyclopedia* contains short articles on writers, scientists, and philosophers of all countries and periods, as well as literary expressions and terms, plots, and characters of famous works. It is a reference that will be extremely useful in a literature course. In it you can determine the pen name of Charles Lamb or find an explanation of *existentialism*.

Call number: _____

Your question and answer:

_____

_____

8. *Bartlett's Familiar Quotations* is arranged chronologically by authors with exact reference to the source of each quotation. The index contains an average of four or five entries for each quotation. You can use it to find a quote about mothers or to find out who said, "We live and learn, but not the wiser grow."

Call number: _____

Your question and answer:

_____

_____

Now take the following matching quiz to see how well you remember.

Matching: To test how well you remember what is in each of the reference books, match the question to the book that would be most useful in finding the answer.

a. Kane's *Famous First Facts*
b. *World Almanac and Book of Facts*
c. *The Statesman's Yearbook*
d. *Congressional Directory*
e. *Statistical Abstract of the United States*
f. *United States Government Manual*
g. *Bartlett's Familiar Quotations*
h. *Benét's Reader's Encyclopedia*
i. *Biography Resource Center*

Using the above list, where would be the most efficient place to find the answers to the following questions? Write the letter in the blank.

_____ **1.** Who are the two main characters in Toni Morrison's *Jazz*?

_____ **2.** For what is Andy Warhol famous?

_____ **3.** What is the source of this quote: "All animals are equal, but some animals are more equal."

_____ **4.** What are the trends in the cost of postsecondary education?

_____ **5.** What U.S. government department issues passports?

_____ **6.** Where was the first ice-cream cone served?

_____ **7.** What is the currency in Bhutan?

_____ **8.** What are the names of the planets in our solar system?

_____ **9.** How many representatives does California have in Congress?

Biographical Resources

Often you will need to find biographical information about someone but may not know where to start. There are probably several electronic databases in your library specifically for finding out information about people. The *Biography Resource Center* combines more than 415,000 biographies on more than 325,000 people from over 880 volumes of more than 135 respected Gale Group sources such as *Contemporary Authors; Encyclopedia of World Biography; Newsmakers; Contemporary Theatre, Film, and Television; Contemporary Musicians; Historic World Leaders; Notable Twentieth-Century Scientists; Contemporary Black Biography; Religious Leaders of America; International Dictionary of Art and Artists;* and *Writers Directory*, with full-text articles from more than 270 magazines including *American History, Christian Century, Saturday Night,* and *U.S. News & World Report*.

Exercise 11.10

Using Biography Resource Center

1. Choose one of the people listed below.
2. Locate that person in *Biography Resource Center* or another electronic biographical database.
3. List three sources referred to by *Biography Resource Center*. Be sure you list the entire name of the publication, not just the abbreviation.

4. Find four specific facts about the person in at least one source listed.

5. List four facts about that person and the source of your information.

Dietrich Bonhoeffer   Maya Angelou

Jeff Bezos   Johnny Carson

John J. Ratey   Jean Piaget

Chet Baker   Ralph Lauren

Benedict XVI   Cleveland Amory

Three sources listed in *Biography Resource Center*. (If source other than *Resource Center* used, list here.)	Four facts about _____ (Name person chosen.)
1.	**1.**
2.	**2.**
3.	**3.**
	4.

Exercise 11.11

Practicing What You Have Learned

Using **learning styles** as your topic, search databases available to you and find information about that topic. You should use a different database for each section.

_____ Database used

_____ How many books found in that database?

_____ Title of one book

_____ Author (or editor) of above book

_____ Call number of above book

_____ On what floor in the library will it be found?

_____ Is it on the shelf?

Periodical Article (*Note:* do <u>not</u> use *New York Times* articles here; the *New York Times* is a newspaper.)

_____	Database used
_____	Name of one article
_____	Author
_____	Name and date of periodical
_____	Is full text given?
_____	Is abstract given?

Newspaper Article

_____	Database used
_____	Headline of article
_____	Name of newspaper
_____	Date of newspaper
_____	Can you read the article from your computer?

Internet Article

_____	Search engine
_____	URL for article (not search engine)
_____	Three facts about your topic found on this site

VIRTUAL FIELD TRIP

Citing Sources

 Visit the College Success CourseMate.

Modeling the Learning Process

Gathering. You learned the steps of the research process and the names of databases.

Analyzing. You analyzed what you would use each database for.

Creating New Ideas. You projected a limit for your topic and projected which databases to use.

Acting. You planned the parts of a research project. Some of you actually wrote a research paper.

SUMMARY

To see if you grasped the major points of the chapter and to make a useful study guide, answer the following questions found in your reading. When you have written your answers, cover them and see if you can say the answer to each question in your own words. If you prefer to type your answers, you will find a Microsoft Word download for each summary on the College Success CourseMate for Practicing College Learning Strategies at **www.cengagebrain.com.**

Name the six elements of information literacy.

1. _____
2. _____
3. _____
4. _____
5. _____
6. _____

What is a database?

_____

Name six steps used to systematically approach a research project.

1. _____
2. _____
3. _____
4. _____
5. _____
6. _____

What are good sources to use to gather background for your topic?

_____

_____

What system of classification for books does your library use?

_____

What advantages may periodicals have over books?

_____

_____

What are three types of periodicals?

1. _____

2. _____

3. _____

Give an example of a web browser.

_____

Define *search engine* and give an example of one.

_____

List some frequently used domains.

_____

_____

What are some elements you should consider when evaluating sources.

A _____

A _____

O _____

C _____

C _____

Name two possible formats for citing sources.

_____

_____

_____

What is the primary database in your library for books?

_____

In your library, what is the primary database for *general* periodicals?

_____

What are some databases for *subject-specific* periodicals?

_____

_____

Name a database you can use to find articles from newspapers.

_____

Choose one search engine and explain how to use it to perform a subject search on the Internet.

_____

_____

_____

Case Study: What's Your Advice?

Nathan is beginning college after working in sales for 10 years and enjoying the challenge. In his English class, Nathan has been assigned a research paper. The paper must have at least eight sources, including a minimum of two books, two periodical articles, one newspaper article, and one authoritative Internet source. From his instructor's suggested topics, Nathan has chosen a subject that interests him. However, when he goes to the library, panic sets in. Nathan has not been in a library in ten years and has no idea where to begin.

You find a worried Nathan in the front of the library. Please make Nathan a list of which databases are available in your library for books, periodicals, and newspapers and give him suggestions for using them efficiently. You will also need to suggest a search engine or two he might use to find an Internet article and explain to Nathan how to tell if it's "authoritative."

Parallel Parking

Complete the following driving occurrences with parallels from researching a topic:

Writing Down Directions

_____

Taking an Alternate Route

_____

Programming Your GPS

_____

Stopping for Fuel and Food

_____

Evaluating Learning Outcomes

How successful were you in making it to your destination in this chapter?

Analyze what you learned in this chapter. Put a check beside each task you are now able to do. Now think of strategies that you learned that will help you save time and study more effectively. List them in the appropriate place on the back inside cover.

☐ **Explain** the elements involved in information literacy

☐ **Identify** library databases used to find books, general periodicals, subject-specific periodicals, newspapers, and Internet sources.

☐ **Follow** a systematic approach to a research topic, including identifying and narrowing the topic; finding book, periodical, and Internet sources; and evaluating each source and listing information that should be cited.

☐ **Access** library resources from an off-campus site.

☐ **Explain** how to evaluate an Internet site for accuracy, authority, objectivity, currency, and coverage.

☐ **Indicate** the appropriate use for *Kane's Famous First Facts, World Almanac, The Statesman's Year-book, Congressional Directory, Statistical Abstract of the United States, Bartlett's Familiar Quotations,* and *Benet's Reader's Encyclopedia.*

☐ **Locate** reliable biographical sources by using various library biographical databases.

☐ **Explain** the learning process modeled in this chapter.

Your Student Tip for This Chapter

Use the space below to write a tip you would give other students about what you have learned in this chapter.

_____

_____

_____

Appendix

A Principles of Studying Math

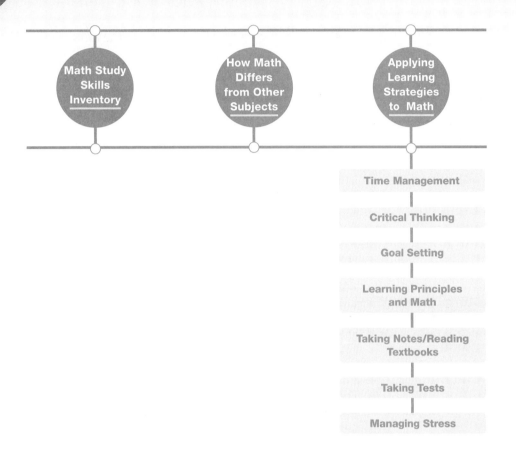

Your Road to Becoming a Better Math Student

It may be that you are actually better at math than you think. I find that when many students say they are not good at math, it's not because they have no math skills; rather, it's that they have poor study skills when it comes to math, which can be easily remedied with a little effort. If you get lost while driving to a specific destination, it may be that you lost concentration or that your trip preparation was not done carefully in your hurry to get there. Even if the directions were complicated, there were probably things you could have done to avoid confusion in the first place. The same is true of getting to your math destination. The principles of learning we utilized in this textbook are applicable to any subject, but they may need to be adjusted a bit for math. You may need to slow down, drive more carefully, and watch out for speed bumps.

Let's begin by evaluating your math study skills.

Math Study Skills: Diagnostic Inventory

Thoughtfully rate your behavior in regard to the following as **3** for **almost always**, **2** for **sometimes**, **1** for **almost never**, and **0** if you have **never even thought about doing** what the statement says.

Selecting a Math Class

_____ **1.** I schedule my math class at a time when I am mentally sharp.

_____ **2.** When I register for a math class, I choose the best instructor for me.

_____ **3.** If I have a choice, I select a math class that meets three or four days a week instead of one or two days.

_____ **4.** I schedule my next math class as soon as possible after I have completed my current course.

_____ **5.** I make sure that I have signed up for the correct level math course.

During Math Class

_____ **6.** I come to class on time and even try to be early.

_____ **7.** I sit as close to front and center of the room as possible.

_____ **8.** Before class starts, I review my notes.

_____ **9.** I never miss class.

_____ **10.** If I must miss class, I get clear, accurate notes and homework assignments and try to work on the assignment before the next class.

_____ **11.** I make a conscious effort to focus each class period.

_____ **12.** My goal for each class is to learn as much as possible.

_____ **13.** I try to find a way to connect new concepts to what I already know.

_____ **14.** I take good notes in class.

_____ **15.** I have a method for taking good notes.

_____ **16.** I ask questions when I don't understand.

_____ **17.** If I get lost, I identify where I got lost.

_____ **18.** I attend additional classes if I need to go through it again.

Time and Place for Studying Math

_____ **19.** I study math every day.

_____ **20.** I try to do my math homework immediately after math class.

_____ **21.** I have a specific time to study math.

_____ **22.** I have a specific place with few distractions to study math.

_____ **23.** I do my math homework in the lab where I can get help.

_____ **24.** I am careful to keep up to date with my math homework.

_____ **25.** I study math at least 8 to 10 hours a week.

_____ **26.** I study in short sessions 45–50 minutes long.

Study Strategies for Math Class

_____ **27.** I read my math textbook before I come to class.

_____ **28.** If I have trouble understanding the textbook, I find an alternative text.

_____ **29.** I take notes in math class.

_____ **30.** I am careful to copy all the steps of math problems in my notes.

_____ **31.** I ask questions when I am confused.

_____ **32.** I go to the instructor or lab when I am confused.

_____ **33.** I try to determine exactly when I got confused and exactly what confused me.

_____ **34.** I review my notes and text before beginning homework.

_____ **35.** I work problems until I understand them, not just until I get the right answer for homework.

_____ **36.** I use flash cards for formulas and vocabulary.

_____ **37.** I develop memory techniques to remember math concepts.

Math Tests

_____ **38.** I preview the test before I begin.

_____ **39.** Before I begin taking the test, I make notes on the test of things such as formulas that I might need or forget.

_____ **40.** I begin with the easy questions first.

_____ **41.** I take the full amount of time allotted for the test.

_____ **42.** I carefully check or rework as many problems as possible before I turn in my test.

_____ **43.** When tests are returned, I correct my errors, and I keep a log of the types of mistakes I made—concept errors, application errors, careless errors.

_____ **44.** I keep up to date so that I don't have to cram the night before a test.

Anxiety

_____ **45.** I believe that I can succeed in math class.

_____ **46.** I have study partners in my math class.

_____ **47.** I find out as much as possible about each test.

_____ **48.** I take practice tests.

_____ **49.** I know several good relaxation breathing techniques.

_____ **50.** I am comfortable asking for help.

_____ **Total score**

Scoring

Now that you have evaluated each item from 0 to 3, total your score for all 50 items. Use that total to determine your strengths and things you need to work on.

If your score is 135–150, give yourself an **A**. You are using the study skills you need in order to be successful in math.

If your score is 120–134, give yourself a **B**. You are using good math study skills. Note items with low scores. Choose a few strategies to work on each day, and you will be well on your way to an A. Make a list and set a time frame for incorporating these strategies into your routine study of math.

If your score is 100–119, give yourself a **C**. Your study skills are average. If you want an A, choose one or two strategies in each category to work on until you are using most of the strategies described in the inventory. Make a list of those items you scored low on and write a goal or plan of action to apply toward those strategies. Remember, a goal should be specific, measurable, realistic, and challenging, and have a specific completion date.

If your score is below 100, you are probably having a difficult time in math class. Math may not be your trouble! More than likely, your main problem is the study strategies you are using (or not using). *Make* yourself do as many of the things listed as you can.

Review this inventory often. It becomes your checklist for improving your math study skills. Highlight those you need to work on first. Now write a goal for raising your score. Remember, a goal should be specific, measurable, realistic, and challenging, and have a specific completion date. Set a specific time to begin each one. The items on the list have nothing to do with how smart you are in math and everything to do with decisions you make about how you will approach math.

Four Reasons Why Math Is Different from Other Subjects

1. Math requires different study processes. In other courses, you learn and understand the material, but you seldom have to *apply* it. You have to apply the material when you do math problems.

2. Math is a linear learning process. What is learned one day is used the next, and so forth. (In history, perhaps you can learn Chapter 2 and not Chapter 3 but still be able to understand Chapter 4. In math, you must understand the material in Chapter 3 before you can go on to Chapter 4.)

3. Math is much like a foreign language. It must be practiced *every day*, and often the *vocabulary* is unfamiliar. Make a list or flash cards of terms you need to remember. Just as the direction words in the test-taking chapter seemed to be simple, understanding what each required makes a difference. Likewise, knowing what each term in math requires you to do could make a real difference in improving your math performance.

4. Math in the university is different from math in high school. Instead of going to class every day, in college you go only two or three times a week. What took a year to learn in high school is now covered in only 15 weeks or less. This basically means that the responsibility lies with you to put in as much time as necessary to understand and reinforce what goes on in each class meeting. And it also means that missing class could spell disaster. If you must miss a math class, make every effort to catch up before the next class period.

Applying the Learning Strategies to Math

Your approach should not be just getting through your math course, but you should also model the learning process you used and become fully engaged in learning. Let's review some things you've learned and apply them to math.

Time Management

Math is simply going to take more time than you really want to spend on it. Use these strategies to make the most of your time spent on math.

- Set a specific time to study math every day. Use distributed practice. Several shorter sessions are more helpful than a long, tiring or frustrating one. One session should probably not exceed 45–60 minutes.
- If there is a math lab or math tutoring center, bring your homework there as soon as possible after class before you have a chance to forget. Use an index card and write the location and hours your math lab is open. Use the card to record when you attended and the names of tutors you like after you use them.

- Even if it you have completed the assigned work, each day work a sample problem to see if you still understand how to do it.
- Reread the textbook section. It may not have made sense the first time because you really didn't understand that type of problem. After covering it in class, you have some background to build on.
- Teach a new concept to your study partner.
- If you need help, get it immediately.

Critical Thinking

In the critical thinking chapter, you learned the steps in the decision-making process. Solving a math problem is not really much different. One reason for learning about math is to develop better problem solving skills to use in all aspects of life. Many math problems are multistep and require a systematic approach. Follow these steps.

- Read the full question.
- Analyze and compute.
- Determine what is **given**, what you need to **find**, and what you need to **do** in each question or problem. (It would be nice to have a math GPS to guide you through it, but with critical thinking, you can solve the problem).
- Draw pictures; they can simplify the problem.
- Use a calculator; do the calculations twice.
- Check your results; do the problem again another way or use methods you've learned to check answers. Make sure that your answer makes sense and that you've used the same terms or units in your answer.

Goal Setting

It is important that you set goals for not just your math class in general, but also that you have a goal for each math class and homework assignment. Review the elements for a SMART goal and apply these elements to math.

Specific	Describe what you want to accomplish with as much detail as possible.
Measurable	Describe your goal in terms that can be evaluated clearly.
Action Plan	Your goal should explain what action you will take.
Realistic	You know you are capable of doing or achieving this goal.
Time Framed	Clearly specify target-completion time—longer goals broken into shorter pieces.

Learning Principles and Math

Let's quickly review the learning principles and apply them to math. Here are some basic ideas. Once you get the basics, you can think of other ways to use each principle.

The first group involves **Starting the Connections**.

- Remember, the principle of **interest** says if you are not interested, you won't remember. It may be that you have not always been successful at math and so the learning principle of interest is difficult for you. What do you need to do to get interested in math? It may be as simple as finding a study group or study partner or asking the instructor what real life situations use this kind of problem. You might compare the steps of a problem to some activity you already know. Chances are that you will use some type of math on your job in the future.

- Second, both in class and when studying, you need to apply the principle of **intent to remember**. What adjustments can you make in your attitude to make sure you really "get it" in class? You might meet with your study partners before class to review and determine questions you may need to ask. Come to class early. Get your material and notes ready. Take notes. Pay attention. Ask questions.

- The third principle will affect just how much effort you must make in order to learn new concepts. Math is linear and your **basic background** is crucial. If you are lost, try to remember the last time you understood and go back and begin there. Your instructor or tutor can help you.

The second group of learning principles deals with **Controlling the Amount and Form of New Information**.

- **Select** the main ideas first. What facts are important and necessary for solving the problem?

- Then **organize** the steps of a new process. Color-code them, draw a flow chart, or make a mnemonic. Make sure the sequence is correct. Always show your work so you can follow the process.

The third group of learning principles is used to **Strengthen the Neural Connections** you have already made.

- Do you self-test by **reciting** the formulas or steps to solving a problem? Try saying the steps out loud as you work a problem.

- Can you **visualize** what you are doing, using real objects? Many times it may be necessary to draw the problem to see if your answer makes sense.

Make an effort to **associate** each new type of problem with something you already know. Determine how it differs from the previous type of problem. Are the steps similar to making a cake, running a play on the football field or basketball court, or finding a lost object?

The last group of principles is used to **Solidify the Connections** you have made in your brain.

- Your brain must have time for new information to **consolidate**. This requires repetition, reinforcing the concepts in as many different ways as possible. But the key word here is *time*. When you learn a new type of problem in math class, keep a chart of how much time you spend getting that concept secure in your brain. Also note how many different ways you used to reinforce it.

- Quickly doing homework just to get it done won't establish the network you need to build. This brings us back to **distributed practice**. You should work in short sessions **every day** to make sure you understand. The sessions don't have to be the same. You could work the problems on your assignment during one session. Reread the textbook explanation and work a sample problem the next. Compare your class notes with a study partner's the next. Try to teach it to someone the next.

Taking Notes and Reading Math Textbooks

The next strategies you learned used the **Question in the Margin system** to **take notes** in class and to **read** textbooks. You have learned the necessity for taking notes in class. Short-term memory won't hold what you need, even if you understood everything that went on in class. The concepts covered in math class are usually linear (one step builds on another) and complex, so it is especially important to take notes. Use the strategies below for math.

- Your first step is to prepare before you come to class. The more you know, the easier it is to take notes. See if you can make up a problem that parallels the ones you worked in your assignment.
- Review your notes and homework immediately before class. Right before you go to math class, meet a study partner and teach each other the concepts from the previous class.
- Read textbook assignments so you have something to build on. Make note of whether the explanation given in the textbook is different from the one the instructor uses and underline the similarities. Mark rules and procedures and make notes of mistakes that the instructor indicates students often make—having the wrong sign or solving in the wrong order, for example.
- Find the style of note taking that works best for you. I suggest that instead of the two-column system we used in the Question in the Margin system, you may want to modify it to three columns. Keep one column for questions and labels, use the second column for examples, and the third one for explanations. Don't just write down what is on the board; listen carefully for directions—the whys and hows. Use the same text message shorthand to record what you need in order to understand the process. Below is an illustration similar to the three-column note page suggested by Paul Nolting in *Math Study Skill Workbook*.

Questions/Rule/Terms	Work the Problems Here	Explanation of Steps and Notes for What to Check For

- Listen actively in class! If you get lost, ask questions. Don't forget to record the answer! Note where you are confused and leave a space to complete later. It is important in math class to review and label your notes as soon as possible after class.
- Compare notes with fellow students. Use the recite and reflect steps of the system and review often. Make summary sheets, maps, and flash cards of each new concept. Time-consuming? Yes, building those connections takes time, especially in math.

Reading a math book is very different from reading a history assignment. Many math students try to depend on the instructor's explanation in class and skip reading the textbook. You will be surprised how much more you understand in class when you read your text before class. Follow the below steps when reading a math textbook.

- You still need to survey and try to determine the main idea before you begin to read. Writers of math books usually are brief and to the point. Make sure you understand each sentence before you go on.
- Pay close attention to diagrams, charts, and problems.
- If you didn't understand, go over it again.
- After class, read the textbook assignment again and use it to clarify or make additions to your notes. As you discovered throughout this text, most learning takes place outside the classroom. You begin the gathering by reading and taking notes in class, but then it is up to you to analyze what you gathered, create situations for using the information, and act by making and working problems.
- Meet with the instructor often. Show her or him your notes. Let her or him help you identify what you did wrong. It is especially important that you state the purpose of the office visit. Not just "Help, I don't get this stuff," but "I understand that I must change the numbers to like terms, but I am having trouble understanding how to do it."

Test-Taking Strategies

Use the below strategies when faced with a math test:

- Just as you would in any other test, preview a math test before you begin.
- Write down any formulas or steps you think you might forget.
- Read directions carefully.
- Work the problems you are sure of first.
- Budget your time; if you get stuck, go to another question and come back.
- Show all your work. This helps both you and the instructor see the process.
- When you finish a problem, analyze your answer. Does it make sense? If you finish early, actually rework each problem.
- When your test is returned, make sure you understand why you missed an answer. Did you read the directions wrong? Was it a careless error? Did you really not understand the concept? Did you study the right things?
- If you are consistent in the type of error you make, be sure that before you turn in the next test, you look for that type of error.

Managing Stress

Math anxiety is real. But just as you learned to manage other stressors in your life, you can learn to manage the stress caused by math class. Repeated lack of success is the cause of most math anxiety. Let's go back to the beginning of this section to the math study skills inventory and seek the cause of your anxiety.

- Is your lack of time and effort in studying math one of the main factors in your anxiety? As the inventory indicates, improving your approach to studying math can control much of math anxiety.
- You must take positive steps to reduce your anxiety.
- You should learn and practice relaxation skills.
- You should immediately find a study partner or join a study group.
- You should attend all classes and do all homework as assigned and seek extra help when necessary.
- This will probably include seeing the instructor during office hours or scheduling an appointment for assistance.
- You should give math at least the same effort you give to other subjects.
- As a competent adult, you have the responsibility to approach math with an open mind rather than fighting it.

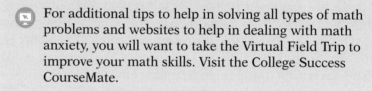

VIRTUAL FIELD TRIP

Improving Your Math Skills

For additional tips to help in solving all types of math problems and websites to help in dealing with math anxiety, you will want to take the Virtual Field Trip to improve your math skills. Visit the College Success CourseMate.

When educators speak of learning, sometimes they emphasize one or two strategies as important. Neuroscientist and educator Eric Jensen synthesizes the findings of brain and learning research, reminding us there are many things we need to consider when seeking strategies for learning.* The following equation terms are areas you need to consider if you want to truly learn something:

Jensen's Equation for Optimal Learning

Meaning

(connecting experience, data, and stimuli to form conclusions and create patterns that give our lives meaning)

+

Present circumstances

(environment, feelings, people, context, goals, moods)

+

Personal history

(beliefs, experiences, values, knowledge)

+

Input

(five senses: visual, auditory, kinesthetic, olfactory, gustatory)

+

Processing

(learning preference, states, left/right hemisphere, abstract/concrete)

+

Responses

(seven intelligences: verbal-linguistic, spatial, bodily kinesthetic, musical-rhythmic, mathematical-logical, intrapersonal, interpersonal)

=

Optimal learning

*From *Super Teaching* by Eric Jensen, 1998, p. 20. Reprinted by permission of the author.
www.jensenlearning.com

Bibliography

Principles for Optimal Learning

Brain-Compatible Strategies for Memory and Learning

Arden, John B. *Rewire Your Brain*. Hoboken, NJ: John Wiley & Sons, 2010.

Chudler, Eric. "A computer in your head." *Odyssey*. March 2001.

Ford, Martin. *Motivating Humans*. Newbury Park, CA: Sage Publications, 1992.

Hart, Leslie. *Human Brain and Human Learning*. White Plains, NY: Longman, 1983.

Hillman, Ralph. *Delivering Dynamic Presentations: Using Your Voice and Body for Impact*. Boston: Allyn and Bacon, 1999.

Horstman, Judith. *The Scientific American Day in the Life of Your Brain*. San Francisco: Jossey Bass, 2009.

Howard, Pierce. *The Owner's Manual for the Brain: Everyday Applications from Mind-Brain Research*, 2nd ed. Austin: Bard Press, 2000.

Jensen, Eric. *Brain-Based Learning*. San Diego: The Brain Store, 1995.

Jensen, Eric. *Completing the Puzzle: The Brain-Compatible Approach to Learning*. San Diego: The Brain Store, 1997.

Jensen, Eric. *The Learning Brain*. San Diego: The Brain Store, 1995.

Jensen, Eric. *Super Teaching*, 3rd ed. San Diego: The Brain Store, 1998.

Jossey-Bass. *Reader on The Brain and Learning*. San Francisco: Wiley, 2008.

Locke, E. A., and Gary Latham. "Work motivation and satisfaction: Light at the end of the tunnel." *Psychological Science* 1 (1990): 240–246.

Markowitz, Karen, and Eric Jensen. *The Great Memory Book*. San Diego: The Brain Store, 1999.

Medina, John. *Brain Rules*. Seattle: Pear Press, 2008.

National Research Council. *How People Learn: Brain, Mind, Experience and School*. Washington, DC: National Academy Press, 1999.

O'Keefe, J., and L. Nadel. *The Hippocampus as a Cognitive Map*. Oxford: Clarendon Press, 1987.

Pink, Daniel H. *A Whole New Mind: Why Right-Brainers Will Rule the Future*. New York: Penguin Group, 2005.

Ratey, John. *A User's Guide to the Brain: Perception, Attention, and the Four Theaters of the Brain*. New York: Vintage, 2002; Corwin press, 2003.

Smith, Allistair. *The Brain's Behind It*. Norwalk, CT: Crown House Publishing, 2005.

Tate, Marcia L. *Worksheets Don't Grow Dendrites*. Thousand Oaks, CA.

Willis, Judy. *Research-Based Strategies to Ignite Student Learning: Insights from a Neurologist and Classroom Teacher*. Alexandria, VA: Association for Supervisions and Curriculum Development, 2006.

Wurtman, Judith. *Managing Your Mind and Mood Through Food*. New York: HarperCollins, 1986.

Zull, James. *The Art of Changing the Brain: Enriching Teaching by Exploring the Biology of Learning*. Sterling, VA: Stylus, 2002.

Index

Note: The locators followed by 'n' denotes note number cited in the text